We Will Remember Them

We Will Remember Them

THE MEN OF TAVISTOCK WHO DIED IN THE FIRST WORLD WAR

ALEX METTLER AND GERRY WOODCOCK

The Tavistock and District Local History Society

First published in Great Britain 2003

Copyright Alex Mettler and Gerry Woodcock
Copyright on individual images remains with the owner

All rights reserved. No part of this publication may be reproduced,
stored in retrieval system, or transmitted in amy form or by any means
without the prior permission of the copyright holders

ISBN 0-9544284-1-2

Published the The Tavistock and District Local History Society

Typeset by TW Typesetting, Plymouth, Devon
Printed and bound by Cromwell Press, Trowbridge, Wiltshire

DEDICATION

A War Memorial in the centre of a Midlands town bears the simple inscription: 'To the Unreturning Brave'. We wish to dedicate this book to the memory of the men of our own locality who went to fight in the First World War and who did not return. It is our hope that their sacrifice will never be forgotten.

LOTS OF LOVE & FOND KISSES TO DEAR FATHER AT THE FRONT

Father dear, we miss you sadly,
Each long day we think of you,
Trusting God will bring you safely,
Back to those who love you true;
So dear Father just keep smiling,
Visions fairer try to see
Of the time when you'll be with us
In the happy days to be.

CONTENTS

Acknowledgements	xi
Introduction	1
Hugh Mockler-Ferryman	6
Thomas Brenton	8
James Watts	10
Percy Adams	12
William Simmons	14
George Tyrrell	16
Samuel Tucker	18
Henry Perkin	20
Christopher Hoskyns-Abrahall Sr	22
Edward Coles	24
Albert Hodgins	26
Sidney Bassett	28
Dingle Martin	30
J. Trick	32
Arthur Gallie	34
Alfred Lethbridge	36
Francis Maker	38
John Westlake	40
Samuel Stacey	42
Henry Barkwill	44
William Garland	46
Cecil Merrifield	48
Robert Wilson	50
John Yard	52
Alfred Coombe	54
James Harris	56
Ernest Davey	58

J. Davey	60
Francis Collacott	62
Francis Harvey	64
Thomas Chenhall	66
James Chenhall	68
Charles Philp	70
Rees Martin	72
Frederick Warren	74
Henry Weaver	76
Frederick Maker	78
William Davy	80
Joe Plummer	82
Theodore Martin	84
Philip Palmer	86
Ernest Friend	88
George Hill	90
Frederick Gawman	92
Henry Pengelly	94
William Parsons	96
John Symons	98
George Rooke	100
Frederick Attewill	102
Francis Skinner	104
Max Teglio	106
Harold Maker	108
Wilfred Lewis	110
John Watts	112
William Raymont	114
William Jago	116
Robert Brooks	118
Francis Harry	120
Reginald Kerswill	122

Frederick Perkin	124
Harold Goodman	126
William Walkem	128
James Craze	130
Edward Skinner	132
Reginald Northway	134
Albert Grainger	136
William Harry	138
Harry Bath	140
Isaac Watts	142
Thomas Edwards	144
Charles Bickle	146
Ernest Harris	148
George Cloak	150
William Gould	152
George Adams	154
Christopher Hoskyns-Abrahall Jr	156
William Holman	158
George Mathews	160
William Hellier	162
Harry Greening	164
William Hayman	166
Harry Waye	168
Ernest Ackford	170
Charles Spooner	172
Bertram Wilkinson	174
Francis Jago	176
William Friend	178
Sylvester Pethick	180
Samuel Brenton	182
Bertie Doige	184
Ernest Collins	186

Reginald Spurway	**188**
Charles Horne	**190**
Leonard Harris	**192**
Alfred Pendry	**194**
Robert Roberts	**196**
Jesse Mitchell	**198**
Claude Blythe	**200**
John Sargent	**202**
Frederick Woodrow	**204**
Henry Maker	**206**
Thomas Trick	**208**
John Palmer	**210**
William Rich	**212**
John Harvey	**214**
William Turner	**216**
Sidney Vinson	**218**
Frederick Hicks	**220**
Wilfred Cruze	**222**
Charles Hawkins	**224**
Percy Coles	**226**
Charles Merrifield	**228**
Reginald White	**230**
Robert Smith	**232**
William Exworthy	**234**
Samuel Miles	**236**
Richard Stranger	**238**
Arthur Whittome	**240**
William Tucker	**242**
Sources used	**245**
Surname index	**249**

ACKNOWLEDGMENTS

We are very grateful to all those people who have helped us with information. In particular, we acknowledge the assistance of:

Roy Acton, Clifford Alford, David Anthony, Bill Antrobus, John Arnold, Kathleen Bhinda, Pauline Bird, Heather Bond, Geoff Boucher, Paul Brough, Juliet Chadwick, Gordon Chenhall, Keith Chenhall, Nellie Cloak, Bill Collacott, Don Connett, Catherine Coombe, A. Cox, Doreen Creber, John Cruikshank, Christine Davey, John Davies, Simon Dell, Diane Dennison, Kevin Dickens, Elizabeth Earing, Charles Edwards, Linda Elliott, Lorna England, Roy Eston, Brenda Faulkner, Robin Fenner, Margaret Fisher, Hilda Frost, J. Garland, Audrey Gaye, Phyllis Geake, Judy Gibson, Betty Gilbert, Sylvia Guthrig, Roy Hammond, Glenda Harvey, Phyllis Hawken, David Holland, Dorothy Horrell, Lillian Jago, Simon Kemp, J.P. Kester, John Killingbeck, William Lethbridge, Capt. N. Louloudis (Greek Embassy), Linda Lowry, Margaret Maker, Roderick Martin, Julia Massey, Eddie McCabe, Jenny Metcalf, Robert Mettler, Mary Mott, J.J.W. Nijssen (Netherlands Embassy), Rory O'Connor, Margaret Papados, Douglas Parkhouse, Bill Parsons, Sheelagh Parsons, Len Perry, Norah Phillips, Jennifer Pooley, A. Prasad, John Rawlings, Donald Roberts, Douglas Roberts, Madge Sargent, Maureen Selly, Janson Skinner, John Skinner, Percy Skinner, Paul Slater-Lindsay, Penny Spackman, Stephen Stratford, Muriel Symonds, Shirley and the late Jim Thorington, Nick Thornicroft, Joyce Trethewey, Bill Tucker, Gladys Tucker, A.W. Tyrrell, Les Watkins, Peter Wernham, Harold White, Margaret Wilton, Pat Wood, Mark Woodcock, Arnold Worbuoys, G.H. Wyatt.

INTRODUCTION

Almost a century ago there appeared, in cities, towns, and villages throughout the kingdom, new features of the local landscape. The 'Great War' was over. Now was the time to memorialise it as the 'war to end wars', and to commemorate the men who had died in it. The sudden burgeoning of memorials in the hearts of the largest municipalities and the smallest communities in the land was accompanied by similar tributes on behalf of organisations, churches, companies, clubs, and schools. It was as if the whole country, recalling the biblical lament that, of past heroes, 'some, there be, which have no memorial', had determined that this should not be allowed to happen this time. Each of the stone monuments, whether on the village green, or in a churchyard, or in the middle of swirling urban traffic, carries the same poignant, direct message, as clear today as it was in the 1920s: 'Here I stand, a reminder of tragic events, of loss, and of sacrifice'. They also convey an appeal that echoes across the generations. In the words of J.M.Edmonds, written for a soldier's grave in France, and published in 'The Times' in July 1918:

> When you go home, tell them of us, and say:
> For your tomorrow, these gave their today.

This book is written in the conviction that for us, as for generations still to come, remembrance remains both a need and a duty.

The Tavistock Parish War Memorial proclaims itself as standing: 'To bear proud witness to those men of Tavistock who died for England in the Great War'. There follow 119 names, limited to surname and initials, arranged alphabetically, and occupying all four faces. There are no references to rank, service, or regiment. The project for its construction was launched in February 1919 when a public meeting unanimously endorsed a recommendation made by a committee that had been set up in the previous month. The meeting resolved that:

> The Tavistock War Memorial should take the form of a rough granite cross, placed in the south-east corner of the churchyard, but railed off and thrown open, with steps approaching it from the square; the names of the fallen to be inscribed on tablets affixed to the cross.

Subscriptions were thereupon invited, and the President of the Royal Academy was consulted about the design. In May the *Tavistock Gazette* revealed that work on the design was going ahead, but that the cost of the project would be £600. In January 1920 a further public meeting confirmed the decisions taken on design and site, and showed sufficient confidence in the scheme to invite opinions on what might be done with any funds raised that were surplus to requirements. By August some of this optimism had drained away as it became increasingly evident that the sum raised was going to fall short of the target by about £150. In October it was decided that the original design and site would have to be abandoned in favour of cheaper options. Not enough attention had been paid to the fact that, for a number of reasons, many of them relating to purely local conditions, Tavistock was a town in the depths of an economic depression. The Urban District Council, into whose court the ball now fell, looked at alternatives. They then commissioned Messrs Rogers, a local firm of monumental masons, to produce a modified version of the original design, incorporating three bases and four panels, the latter bearing the inscription and the names cast in black letters. Above this, the granite would taper off to an octagonal shaft, the cap of which would support a cross. The monument, of Cornish granite, would occupy a site owned by the Council, in a corner of Guildhall Square. On this basis, work began in November 1920. The Memorial was unveiled and dedicated in a ceremony on the afternoon of Sunday 22 May 1921. There were then 101 names. A further eighteen were added subsequently in the light of further information. The list was finally closed in November 1923. Since the late 1940s the 119 names of the First World War fallen have shared the Memorial with the forty local casualties of the Second War.

In recent years, and increasingly during the last quarter of the century, doubts have been raised about the suitability of the site. In the discussions that ensued, our contribution was limited to pointing out that the original desires and intentions with regard to the Monument had not been carried out. In September 2001 Tavistock Town Council conducted a poll of town residents which produced an overwhelming majority in favour of reverting to the original intention to seek a site in a corner of the churchyard.

The criteria to be applied before a name was included in the list to be commemorated and displayed do not seem to have ever been clearly established. It appears that the wishes of the next-of-kin constituted the overiding qualification, and that the responsible committee drew up a list of names based on family requests and supplemented from a narrow range of other sources. Of the 119 named casualties, fifty-four had been born in the parish, and a further twenty-seven had Tavistock addresses at the time of their deaths. Thus eighty-one men were included on the basis of clear qualifications of birth or residence. Of the remaining thirty-eight, thirteen were Tavistockians by marriage, and fifteen had close relatives living in the town. A further four signed up for service here and another two were buried here; the connection of each of these six with Tavistock almost certainly extended beyond these occasions of enlistment and interment. There remain four for whom a link, however tenuous, remains hidden. We had to decide whether, in these circumstances, we should limit our investigations to those cases where the link was of the most clear and direct kind, by applying, for example, only the criterion of birth. We quickly discovered that a very considerable number of men thus qualified did not feature in the final list of 119. We cannot speculate on why this was so. Nor can we, or should we, challenge the decisions or wishes of the bereaved families at the time. Our findings, therefore, relate to the 119 whose names are on the Memorial, and who were so recorded because of the clear wish of those left behind, who included forty-six wives, seventy children, ninety-eight parents, and, in the absence of anyone in the above categories, next-of-kin or close relatives.

There are three unknowns when it comes to establishing, among the 119, affiliations within the services. Eighty-five men were in the British Army, of whom twenty-seven belonged to the Devonshire Regiment. Of the seven other soldiers, six were members of the Canadian forces and one fought in the Indian Army. There were three Royal Marines, nineteen Royal Navy personnel, and two members of the infant Royal Flying Corps. These were, of course, predominantly young men. It is, however, misleading to follow the notion, often expounded, that they were all little more than boys when they died. The youngest was sixteen, and there were eleven who were still in their teens. There were, on the other hand, nine who were over forty, and the oldest was fifty-three. The average age of death was twenty-nine. Those aged below twenty represented 10% of the casualties. The figures for those in their twenties and their thirties were 43% and 39% respectively. This left 8% who were over forty.

Of the eighty-five soldiers identified as being in the British Army, fifty-one were killed on the Western Front. One-third of those have no known graves. Each man is either buried in, or commemorated on, one of the large number of cemeteries and memorials that, now quiet and peaceful, mark lines and places that were once scenes of indescribable horror and destruction. The Commonwealth War Graves Commission tends these places with care, as it does the other sites worldwide that hold the graves of Tavistock warriors. These include Niederzwehren and Hamburg in Germany, Salonika and Karasouli in Greece, Jerusalem and Ramleh in Israel, Baghdad and Basra in Iraq, Cairo in Egypt, Barrackpore in India, and Brisbane in Australia, as well as seventeen graves in Britain, one in Ebrington, one in Lambeth, and the others at home, in either Gulworthy Churchyard or Tavistock Cemetery. There were, in addition, seven other men with strong Tavistock connections who died fighting in colonial armies. One, who served in the Indian Army, is commemorated on the Basra Memorial in Iraq. The other six were Canadian soldiers, albeit Tavistockians by birth, two of whom returned to Canada with ailments from which they were thought to have died, while the other four ended their days on the Western Front, two of them in marked graves. The three Royal Marines met rather different ends, as perhaps was fitting, given their versatility and amphibiousness. One went down when his ship was torpedoed, while another was killed in the early stages of The Gallipoli Campaign. The third died off Bermuda, and was taken there for burial. Of the nineteen sailors who lost their lives, five were destined for graves ashore, two in Tavistock, one in Portsmouth, and one each in Malta and Holland. The others went down with their ships. All but one of the latter group ultimately found places on the National Naval Memorial at Plymouth, the one exception appearing instead on the sister monument at Portsmouth.

The great majority of the men concerned joined up at recruitment offices in the immediate area, with approximately 40% enlisting at Tavistock and a further 27% at either Plymouth or Devonport. The pressures to take the king's shilling were formidable. National and local campaigns were waged and powerful influences applied by communities, churches, organisations, friends, relations, and women with their white feathers. The need to prove your manhood and to deflect charges of cowardice was matched by the appeal of adventure and of comradeship and by the prospect of starting afresh if civilian life had proved unsuccessful or boring. The uniform offered an escape from unemployment, from stifling routine, and from the limitations of small town life. In 1916 these strong influences were buttressed by the law. Those who were involved in the war in its first eighteen months had volunteered for duty in one way or another. They were either professionals continuing their prewar service, or reservists called back into action, or former territorials, or volunteers responding to the call to swell the numbers in

'Kitchener's Army.' In January 1916, under the Military Service Act, conscription was introduced. It applied initially to unmarried men between eighteen and forty-one who were not in reserved occupations. The extension of these provisions to married men within the same age-range came five months later. Over the course of the war the parishes of Tavistock, Tavistock Hamlets, and Whitchurch, with a combined population of some 6500, provided a total of 815 men for the armed forces. The Service Records that we have consulted do not indicate whether individual servicemen were volunteers or conscripts.

Subordinate only to his loyalty to the crown was the individual soldier's attachment to his regiment. The regiments each provided an administrative and pastoral framework in a context of almost clan-like loyalties. But in operational terms the most important fighting unit was not the regiment but its principal sub-division, the battalion. Consisting of up to 1000 men, each battalion was commanded by a colonel. The units larger than battalions were not exclusively made up of men from a particular regiment. Four battalions made a brigade, led by a brigadier assisted by three staff officers. Three brigades formed a division, under a general. Moving in the opposite direction along the ladder of formations, a battalion was divided into four companies, commanded by captains, and each company would contain four platoons, led by subalterns or non-commissioned officers. For the majority of men who made up the 'Other Ranks', such heights were unimaginable. For them, Privates were at base camp, Lance Corporals occupied the foothills, Corporals attained some appreciable altitude, and sergeants stood on the summit. Rankings in the navy were more complex. Officer ranks covered the range from Admiral of the Fleet to Petty Officer via Vice Admiral, Rear Admiral, Commodore, Captain, Commander, Lieutenant, Sub Lieutenant, and Midshipman. Below was a myriad of grades based on responsibility and function. No more hierarchical system could be imagined. And yet, Admiralty Instructions were quite clear about how to despatch its own in a classless way. If the burial was to be in the United Kingdom, then the coffin would be made of 'one-inch elm board, half inch wood-hooping round the covers, pitched and oil-polished, with screws complete; to be provided with black japanned tin breastplate with names, date of death and age written thereon in bronze, with four pairs of iron sidehandles with japanned tin plates and one pair of ornaments'.

The hostilities that began on 4 August 1914 ended with the armistice on 11 November 1918. At the beginning of the war the size of the British Army was about 750,000, divided roughly into three equal parts, regulars, reservists, and territorials. The Royal Navy had a strength of about 150,000. The equivalent figures for the last days of fighting were approximately 3,500,000 and 400,000. Army casualties amounted to 662,000 dead, 140,000 missing, and 1,650,000 wounded. The Navy lost 35,000 dead and 5000 wounded. Tavistock suffered its first fatal casualty on 16 September 1914, and there were five more before the end of the year. The succeeding years, 1915, 1916, and 1917, brought deaths totalling, respectively, ten, twenty-four, and thirty-nine. In 1918 a further twenty-nine died before the armistice, the last on 9 November. The remaining eleven fatalities occurred after the end of the war, but from war-related causes. This pattern, of the number of casualties mounting as the war proceeded, reflected the national picture. The remorselessness of this seemingly unstoppable trend contributed to a sea-change in public attitudes. In 1914 all the talk was of honour and glory, the metaphors were sporting ones, and the prospect was of the war ending by Christmas. Rupert Brook wrote:

> Now God be thanked Who has matched us with His hour,
> And caught our youth, and wakened us from sleeping.

Four years on, and the mood is very different. Wilfred Owen had spelt it out when, in bitter anger, he had warned those at home that, if they had seen what he had seen, then:

> My friend, you would not tell with such high zest
> To children ardent for some desperate glory,
> The old lie: 'Dulce et decorum est
> Pro patria mori'.

Families were informed of losses through official channels, telegrams, or letters, although on occasions they received the news from the published lists that appeared in the press. Considerable efforts were made to ensure that more detailed, and personal, letters were sent to wives and/or mothers from Commanding Officers, who were advised that, whatever else they wrote, they should give to the grieving family the confirmation that their loved ones had died instantaneously and had received a proper burial. The circumstances did not always make it easy for those assurances to be freely given. To ten Tavistock families the heartbreak occurred twice. In the case of one family it happened three times. For most of those who received these dreaded messages the prospect was of a period of great hardship. For all of them there was the heartache and the sense of loss and waste. There remain a few for whom, after all these years, the pain persists. We, who came later, and who take for granted the liberties that were in fact hard won by the sacrifices of those who went before, should, perhaps, reflect that the debt we owe both to the war dead and to their surviving dependents has never been fully paid. This book is a small contribution to that payment. We will remember them.

Alex Mettler
Gerry Woodcock

HUGH MOCKLER-FERRYMAN
Died Wednesday 16 September 1914. Aged 22.

Hugh Mockler-Ferryman

On the morning of Tuesday 22 September 1914, which happened to be the fiftieth day of what was to become known as the Great War, a telegram was delivered to St John's House in Tavistock. Its contents quickly became public knowledge. Colonel Augustus Mockler-Ferryman and his wife Evelyn had lost their elder son in the war, and the town had suffered the first in a series of losses that was eventually to mount beyond three figures. Three days later the *Tavistock Gazette* reported that 'the news has been received with great regret as he and his family are much respected in the town'.

The Mockler-Ferrymans had settled in Tavistock in the previous decade when Hugh was in his mid-teens and a schoolboy. His father was a professional soldier who, after retiring from regimental duties, became a lecturer at the Military Academy at Sandhurst, a military historian, and a writer of travel books. The son of Edward Mockler of County Cork in Ireland, Augustus had, in 1881, decided to add 'Ferryman', which had been his mother's maiden name. He married Evelyn, the daughter of Sir Charles Whitehead, one of the foremost authorities on agriculture of his age. St John's, the retirement home chosen by Augustus and Evelyn, had been built half a century earlier to accommodate the Duke of Bedford's steward. It was impressive in scale and appearance, and overlooked the town centre from its position near the foot of Whitchurch Road.

Hugh had been born at Sandhurst in May 1892. He had attended schools in St Neots, in Eversley, and finally at Wellington College, where he shone in a variety of sports, enjoying his shooting and fishing and excelling as a curler, a craft that he developed during winter holidays in Switzerland. As a cricketer, he represented Berkshire, and in 1913 played some games for Tavistock. There was never any doubt that his career would be a military one, and this was confirmed when he went on to Sandhurst. In September 1911 he received his commission as a 2nd Lieutenant. He joined his father's old regiment, the Oxfordshire and Buckinghamshire Light Infantry. Within four years, regiment, army, and country were to become embroiled, for the first time for ninety-nine years, in a war in Europe.

The Great War was triggered by events in the Balkans, but its fundamental causes were to do with rivalries between the Great Powers. These rivalries spilled over into conflict in the first few days of August 1914, when, in turn, war was declared by Austria and Germany on the one side, and Russia and France on the other. Britain, uncommitted by treaty but leaning towards the Franco-Russian Alliance, hesitated briefly. The German invasion of Belgium ended the uncertainty. Britain entered the war in order to uphold the principle of Belgian neutrality, a principle embodied in an international treaty signed in 1839.

The Second Battalion of the Oxford and Bucks, in which young Mockler-Ferryman had been promoted to the rank of full Lieutenant in April 1914, was at Aldershot when war was declared on 4 August. Ten days later they landed at Boulogne. They were part of the British Expeditionary Force, seven regiments of regular troops who were sent out to France at the beginning of the war, and who were to glory in the title 'The Old Contemptibles'. The young subaltern soon got his first taste of action in early engagements between German and British forces, including the retreat from Mons and the battles of the Marne and the Aisne. But it was to be, for him, a short war. The Battalion War Diary records that, in the middle of the battle of the Aisne, on the afternoon of 16 September, 'C and D Companies with half the regimental scouts were sent up in support of the 4th Brigade. Near La Cour de Soupir, one big shell caused the following casualties – 3 officers, 8 men'. One of the officers was Hugh Mockler-Ferryman. He was buried that night in the nearby churchyard of La Soupir. A corporal in his company described him, in a letter home, as 'a thorough sportsman, liked by everyone and loved by his company'. And a senior officer wrote that 'the whole regiment mourns the loss of one of its best and most popular officers'.

Hugh's family, back in St John's, received a letter from his Commanding Officer suggesting that 'you would be proud if you could hear the way in which the NCOs and men speak of him'. No doubt that pride was already there. And it was soon to be extended also to the younger son, Eric, who served in France and won the MC, and who was destined later to enjoy a glittering career in the code-breaking world associated with Bletchley Park, followed by a long Eastbourne retirement. Meanwhile a memorial appeared on the south wall of the Clothmakers' Aisle in Tavistock Parish Church. It reads: 'To the glory of God and in ever loving memory of Hugh Mockler-Ferryman, Lieutenant 52nd Oxfordshire and Buckinghamshire Light Infantry, killed in action at The Aisne, 16th September 1914, Aged 22. Elder son of Lt Colonel A.F. Mockler-Ferryman of St John's House in this parish, and Evelyn, his wife'.

THOMAS BRENTON
Died Tuesday 13 October 1914. Aged 25.

Guards Memorial, Horse Guards Parade, London

German hopes of a speedy advance to Paris and a rapid military victory were dashed when the Battle of the Marne failed to produce a conclusive outcome. The Germans were forced to take up new defensive positions, against which a series of allied attacks was made, developing into what became known as the Battle of The Aisne. The most intense of the fighting raged for sixteen days in September 1914 before the area became the scene of static trench warfare. On 19 September, three days after the death of Hugh Mockler-Ferryman, and at the height of the battle, Thomas Brenton received gunshot wounds to his head and back from which he was never to recover. Two weeks later the news reached William Brenton at his home, 61 West Bridge Cottages, that his son was in a Versailles hospital and was dangerously ill. Lance Corporal Thomas Brenton of the 1st Battalion of the Coldstream Guards died on 13 October, and was buried in the Les Gonards Cemetery at Versailles two days later. He was accorded full military honours and it was reported in the *Tavistock Gazette* that a number of floral tributes were placed on the coffin.

Tavistock's second casualty of the war had been born at 61 West Bridge Cottages on 30 October 1888. His father, William, was a quarryman at the time of the birth, but in 1894 he secured a job as a labourer with the newly-established Rural District Council. William had two hobbies that absorbed all his spare time. One was gardening; he was a prolific prizewinner at local flower shows. The other was cycling. This was an interest that he was later to pass on to his sons. During a period when cycling became an immensely popular activity, and when there was a town Cycling Club holding regular meetings at its track above Green Lane, the

Brentons were in the forefront of promoting and organising the sport locally. In 1880 William married Mary, a dressmaker, who was the daughter of a farm labourer called Samuel Knight. Mary was twenty-seven at the time of the marriage, four years older than her husband. She already had a five year old son called James. She and William had four children, Ethel, William, Samuel, and Thomas. Thomas was the youngest. With the exception of the father, who hailed from St Dennis in Cornwall, all the members of the family were born in Tavistock. No. 61 West Bridge Cottages was to remain the family home for many years. Father William was to die there at seventy-four in 1930, having failed to recover from an accident when he was thrown from his cycle in a collision with a lorry. His wife Mary died within a year at the age of seventy-eight.

Thomas had four years of schooling at the Plymouth Road Council School, one of the two elementary schools in the town. Of his two elder brothers, one, William, became a policeman and the other, Samuel, a prison officer, but Thomas's ambitions seem always to have been focused on the army. In his teens he joined the local Territorial Force, the 3rd Devonshire Battery, 4th Wessex Brigade, Royal Field Artillery, headquartered at Crelake. During this period he worked in a local quarry, but it was clear that he saw this as merely filling time before he could become a professional soldier. In August 1912 his hopes were realised. He enlisted in the Regular Army, becoming 9722 Private Thomas Brenton, 1st Battalion, Coldstream Guards. He gained his stripe twelve months later when he extended the period of his commitment to the colours from three to seven years. The army records describe him at the time of his enlistment as 5′ 9″ tall and weighing 140 lbs, with a fresh complexion, grey eyes, and brown hair. He was a good sportsman, and gained swimming qualifications during his time in the service.

Thomas had dreamed of the military life when, as a schoolboy, he had read about the exploits of British troops in South Africa. He had gone on to prepare himself for war in his four years as a part-time soldier, followed by his two years as a proud guardsman. Now, in August 1914, the moment had come for this young Lance Corporal to experience the real thing. His war lasted for sixty-two days.

The suffering and loss that the war brought to the Brenton family did not end with the grieving for Thomas. Having lost one son in the early stages of the conflict, they were to lose another in the last summer of the war, when Samuel was killed in action. The Brentons were one of ten Tavistock families to whom the dreaded telegram arrived more than once.

On 1st June 1917, with still no end of the conflict in sight, it was decided that a memorial, albeit a provisional one, should be placed in the Parish Church, and should bear the names of those who had already made the sacrifice. The details of the twenty-seven who then qualified were necessarily bare. Near the top appeared 'Thomas Brenton. Versailles. 13-10-14'. For the family there remained for many years the opportunity, taken every year on the anniversary of his death, to insert in the *Tavistock Gazette* a modest, but heart-felt 'In Memoriam.'

JAMES WATTS
Died Friday 23 October 1914. Aged 23.

Gulworthy War Memorial

For eight local families the tragedy of losing a son in the war struck twice. The pain and anguish that those parents had to endure is difficult to imagine. But for John and Susan Watts it was even worse. They lost three sons. James, in the Royal Navy, died at sea in October 1914. John, a private in the Royal Fusiliers, was killed in France in May 1917. And Isaac, in the Prince of Wales's Own Regiment of West Yorkshire, fell at the Third Battle of Ypres in October 1917. John was the eldest; born in 1888, he was twenty-eight when he died. James, born in 1891, died at twenty-three. Isaac was the youngest: he was born in 1894 and also died at the age of twenty-three. Even before this series of blows, John and Susan had had to cope with bereavement. Their daughter Emmie had died in 1907, of tuberculosis, at the age of twenty.

   John Watts senior was a labourer who had been born in London in 1853. His wife Susan was the daughter of Roger and Ann Duke of Ashwater. John and Susan moved about a fair bit during the early years of their married life. John, their eldest son, appeared at Thrushelton, while James and Isaac were born in the parishes of Calstock and Tavistock respectively. The family then settled in Morwellham, where John senior got a job as a forester. James, or Jim as he was commonly called in the family, had been born on 13 February 1891 in the parish of Calstock on the Cornish bank of the Tamar, but his most formative years were spent at Morwellham. Here he shared with his brothers the experience of living in a community which, a generation before, had sustained a busy, thriving river port, but which now, by the early years of the new century, had declined along with the copper mining industry with which it had for so long been associated. Morwellham in the early 1900s had become a backwater, decaying and largely depopulated. The limited career opportunities that were available in the local area at that period brought many young men to consider one of the two available escape routes, emigration or a service life. For young James, working as a farm labourer, the inspiration lay only a few miles from his home down the Tamar. It is not fanciful to suppose that the experience of seeing a fleet at anchor in Devonport, or of watching from the Hoe as these mighty vessels steamed in and out, must have fired both imagination and ambition. In 1909, at the age of eighteen, he joined the Royal Navy.

When James Watts enlisted he was joining a service that had, for a century, upheld Britain's position as the world's leading naval power. Maritime supremacy had been secured at Trafalgar in 1805 and had been unchallenged thereafter. And then, in the last years of the nineteenth century, this dominance was believed to come under threat from a German navy that was expanding rapidly, and that was developing new weaponry in the form of the torpedo and the mine. A programme of naval rearmament, featuring a new battleship design known as the 'Dreadnought', was hastily launched to combat this menace. In the event, the war did not produce the gladiatorial duels between the two mighty fleets that were anticipated. Only one major set-piece battle was fought, at Jutland in 1916. For the rest, navies busied themselves in minor engagements, in patrol and support duties, and in disrupting enemy trade routes. In particular, the Royal Navy found itself playing a key role in support of ground forces in Europe and beyond. In the opening phases of the war this meant that a lot of attention was paid to the continental coastal waters of the North Sea.

When the war began, Leading Stoker James Watts K/3028, one of some 150,000 naval personnel, was aboard H.M.S. 'Exmouth'. A battleship of 14,000 tons with a complement of about 750 men, the 'Exmouth' had been built at Birkenhead and launched in 1899. She was commissioned at Chatham in 1903 for service in the Mediterranean, and was for eight years a flagship. Following re-commissioning at Devonport in 1913 she became a Gunnery Training Ship. When the war came she was employed on patrol duties in the North Sea, and saw action off the coast of Belgium. A particular mission was to search for the large German cruiser the 'Berlin'. It was while he and his crewmates were involved in such exercises that James Watts died of nephritis, a kidney disease, on 23 October. He was buried at sea on the following day.

James is commemorated on the Plymouth Naval Memorial. His name also features on the Gulworthy War Memorial. St Paul's Church Gulworthy, in the yard of which the memorial stands, serves the western parts of the parish of Tavistock, including such outlying settlements as Morwellham. Its memorial includes the names of thirteen of the men who appear also on the Tavistock Parish monument in the town centre, and who came from the Tamarside part of the parish.

Soon after James's death, H.M.S. 'Exmouth' was transferred to duties in the Channel. Her service continued throughout the war, and included action in the Dardanelles. She was sold off in 1920, and broken up.

PERCY ADAMS
Died Sunday 1 November 1914. Aged 20.

Adams family memorial in Plymouth Road Cemetery

On 1 November 1914 the British Navy suffered its first defeat at sea for more than a century. The Chilean port of Coronel was the rather unlikely setting for an engagement that resulted in the loss of 1600 British lives and created an atmosphere at home of alarm bordering on panic. Among the casualties, aboard H.M.S. 'Monmouth', were two Tavistock men, Percy Adams and William Simmons.

Percy Adams came from a large family. Born on 15 November 1893 at 10 Bannawell Street, the family home, he was brought up there, the ninth of ten children. He followed his five elder brothers and three sisters in attending the Plymouth Road Council School, one of the two elementary schools in the town. The school was, in the evenings, used to house a variety of classes, mainly of a vocational and practical nature, for those who wanted to widen their skills and job opportunities. Percy, while working as a railway porter, sought this path to self-improvement, before deciding, in March 1914, to enlist in the Royal Navy.

Percy's father, William, was a Permanent Way Inspector employed by the London and South Western Railway Company. He and his wife Elizabeth had begun their married life in Broadclyst, where her father, George Clarke, had roots, and where the marriage had taken place in 1875. The two fathers at the wedding, Thomas Adams and George Clarke, were both labourers. Thomas had re-married, following the death of his first wife Maria, who was William's mother, and who had died at the age of forty-six, soon after giving birth to twin boys. William and

Elizabeth moved to Tavistock with their (then) seven children in 1890, when the LSWR opened its line through the town. William died in 1904, when Percy was only ten. By then, however, the six eldest children were earning a living, so that Elizabeth was able to cope, in spite of having four of school age.

One feature of the education that Percy and his contemporaries received at Plymouth Road about the turn of the century was a strong thread, running through the curriculum, of patriotic pride. Queen Victoria's Jubilees, in 1887 and 1897, were occasions for celebrating British achievement, and for instilling into the young the virtues of loyalty and duty. Also the Boer War (1899–1902) provided an opportunity to remind the youth of Britain that the role of a world power occasionally required sacrifice and a call to arms. This being Tavistock, there was also a heady concentration on the sea. This was, after all, Drake's town. And if any reminder of this were needed, it could be found in the statue of the great hero, which had, in 1883, become such a welcome addition to the local landscape. It is not fanciful to see, in such experiences, potent influences which must have guided many young men like Percy to their particular calling. They had already led his eldest brother William towards a career as a master mariner.

H.M.S. 'Monmouth', on which Percy Adams served, was an armoured cruiser of 9800 tons. She had been built in 1901 and was based at Devonport. One of four such ships in the First Cruiser Squadron, she had, by 1914, become somewhat outclassed as a result of changes in design that had taken place since her launch. She certainly paid, on 1 November, for her lack of both speed and firepower.

Commanded by Admiral Cradock, head of the South American Station, a British squadron had sailed through the Straits of Magellan, with a speedy light cruiser leading the way and gaining the Chilean Pacific port of Coronel. 'Monmouth', along with H.M.S. 'Good Hope' lumbered up behind, to find the German Admiral von Spee waiting for them near the entrance to the port. When darkness fell on the evening of Sunday 1st November, the German cruisers opened fire. 'Good Hope' was sunk, while 'Monmouth', badly damaged, broke away in an attempt to escape to the north. At 9 o'clock the German cruiser 'Nurnberg' found herself to the port side of 'Monmouth'. The British cruiser had such a steep list to that side that she was unable to use her guns. Under uninterrupted fire the 'Monmouth' went down. The rough weather prevented the German ship from lowering her boats. The only four survivors from the crew of the British cruiser were the men who had earlier been landed on the Albrohos Rocks to establish a look-out station. Their 900 crewmates were lost. They included K/22243 Stoker Second Class Percy Adams. He was two weeks short of his twenty-first birthday. Percy, and his friend and fellow-townsman William Simmons, were Tavistock's first naval casualties to be lost in combat during the war. They were not to be the last.

When Percy died, his mother had two other sons serving in the forces. George, a stoker on Torpedo Boat Number 14, was to die in December 1917. John, the youngest of the family, who was in the 5th Battalion of the Devonshire Regiment, was to survive. Percy is commemorated on the Plymouth Naval Memorial. He also has an entry on the tombstone marking the family plot in the Plymouth Road Cemetery. Immediately below the details of the deaths of his parents, the stone records the loss of 'Percy, 6th beloved son of the above'.

WILLIAM SIMMONS
Died Sunday 1 November 1914. Aged 28.

No. 38 Exeter Street, Tavistock

Paull's Buildings were demolished in 1935. Occupying a cramped site between Brook Street and the River Tavy, this small complex of slum dwellings had, for the best part of a century, had a reputation for sheltering some of the poorest and most deprived local families. Originally Palk's Buildings, they had been erected in the middle of the nineteenth century by the mining entrepreneur Captain John Palk. The 1891 census recorded that there were sixteen numbered dwellings housing eighteen different households, and that the number of residents was sixty-six. The whole complex consisted of dwellings in cramped conditions, with only the most basic of facilities. Here William John Simmons was born on 18 June 1886.

One of the difficulties in tracing a family with a name like Simmons is that the name can be spelt in a number of ways. There is a tendency for 'i's and 'y's to slip in and out, for a 'd' to appear and then vanish, and for the number of 'm's to be random. Such variations of usage, which have been largely ironed out in the last two or three generations, were common in the nineteenth century, in the mouths and on the pens, not only of registrars, recorders, and reporters, but of members of the families themselves. Thus it was that when the birth of the boy known to us as William Simmons was registered on 27 July 1886, the name of the mother was recorded as Annie Symons.

Annie entered her occupation as chambermaid. The space for the father's name was left blank. William was illegitimate. Annie Simmons was born in the Tavistock Workhouse in October 1853, the eldest of four illegitimate children born to Maria, the daughter of Robert Simmons of Lumburn. John, Annie's younger brother, arrived four years later. Sarah Jane, who came next, died in infancy, to be followed by Sarah Ann. In 1874 Maria, now in her mid forties, and with her two elder children grown up and working, married fellow Lumburnian James Henry Coombe, widower, journeyman miller, and now in his sixties. The middle aged couple had two children, Henry and Elizabeth, before James Henry died at eighty. The 1891 census, coming eleven years after James Henry's death, found his widow Maria living in Paull's Buildings with her younger children, Henry and Elizabeth, and also looking after her four year old grandson, Annie's son William. Annie had died during her son's infancy. Maria had immediately taken responsibility for the parentless infant, and had brought him up in her Paull's Buildings home. He was still living there in 1901, when the census recorded him, at the age of fourteen, with his seventy-nine year old grandmother, and working as an errand boy.

Maria's younger son, Henry Coombe, married, in 1899, Mary Lang, the son of John Lang, a labourer, and it was this couple, Henry and Mary who as 'H and M Coombe' featured prominently in William's later years. Following the death of his grandmother, who had been his surrogate mother, William saw his Uncle Henry's home at 38 Exeter Street as his remaining base in his home town. When he died, a death notice appeared in the *Tavistock Gazette* that described him simply as 'William John, the dearly beloved nephew of H and M Coombe'. The significance lay, not so much in the establishment of Henry and Mary as next-of-kin, but in the way in which Annie had paid her penance. She had been written out of her sailor son's obituary.

On 15 April 1904 William John Simmons appeared at Devonport to enlist. The pretence that it was his eighteenth birthday (he was in fact two months short of that landmark) was almost certainly shared with the enlisting officer. He was described at the time as 5′ 5″ in height, with brown hair, blue eyes, and a fresh compexion. In 1910, halfway through the period of service for which he had enlisted, which was the normal twelve year commitment, he became an Able Seaman. In 1912 he began his service aboard 'Monmouth'.

The Devonport-based cruiser 'Monmouth', on which both Simmons and his fellow Tavistockian Percy Adams found themselves sailing the waters of the South Atlantic in October 1914, was a somewhat ageing ship, which received a battering from German cruisers lying in wait for it at the entrance to the Chilean harbour of Coronel. Its efforts to escape were thwarted by the German cruiser 'Nurnberg', which maintained such an effective fire that the 'Monmouth' finally capsized. Only four of the 900 crew survived. The twenty-eight year old able seaman, No. 2246898, went down, along with Percy Adams from Tavistock and Chief Petty Officer Fay from Mary Tavy. They are commemorated on the Plymouth Naval Memorial. That fine monument lists the names of 672 casualties of the 'Monmouth'. Others of their shipmates are honoured on the two other national naval memorials, at Chatham and Portsmouth.

The Battle of Coronel may not be as well remembered as some of the land battles of the war. It did, however, at the time, affect opinion at home in a very significant way. British naval supremacy had been unchallenged for a century, and the feeling had persisted that this was an enduring condition. The bodies of 1600 British sailors at the bottom of the Pacific provided some kind of antidote to such complacency.

GEORGE TYRRELL
Died Thursday 24 December 1914. Aged 31.

Panel on Menin Gate Memorial with commemoration for G.H. Tyrrell

'Tyrrell' is another example of a name that has been spelt in various ways, at different times, and by different people including family members, resulting in some confusion about the details of family history and relationships. In the case of George Henry Tyrrell there are added complications.

In 1887 a George Tyrrell married an Emily Metters. They lived at 27 Exeter Street, with Emily's seven children, who were to be described in the 1891 census as stepchildren of George. They were called Metters. George Henry was the fifth of these. Register Office records confirm the birth on 29 September 1883, in the Tavistock Workhouse, of a son, George Henry, to Emily Metters. It is, of course, possible that his mother's new husband was his father. Indeed, it is conceivable that George senior fathered all seven.

Emily had been born at Grenofen, the youngest child of a miner called William Metters and his wife Louisa, nee Brown. When her father died at their home in Paull's Buildings, Emily was sixteen, and was carrying her first child. She continued to live there with her widowed mother for the next ten years, during which time she had five illegitimate children, all born in the Workhouse Infirmary. Two more were subsequently born in Exeter Street after Emily, earning money as a charwoman, moved her family there. A few doors along lived George Tyrrell. He had been born in Plymouth, but his parents, Samuel and Elizabeth, had moved to Tavistock, where his father had become a well-known figure as newsagent, bill poster, and town crier. In February 1887 George and Emily were married. Seven more children appeared over the next twelve years, bringing Emily's final tally to fourteen. By the time it came to registering the last one in 1899, George senior was no longer being listed with a civilian occupation, but was entered as 'Private in the

3rd Battalion, Devonshire Regiment'. There were now seven Tyrrells, and seven Metterses, reduced to six by an early death. The latter adopted, at an early stage, the majority name. The problem of why the George Tyrrell of the Devonshire Regiment who was killed on Christmas Eve 1914 appears to have no birth record is, therefore, solved. He was the George Metters who first saw the light of day through the workhouse window in 1883.

By 1914 the family had moved from Exeter Street to Taylor Square. But by that date young George had fled the nest. As a teenager he had worked as a groom, after which he had served in the army, in his own county regiment. While still in uniform he had married, in 1908, Annie Crook, the daughter of a labourer from Milehouse in Plymouth. By 1914 they had settled in Tamerton Foliot with their three children. But the army had not finished with him, and, as a reservist, he was called up when war was declared. A condition of military service, which had been instituted by the Cardwell reforms of the 1870s, was the acceptance of a fixed spell of duty in the reserve following a period of service in the colours. On the first day of the war he re-enlisted at Tavistock as a Private, No. 7533, in the 1st Battalion of the Devons. He was soon to find himself at Ypres.

The Belgian town of Ypres became a key objective for the German armies in the first weeks of the war, and remained so throughout the conflict. British determination to resist was related to the need to protect the nearby channel ports. The front line at this point left the British holding a salient which was under constant threat from three sides. Here, in the place they called 'Wipers', British Tommies were to die in their hundreds of thousands, in campaigns featuring three major battles and an unceasing period of attritional warfare. The gains achieved by the huge sacrifices on both sides could be measured in yards rather than miles. The stalemate that developed along the western front provides a stark contrast with the spirit of optimism which the first British troops showed when they arrived in France in August 1914. Private George Henry Tyrrell probably shared with his mates, as well as with public opinion at home, the belief that it would all be over by Christmas. Sadly, for George himself, it was to be so.

When, on 22 November 1914, the fierce fighting of the First Battle of Ypres gave way to the steady slaughter of trench warfare, the British Expeditionary Force had already suffered 50% casualties. The 1st Battalion of the Devonshires was at this point given responsibility for a section of the front line. In the six weeks that followed, it lost about 100 men. One of them was Private Tyrrell, who died at Neuve Eglise on Christmas Eve. The news, it was said, reached father George on a postcard from his youngest son, Henry, who was also serving at the front with the 1st Battalion. Henry survived the war, as did the only other brother John, who was wounded in the Palestine campaign. The parents both died in their sixties in the early 1920s. George Henry himself is commemorated on the Menin Gate Memorial at Ypres.

SAMUEL TUCKER
Died Wednesday 13 January 1915. Aged 22.

Foresters' War Memorial, Tavistock

Official reports and sober obituaries called him Samuel. Everyone knew him as Sam. On the War Memorial he is initialled 'SA'. In fact he was baptised as Alexander Samuel, taking his first name from his paternal grandfather, a blacksmith who had lived in Exeter Street. It appears that filial, or grandfilial, duty having been done, no more was heard of the name 'Alexander', and the young man remained, throughout his short life, Sam.

He was born on 12 January 1893, at the family home, 40 Bannawell Street, one of those houses in the terrace at the top of the street that faced the workhouse and enjoyed the enigmatic name 'Gold Diggings'. His father, John Thomas Sambles Tucker, a saddler and harness maker, had married his mother, Mary Jane Dodd of 44 Exeter Street, in 1879. John had been born in Tavistock in 1852, the eldest son of a blacksmith, Alexander Tucker, and his wife Mary Ann. Mary Jane was two years younger than her husband, and had been born in Peter Tavy, the daughter of a labourer called Samuel and his wife Elizabeth nee Gloyne. When he married Mary, John had a secure job with John Davy Williams, whose saddlery and harness making business was in West Street. Following a pattern that was still quite commonly followed well into the twentieth century, John was with the same employer for more than half a century. When he died, in 1923, it was pointed out that fifty-two of his seventy-one years had been spent working in the same place.

Married in 1879, John and Mary started a family in 1880, when Ellen came along, to be followed at regular intervals by John, William, May, Ernest, and finally Alexander Samuel. Sam's arrival provided his parents with the stimulus to catch up on a backlog of christenings. The last four were all baptised on 15 May 1893.

Although they had been married at the Register Office, John and Mary arranged for their children to be baptised in the Parish Church, and to be enrolled at the Church School in Dolvin Road. Samuel, in what was probably his final year at the school, in 1906, received special mention for his performance in the annual Religious Instruction Examination. That apart, little is known of his life in Tavistock before the outbreak of war.

The Territorial Army was established in 1908 as part of a programme of fundamental military reforms carried through by Lord Haldane, the Secretary of War. It was a volunteer support force, replacing the old militia and volunteer organisations. Its members were part-time soldiers, who maintained a level of preparedness that made them ready for immediate mobilisation in the case of an emergency. One of the units of this new county-based organisation was the Third Devonshire Battery, Fourth Wessex Brigade, Royal Field Artillery. On 4 August 1914 the strength of this Battery, housed at the Crelake Barracks, was low, but within days the full establishment target of five officers and 140 men had been reached. One of the new recruits was Samuel Tucker. On 15 August, to the accompaniment of the cheers of a large crowd of well-wishers, the Battery left for Salisbury Plain. After some weeks of training the unit was divided into two, the men having been required to opt for either home or foreign service. On 9 October those going abroad left for India. Those who had chosen home service, including Samuel, had, as one of their responsibilities, the care of the horses that the Battery had brought with them. Their unit was soon after transferred to Slough, which was where Gunner Tucker found himself in January 1915. On the 15th, the *Tavistock Gazette* carried the following report:

> Much sympathy will be felt with Mr and Mrs John Tucker of 40 Bannawell Street, Tavistock, on the death by accident of their youngest son Gunner Samuel Tucker of the Tavistock Battery, which is stationed at Slough. On Monday they received a letter from him stating that he was in splendid health. The same day he was kicked by a horse. He was removed to the hospital and operated upon by a specialist from London, but the case was hopeless from the start, and he died at 5 a.m. on Wednesday.

The day that he lay in hospital, between the accident and his death, was his twenty-second birthday.

John and Mary had the body of their youngest son brought back to Tavistock, and it was laid to rest in the Plymouth Road Cemetery. A further commemoration came through his membership of the Ancient Order of Foresters. The local Court of this nationwide Friendly Society designed their own memorial, on which Samuel's name features, and unveiled it in February 1921. For some time it hung in the Town Hall, but was later moved to the Magistrates' Room in the Guildhall, which the Court used for its meetings. It is now in the custody of the area branch office of the Order.

After Sam's death his brother, Ernest, who was a driver in the same battery, remained in the service. Another brother, William, though far away in Canada, was also wondering whether he ought to respond to the call. For John and Mary the agony was far from over.

HENRY PERKIN
Died Friday 25 April 1915. Aged 35.

Henry Ernest Perkin

Six of the names on the Tavistock Memorial are of men who fought, not in the British, but in the Canadian forces. Alfred Coombe, Reginald Kerswill, Henry Perkin, John Sargent, Francis Skinner, and William Tucker, had all been born in or near Tavistock between the years 1878 and 1895. They had all emigrated to Canada in the years before the war, when depressions in mining and in agriculture tore the heart out of the local economy. When war came they, like thousands of others, volunteered in their adopted land for active service in Europe. The first of the six to die, in April 1915, was Henry Ernest Perkin.

Henry Perkin had been practising his profession as a surveyor in Quebec Province for some years before the outbreak of war. He enlisted at Valcartier on 23 September 1914. Among the miscellaneous information that the army authorities recorded about him at the time were the facts that he was single, was 5' 9" tall, was a member of the Church of England, and carried scars on knee and buttocks. He joined the 8th Battalion of the 90th Winnipeg Rifles, and travelled to England with them in February 1915.

The first volunteers for the Canadian Expeditionary Force had begun to assemble within days of the outbreak of war. The first recruits reached Britain in mid October. By February 1915 the 1st Canadian Division under General Alderson was ready for duty on the Western Front. It immediately distinguished itself by playing a key defensive role in the Second Battle of Ypres in April. For Henry Perkin, and for thousands of his compatriots, this battle was the first experience of armed conflict in the raw. For many it was the prelude to a brutal, pitiful, and painfully prolonged drama. For Henry it was prologue and epilogue rolled into one. On 25 April, at a spot known as Hill 60, he was shot through the head. A relative wrote to Henry's old school, Kelly College, to tell them that 'he died, as many others have done, in saving his comrades, though wounded himself'. And Christopher Postlethwaite, a Brentor doctor, told the bereaved father of a conversation that he had had with a wounded soldier: 'He told me of the wonderful bravery of one of the Canadians, who ought to have been awarded the VC. He was wounded, but still went on trying to save the lives of his comrades'. The name of the hero was said to be Henry Perkin.

The name of Henry Perkin is one of the 54,896 inscribed on the Menin Gate Memorial at Ypres, that impressively moving combination of arch and tunnel under which buglers to this day pay their nightly tribute to the dead. At home he is commemorated also on the monument that stands in front of the church at Gulworthy, where he was baptised back in February 1880, and near the spot where the family plot holds the remains of his father, mother, brother, and sister. Inside the church, a plaque on the south wall records, under the insignia of maple leaf and crown, that 'Henry Ernest Perkin, son of Henry Rundle Perkin of this parish, was killed in action at Ypres, 25th April 1915, whilst serving with the 90th Winnipeg Rifles C.E.F.'

The Perkins were a well-known Gulworthy farming family. Henry's father, Henry Rundle Perkin, inherited a 500 acre farm from his father Robert. He then further strengthened the family's fortunes, and its social standing, as a result of a marriage to Annie Ward, the daughter of Daniel Ward, a prosperous Milton Abbot farmer and land surveyor, in 1876. By 1891 there were six children, aged between four and thirteen. A cook and a housemaid lived in. The two eldest children died in their teens, leaving Henry, who had been born on 14 January 1880, as the eldest surviving child. He attended Kelly College, as a day boy, from 1890 to 1896, and was the first of four Old Boys of that school to die in the war and be commemorated on the parish memorial. The school has its own memorial tablet in the college chapel, which contains, among more than fifty names, those of the four local Old Kelleians who fell, Henry Perkin, Christopher Hoskyns-Abrahall, Max Teglio, and Edward Skinner. There is also, in the grounds of the school, a large granite cross, with a plinth bearing the inscription 'In proud and loving memory of our glorious dead'.

Henry's sadly fore-shortened military career contrasted sharply with that of his brother Dan Ward Perkin, who was one year his junior. For some time their lives seemed to run in parallel, both moving on from Kelly to be articled to a surveyor, and then both seeing their future in the colonies, Henry emigrating to Canada in 1900 and Dan re-settling in South Africa soon afterwards. But then came the war. Henry died in the mud of Flanders. Dan enlisted in the Yeomanry, saw service in Mesopotamia, was mentioned in dispatches, rose to the rank of captain, and was demobilised in 1920. This was much to the relief of his father and mother. Henry Rundle lived on to 1924 and died at the age of seventy-two. Annie was well into her nineties when she died in 1944.

CHRISTOPHER HOSKYNS-ABRAHALL Sr
Died Tuesday 4 May 1915. Aged 43.

Hoskyns-Abrahall family grave in Plymouth Road Cemetery

In Tavistock's Plymouth Road Cemetery there is a plot for the Hoskyns-Abrahall family. Commemorated here is Christopher Henry, a major in the Royal Marine Light Infantry, who had been born on 23 July 1871 and who, on 4 May 1915, at the age of forty-three, died of wounds received in the Dardanelles Campaign. His father James and his mother Ellen are both buried here. So is his wife, Alice, who died in 1904 at the age of twenty-three. And so also are two of his three children. Ellen, the only daughter, died in 1926, aged twenty-four, while Christopher, the second son, was killed in 1917 at the age of eighteen, so providing the story of Tavistock in the First World War with its only father and son victims. Of the immediate family, it seems that only the eldest son, James, has been omitted. He lies in faraway Australia.

The Hoskyns-Abrahall family first appeared on the Tavistock scene in the 1890s, when father James, at the end of a career in the War Office, retired to a house in West Street called Stepton. He then bought Rosebank, on Butcher Park Hill, later to be re-named Quarry House, where he died in 1913 at the age of eighty-three. His wife Ellen died four years later at the age of eighty-two, having moved, on James's death, to more modest accommodation on Spring Hill. Meanwhile John, their elder son, a retired army officer, had installed himself at Malvern Villa on Watts Road, and this house became the 'family seat'.

Christopher was the younger son of James and Ellen. He was born in the Bayswater district of London in 1871, and followed his brother John into a military career. In 1890 he was commissioned as a regular officer in the Royal Marines, and in the same year he saw his first action when he landed in East Africa to take part in a punitive expedition against the Sultan of Vitu. Serving in the Marme Battalion of the Naval Brigade, he participated in an exercise to assert British control over a strip of coastal territory. His conduct, in what was a typical Victorian punitive expedition, during the period when Africa was partitioned between the European powers, earned him the Vitu Medal with Clasp. For the next twenty-three years his career unfolded as he gained promotion, ultimately to the rank of major in 1910. His service afloat during that period included periods on three battleships, five cruisers, and a frigate. The 1901 census provided a snapshot of him living at Gillingham in Kent with his twenty-one year old wife and two year old son. But the course was not an even one. In 1898 a promotion was cancelled following a case of drunkenness. In 1904 his wife Alice, whom he had married in 1897, died at the age of twenty-three. In 1906 his Commanding Officer wrote that he had 'had occasion to caution him not to give way to habits of intemperance'. There were occasional difficulties in the payment of mess bills. This was one side of the man. Of his courage, tenacity, and sense of duty, there was nothing but the highest praise.

In September 1913, when he was forty-two, Major Hoskyns-Abrahall was, at his own request, placed on the retired list. Appointed to the Officers' Reserve, with a pension of £250 per annum (half of which, in a characteristic decision, he commuted for a lump sum of £1677) he carried out his wish to retire to Australia, to live with his elder son James. It proved to be a short retirement. Within a year the war came and he was recalled to service. In January 1915 he was appointed second-in-command of the Portsmouth Battalion of the Royal Marine Brigade. The Battalion was soon to see action in the Gallipoli Campaign. This was an imaginative attempt to alter the military balance resulting from the stalemate into which the Western Front had degenerated. The idea, the brainchild of Winston Churchill, was to force a passage through the Dardanelles, to secure Turkey's withdrawal from the war, and to thereby effect a transformation of the balance of forces on both land and sea. The aims were not achieved and the casualties were heavy. The first landings, on 25 April, managed to establish two beachheads, but the resistance was fierce and sustained. The Portsmouth Battalion operated on one of these, the Anzac Front, in support of hard-pressed Australian and New Zealand Divisions. On 3 May, after occupying trenches there, the Battalion went into action as part of a major attack on the Turkish lines on the high ground known as Baby 700. Severely wounded by machine gun fire, Major Hoskyns-Abrahall died the next day of his wounds. It was an end of which, perhaps, he might have been proud: struck down in an act of derring-do far from home, making a defiant and brave gesture as he gambled for the last time. He is commemorated on the Portsmouth Naval Memorial, but, strangely, has no known grave.

Christopher passed on to both his sons the qualities of courage and boldness that had characterised his career. His younger son and namesake lost his life in 1917 as a pioneer airman. James, the elder son, served in the Australian Expeditionary Force, received the Military Medal, was severely wounded, but survived.

EDWARD COLES
Died Thursday 13 May 1915. Aged 30.

Plymouth Naval Memorial

Tavistock's relationship with the sea has been a factor in her development from the time of Drake to the present day. Every generation has given something to this relationship, whether in peace or war. As regards the World Wars, there is no more telling source of confirmation for this claim than the strikingly impressive Naval War Memorial on Plymouth Hoe. Unveiled in 1924, it commemorates, along with similar monuments at Portsmouth and Chatham, 'the names of those officers and men of the navies of the Empire' who had died during the Great War, and who 'have no other grave than the sea'. Among the names are thirteen that feature also on the Tavistock Memorial. Percy Adams and William Simmons died at Coronel, and Cecil Merrifield, Robert Wilson, and John Yard at Jutland. Edward Coles, Albert Hodgins, and Sidney Bassett went down aboard the 'Goliath' in the Dardanelles Campaign. The others were lost in various engagements in the North Sea. A further two names, William Gould and Christopher Hoskyns-Abrahall Senior, appear on the sister-monument at Portsmouth.

Edward Coles was not born in Tavistock. The town's Memorial honours adopted sons as well as natives. In Edward's case the connection was formed through marriage. He was born in the village of Asney Overton in the County of Flint, close to the English border, on 20 February 1885. His father, also Edward, was a gamekeeper. His mother was Mary Elizabeth, and her maiden name was Davies. The 1901 census found father, mother, and son, living on the Hardwick Estate, near Ellesmere in Shropshire, where Edward senior worked. Young Edward was then working as a gunsmith's apprentice. On 22 January 1904, four weeks short of his nineteenth birthday, he enlisted in the Royal Marine Light Infantry. He was at the time living in London, where he had been working for about a year for a surgical instrument maker in Seaton Street. After enlistment, which was for the statutory twelve year period, he remained at the London Depot for some months before tranferring to the Plymouth Division in October 1904. Thereafter, Plymouth remained his base through the remainder of his marine career, and his life. He was described, on his arrival at the Stonehouse Barracks, as 5′ 8″ tall, with a dark complexion, black hair, and brown eyes. Over the years he served on a number of ships. At some point Edward met, and subsequently married, a Tavistock girl called Mabel Mary. This is the probable circumstance that led to his facing, between 1908 and 1912, five charges of either desertion or going absent without leave.

Edward and Mabel set up home in Tavistock, at 40 Westbridge Cottages. Mabel was still living in the same house in 1927. It appears that at some point Edward's widowed mother moved to Tavistock, presumably to be close to her daughter-in-law. This would provide an explanation of the fact that, in August 1942, Mr W.H.F. Soper registered the death of his grandmother Mary Elizabeth Coles, at the age of seventy-nine. Mrs Coles, described as the widow of Edward Coles, a gamekeeper, had died at the Gardener's Cottage at Mount Tavy, where she and her grandson both lived. Her grave, in the Plymouth Road Cemetery, bears an inscription describing her as 'the beloved wife of Edward Coles'.

Private Edward Nelson Coles, Ply/12418, R.M.L.I., was aboard H.M.S. 'Goliath' when he was killed in an action with a Turkish Destroyer on 13 May 1915. Albert Hodgins, was a Royal Naval Petty Officer aboard the same ship, and suffered the same fate. So did Cook's Mate Sidney Bassett. 'Goliath' was a battleship of 12,950 tons, belonging to the Third Fleet. Built at Chatham in 1898 at a cost of £866,000, she was one of the first five of a new class of 'Canopy' battleships to be built. According to A.A. Hoehling, she was, by 1915, an old lady, and little more than 'a creaking contrivance of bolts and museum-piece weapons', when she 'waddled off' to give any support that she could to the Gallipoli landings. In the Spring of that year she took part in a combined military and naval operation in the Eastern Mediterranean which, if it had succeeded, would have forced a passage through the Dardanelles Straits, and compelled the Turks to withdraw from the war. On 12 May 1915 she had been bombarding Turkish positions on Cape Helles, a strategically important spot on the tip of the Gallipoli peninsular, where some of the initial landings by British and ANZAC (Australian and New Zealand Army Corps) forces had taken place in recent days, and where there had been some of the most bitter, if inconclusive, fighting. During this period, immediately following the landings, naval operations in the area were concerned with supply and transport duties, and with giving ground troops any artillery support that was possible. On the night of the 12th 'Goliath' anchored in Morto Bay, a rather exposed anchorage. The joint German and Turkish command, alarmed at the damage that the British ship was inflicting, ordered the Turkish Destroyer 'Muavemet' from the Dardanelles to find her. The search was successful. 'Goliath' was torpedoed. There were 570 casualties and 180 survivors. None of the Tavistock men aboard were among the lucky ones. Their names are among 395 casualties of 'Goliath' who are honoured at Plymouth. Others are commemorated at Portsmouth and Chatham.

ALBERT HODGINS
Died Thursday 13 May 1915. Aged 38.

The Abbey Chapel, Tavistock

Three men whose names are on the Tavistock Memorial were among the 570 who went down with H.M.S. 'Goliath' following an engagement with a Turkish destroyer in the Eastern Mediterranean on 13 May 1915. Edward Coles, a Royal Marine whose home was at Westbridge, was one of them. Albert Hodgins, who came from the other end of town, was another. It is not clear whether the two men knew each other before they found themselves fellow shipmates aboard the 'Goliath'. Neither of them had been born in Tavistock: Edward was a Shropshire lad while Albert was probably born in Madras in India. In both cases their careers in the services had brought them to Devon, where they each met, and married, a Tavistock girl. Having settled in the town, they both became adopted sons of Tavistock. Whether their paths had crossed on occasions during their Tavistock days, there can be little doubt that tales of home and mutual acquaintances would have helped to fill any spare time they might have had in those last days as their ship went about its task of bombarding positions on the Turkish coast, in support of the Gallipoli landings. The 'Goliath' fell a victim to a torpedo attack after a Turkish destroyer had located her seeking shelter in Morto Bay.

Born on 9 December 1876, probably in India during his father's spell of service in the army there, Albert Hodgins enlisted at Devonport on his eighteenth birthday. He was described at the time as being 5' 4" high with brown hair and grey eyes, as having previously worked as a labourer, and as featuring three scars on his forehead and tattoos of a sailor and a woman on his forearm. He was the son of James Hodgins, a labourer and former soldier. Rising through the ranks, Albert emerged from his twelve year period of service as a Stoker First Class, No.

173928, with the experience of service on eighteen ships or shore establishments. Re-enlisting at Devonport in 1906, he clocked up a further eight years of peacetime service before finding himself, when war broke out, aboard 'Goliath'.

On 30 January 1905, at the Abbey Chapel, the oldest place of nonconformist worship in the town, and, at that time, the home of the Unitarian Church in Tavistock, Albert married Mary Ellen Down, aged twenty-one. Mary Ellen had been born at 72 West Street on 29 January 1884, the daughter of James Down, then a general labourer, and his wife Esther. Esther had been born in Whitchurch in 1847, the daughter of a labourer called Justham. At the age of nineteen she married a farm labourer called John Down. John died, at the age of thirty-three, 'from injuries accidentally received'. Esther was left a young widow with five children. In 1883 she re-married. Her second husband, called James Down, had been born in 1849, and was probably John's brother. James was the father, and Esther the mother, of Mary Ellen Down, the new Mrs Hodgins.

At the time of her marriage to Albert, Mary Ellen lived at 38 Brook Street. Her new husband had on a number of occasions lodged there when on leave. In 1901 it comprised a household of fourteen people, of whom five were lodgers. The address was a well-known one. It housed a popular cafe, run by Mary Ellen's father. James Down was an enterprising man who had started in business in the 1880s, when he was described as an 'eating house keeper'. From his original premises in Market Street, he moved, in the early nineties, to a new emporium in Brook Street. For the next twenty-five years or so James ran this coffee house with help from his daughter. Eventually Mary Ellen took it over, re-designated it as 'refreshment rooms', and operated it through to the late 1920s, when she sold out to a Gilbert White, who converted the premises to a general store. Mary Ellen died in November 1936. She had been a widow for twenty-one of her fifty-two years.

Albert and Mary Ellen had three children. William Albert was born in 1907, Esther Elizabeth in 1910, and Reginald James in 1912. They were all born at 37 Brook Street, next door to the shop, and, for a time, when the children were small, the family continued to live there. The children were, respectively, eight, four, and two when their father died. Their grief and loss must have been tempered by the fact that he had been away from them for most of their lives. Their grandmother, who shared the home with them, was to play a positive part in their upbringing. This was particularly so since she now shared No. 38 with them. She and Mary Ellen could provide mutual support, both emotionally, and practically, in terms of both looking after the children and running the business.

Most of the casualties of World War One were young men who were unmarried and childless. They did not have that particular form of immortality that is expressed through having children. Albert would no doubt think that his most cherished memorial was not the inclusion of his name on the Plymouth Naval Monument, gratifying as that was, but the perpetuation of the family, passing such milestones in the 1930s as William marrying Florence Mulvihill and Esther becoming Mrs John Craze.

SIDNEY BASSETT
Died Thursday 13 May 1915. Aged 19.

Tavistock War Memorial west face

On 4 January 1918 the *Tavistock Gazette* reported, briefly, the death of a Private S. Bassett of Tavistock. He was said to have been in the East Surrey Regiment, and to have died of wounds. R. Richardson, in his book 'Through Peace to War' reproduced this information, though without date. The Devon County Roll of Honour's entry is identical. The Commonwealth War Graves Commission, when first consulted, gave 13727 Private S Bassett as belonging to the 2nd Battalion, the East Surrey Regiment, with a date of death as 4 January 1918 and a burial place as the Masnieres British Cemetery at Marcoing. An immediate doubt arose in that this particular cemetery was not opened until October 1918, and the Commission states that all burials within it were of casualties incurred in September and October 1918. The 'Soldiers Who Died in the Great War' source has a Samuel Bassett, Regimental Number 13727, as belonging to the 2nd Battalion, Suffolk Regiment, as having been born at West Row, Mildenhall, Suffolk, and as having enlisted at West Row. The date of death is given as 1 October 1918. The most recent enquiry of the CWGC, made in November 2000, has S. Bassett, Lance Corporal, 13727, 2nd Battalion, Suffolk Regiment, as dying on 1 October 1918, and as having been buried at Masnieres. All attempts to provide any kind of link between Lance Corporal Bassett and Tavistock proved abortive.

Searches of records relating to local families have proved equally unproductive. Marriages that appeared to offer a possibility of a son of the appropriate age, such as that between Samuel Bassett and Susan Wakem at Gulworthy in 1885, provided no conclusive leads. St Eustachius Church saw no Bassett weddings between 1861 and 1899, and neither of the censuses in 1891 and 1901 recorded anyone of that name residing in the parish. Searches originating with local families have as yet yielded nothing.

The Commonwealth War Graves Commission lists eighty-seven soldiers named Bassett as having fallen in the Great War. Three have obvious Devon connections: Albert had been born in Littleham and lived in Exmouth, Henry was a Devonport lad, and John came from Torquay. There is no indication with any of the three of either a Tavistock link or a Christian name beginning with S. There are five others who qualify on the latter test, but appear to have no local connections. This is confirmed by the 'Soldiers Died in the Great War' source, which gives us a Samuel, a Spencer, and three Sidneys, coming, respectively, from Suffolk, Kent, Lincolnshire, Hampshire, and Birmingham. Included in this latter group is the Samuel Bassett of the 2nd Suffolks, who was, erroneously as it seems, referred to as a local man by the *Tavistock Gazette*. One can only guess at the circumstances that produced the ten-word notice in that newspaper on 4 January 1918: 'Died of wounds-East Surrey Reg't- Pte S Bassett, Tavistock'. No clarification appeared in subsequent editions.

Who, then, was the S. Bassett, whose name appears on the West Face of the Memorial? For the most likely candidate we must turn to the navy, to an old ship described as 'a creaking contrivance of bolts and museum-piece weapons', and to an engagement that claimed the lives of two other men, Edward Coles and Albert Hodgins, whose names appear on the Monument.

Sidney Bassett was born at 69 Tavistock Road, Devonport, on 16 May 1895. His father George, a coachman who had been born at North Hill, and his mother, Lewannick-born Asenath, had been married in the late 1870s. Sidney was their sixth child. After leaving school he worked for a time as a horseman. On 9 February 1914 he walked down the road and enlisted at the nearby naval recruiting office. He was eighteen years old, 5′ 4″ high, and in good health, with auburn hair, brown eyes, and a fresh complexion. The recruiting officer was impressed by his character references, and noted that he had an elder brother in the service who was a Stoker. Sidney entered the navy as a Second Cook's Mate. This was the lowest rung of the appropriate ladder, and attracted a weekly wage of 1/8 (8p). A year later, following twelve months service, having passed 'the requisite examination' (where a good knowledge of bread-making was particularly tested), and having given further evidence of his 'very good character', he was promoted to the rank of Cook's Mate, and was given a pay rise, bringing the daily rate up to 2/- (10p).

War broke out within six months of the beginning of Sidney's projected twelve years of service. His first major wartime assignment was aboard H.M.S. 'Goliath', an ageing battleship which, in the early Summer of 1915, was assigned to the Eastern Mediterranean. Its principal duties related to the Gallipoli Campaign, and to the support of the landings being made there by British and colonial troops. On 13 May a Turkish Destroyer found 'Goliath' in a rather exposed anchorage, and the limping old lady was torpedoed. Three men whose names appear on the Tavistock Monument, including Cook's Mate M/7259 Sidney Bassett, went down with her.

Sidney's name appears on the Plymouth Naval Memorial. The link with Tavistock, which would explain its appearance on the Tavistock Memorial, has yet to be established.

DINGLE MARTIN
Died Monday 16 August 1915. Aged 21.

The Madras War Cemetery, shown here, contains a memorial wall which includes the name of W.D. Martin among those 'honoured here but buried elsewhere in India'

It was natural that during the First World War the folk of Tavistock should feel particular pride in the activities of that group of home-grown lads who belonged to what was known locally as simply The Battery. This volunteer force of part-time soldiers had been formed under the terms of the 1908 Army Reforms, which had included the establishment of the Territorial Army. Its full title was the Third Devonshire Battery (Tavistock), Fourth Wessex Brigade, of the Royal Field Artillery (Territorial Force). On the day that war was declared the unit mobilised at its headquarters, the barracks that had been recently built on the old mine site at Crelake. A rapid recruitment operation in the next few days brought its strength up to the 145 which was the establishment target. There followed some weeks of training on Salisbury Plain before the numbers were divided into two on the basis of individual choice of either home or foreign service. Additional recruits from home during this period brought the foreign service element up to 145, and, on 9 October, aboard the Union Castle liner 'Alnwick Castle', this unit sailed from Southampton for India. The destination was Barrackpore, a few miles from Calcutta in the province of Bengal. The journey took thirty-seven days.

The Tavistock Battery formed one element of a force of Wessex Divisional Troops, some 12,000 strong, who made the voyage to India at that early stage of the war. They were sent to contribute to the defence of the frontiers of the British Empire in India, a task that the Army had carried out throughout the nineteenth century. They could also release battle-hardened troops for redeployment in

Europe. It was not until the new arrivals reached Barrackpore that news was received of the entry of Turkey into the war. This development opened up the possibility of using some of the India-based troops in a new theatre of war, against the Ottoman Empire. Such possibilities did not materialise in the case of Driver Wesley Martin. He experienced the settling-in period, following the arrival at Barrackpore on 14 November, and took part in the New Year's Day Parade in Calcutta. In January, along with the rest of the Battery, he undertook a two months' training period, 500 miles away to the west. Back in Barrackpore the hot season arrived, and with it the humidity of the Bengali monsoon period, relieved, for the British troops, only by short recuperative visits to Darjeeling, up in the hills. On 13 August Mrs Martin received a letter from her son saying that he was in the best of health. The following week she heard that he had died of malarial fever. Three months later she received a photograph of his inscribed headstone. He had been buried in Barrackpore New Cemetery.

Born on 5 December 1893, Dingle Wesley Martin (he preferred to use his second name, but accepted the nickname Dinnie that had attached to him since his schooldays) was the son of Thomas Dingle Martin, a mine labourer, and Bessie nee Willis, a domestic nurse. Thomas, from Morwellham, and Bessie, from Gunnislake, had been married at Tavistock Wesleyan Church in 1890. They settled first in Gunnislake and then in Morwellham, where they brought up four children. Wesley was the third. The name 'Dingle' was passed on to him from his father. Thomas had inherited it from his mother, whose maiden name it was. The Martins were Methodists, as their decisions to wed in the Wesleyan Church and to give their second son the name Wesley, would confirm. They appear, however, to have experienced a change of allegiance. Young Dingle, or Wesley, was, at the age of four, baptised in the Parish Church. He then became a pupil at the Church of England School on Dolvin Road. His father, Thomas, died in March 1903 at the age of thirty-nine. He was killed in a mining accident. At the inquest the coroner returned a verdict of death caused 'by injury through the neglect of another'. Bessie was left with four young children. Soon after that the family moved into Tavistock, to re-settle at No. 9 Dolvin Road.

After leaving the Dolvin Road School, Wesley was employed as a driver by Messrs Truscott and Sons and by J. Backwell, both of whom were pioneer motor car dealers and organisers of excursions and taxi services in and around the town. When he joined the Tavistock Battery his skill as a driver was of particular value to the unit, and this proficiency and experience he took with him into a war career that began for him at the age of twenty and ended in a distant cemetery nine months later.

The oldest brother in the family was Theodore, and he also was a casualty of the war. He was born one year before Wesley and died one year after him. The two brothers had shared much in their early lives: an upbringing in a small community, the same school, similar employment, involvement in the local Battery, the experience of going to war. Ultimately, they shared a similar fate. They were survived by a brother and sister, Thomas and Ivy, and by their mother. Bessie, after forty-three years of widowhood, died at 18 Chapel Street, Tavistock, on 15 August 1946.

J. TRICK
Died Saturday 18 September 1915 ? Aged ?

He whom this scroll commemorates was numbered among those who, at the call of King and Country, left all that was dear to them, endured hardness, faced danger, and finally passed out of the sight of men by the path of duty and self-sacrifice, giving up their own lives that others might live in freedom. Let those who come after see to it that his name be not forgotten.

Royal Scroll for the Fallen

The name 'Trick' is relatively uncommon. This is true in local, regional, and national contexts. The search for a J. Trick should not, in these circumstances, have proved difficult. He has, however, remained resolutely elusive.

R. Richardson, in his 'Through War to Peace', has, in his list of Tavistock casualties, a Private J.F. Trick, of the 6th Battalion of the Dorsets, being killed in action at Loos on 18 September 1915. The Devon County Roll of Honour, possibly following this lead, has J. Trick dying in France in September 1915. None of the military sources consulted, including the Commonwealth War Graves Commission, provide any supporting evidence for this. There might be some confusion here with T.F. Trick, who was in the 6th Dorsets, and who died on 18 September 1918.

In the apparent absence of evidence from military or naval sources about a J. Trick (the CWGC lists only five Tricks) it was necessary to concentrate attention on family history. The first, and most obvious, line of enquiry was to discover any possible link with Thomas Frederick Trick. No such connection has been established, and the conclusion has been drawn that the two Tricks whose names are on the Monument are probably unrelated.

Searches of the relevant census returns and of records of births and deaths have provided no leads. In studying this documentary evidence, acknowledgment was given to the fact that the initial given on the Memorial may not have corresponded with that of Mr Trick's first Christian Name. This had the effect of widening the search, but not to an appreciable degree. For example, the 1881 census lists, throughout Devon and Cornwall, fourteen Tricks with J as a first initial, and only a further six with a second name beginning with that letter. All forty-four Devon Tricks who feature in the 1901 census were followed up, without profit.

The main avenues of enquiry having proved to be cul-de-sacs, and no information having been gleaned from local sources, there remained two directions in which the search might proceed. Both rested on scenarios which, while uncommon, were not unknown in Edwardian England. The first concerned the possibility of a name-change. The second related to emigration.

In November 1864 at the Tavistock Register Office Sarah Mallett married Samuel Trick. They already shared a son called Jethro. Samuel died soon after, and in December 1868 Sarah married John Cross. Jethro was at that point seven years old. He might have been brought up as either a Trick or a Cross. Either name might have featured if he, or one of his descendants, had fought in the war. Military records do not reveal a J. Cross with the relevant connections. No other appropriate name-change involving the name of Trick has yet come to light.

One of those comparatively rare events, the birth in the area of a child called Trick, occurred in Okehampton in 1900. The child was, moreover, given a first Christian name to match, in terms of rarity, his surname. He was named Irwin John. On 27 August 1918 Private Irvin John Trick, aged nineteen, was killed in action during the final months of combat on the Western Front. He belonged to the 116th Battalion of the Central Ontario Regiment. He had enlisted in the Canadian Army near his home of Oshawa, Ontario, in March 1916, and had arrived in England one year later, and in France one year after that. Described as a core maker by trade, he was 5′ 3″ tall. His father, John, was, at the same time, also in uniform. His mother's name was Emma. If the Canadian chain is to be shown to be the one to lead us to the real Trick, then two further links must be forged, one identifying Irwin John of Okehampton with Irvin John of Ontario, and the other providing a Tavistock connection. No such links have as yet been made.

Two further wildcards might be chased. James Trick was born in the parish of Stoke Damerel in 1886. And the 1901 Census found William and Annie Trick living at Tithington in Whitchurch Parish, but, at that stage at least, childless. In the latter case the appearance of a male heir soon after the census could conceivably have produced a young man old enough to fight and die. With this chain, as with others, there remain too many missing links.

A final possible explanation deserves at least passing attention. No record survives of the precise way in which those who compiled the list for inclusion on the Monument went about their task. Could it be that a mistake was made at the time? This interpretation was examined, and rejected for four reasons. Firstly, it seems inconceivable that the people involved in the administration of the project, in a matter as serious as this, did not go to some lengths to establish the genuineness of each application. Secondly, they were all local people with deep roots in the community and a knowledge of local families. Moreover if a mistake was made in including a name that related to another place, then the name would still appear in military or naval records. And finally, an error is surely less likely with a rare name than it would be if you were dealing with names that are common and might more readily be confused.

ARTHUR GALLIE
Died Thursday 23 September 1915. Aged 53.

Arthur Lockhart Gallie

Down Road, 'the new thoroughfare from the cattle market to the golf house', as it was known before a name could be decided upon, was laid out in the years immediately before the First World War. The first residence to be built on it was a three-storey house with fifteen rooms built of Hurdwick stone and granite and designed by the eminent architect Sir Edwin Lutyens. It was called Littlecourt. Pevsner, in his 'Buildings of England', called attention to its 'symmetrical north elevation with two steep stepped gables and a central pedimented porch', and its 'entrance hall with main staircase leading out of it at right angles through an arch'. A distinctively designed water tower, which speedily acquired the affectionate name 'The Pimple', offered a continuous supply of water from the reservoir beneath. The first occupant of the house was a retired officer, Major Arthur Lockhart Gallie.

Major Gallie came to Tavistock in 1907, living at Far View in Watts Road and then at Buctor Cross. Littlecourt was built for him, and, when it was completed, he happily settled into it with his wife Edith and their daughter Betty. It should have been the start of a long, satisfying retirement in an elegant home next door to the golf course where he spent so many happy hours, and where he served a term as Club Captain. This was not, however, the fate that was in store for him.

The Gallies had been a military family for as long as anyone could remember. Both of Arthur's grandfathers had fought at Waterloo. His father was John Lockhart Gallie of Broughty Ferry in Scotland (or North Britain, as his tomb inscription insists). His mother was Lucy Ellen nee Amos. Arthur was born in Plymouth on 3 September 1862. He was among the first pupils to attend the United Services College at Westward Ho!, which was opened in 1874 to provide an education for the sons of officers. A contemporary at the school was Rudyard Kipling, who was later to describe his time there in his schoolboy tales 'Stalky and Co'. Arthur's father died during that period. The 1881 census found Arthur, at the age of eighteen, living with his widowed mother on Douro Terrace, St Helier, on the island of Jersey. After leaving school he joined the Gordon Highlanders; according to his service records he was commissioned in 1884 into the 1st Battalion. In August of that year he landed in Egypt to take part in the Nile Expedition. This was the extraordinary operation designed to rescue an eccentric British General of Engineers, Charles Gordon, who had disappeared in Khartoum. After a 1,600 mile journey up the river, the relieving force arrived to find that Gordon had died, at the hands of the Mahdi, two days previously. Safely back in Cairo, where he was awarded the Egypt Medal with Clasp, Gallie proceeded to serve for a year in Malta. Then in 1886 he went to India, where he transferred to the Indian Army, joining the Madras Staff Corps and serving with the 7th Regiment Madras Infantry. Retiring from the army in 1891, he re-appeared in the colours during the Boer War. Thereafter he devoted himself for some years to establishing himself in his adopted town. He became a member of the West Devon and the Constitutional Clubs. He enjoyed a variety of sports, particularly golf, but also cricket, billiards, shooting, fishing, and deer stalking. And he worked on his plans for Littlecourt. Meanwhile his wife, Ethel Miriam, whom he had married in East Devon in 1888, during the period of his Indian service, developed her twin interests in supporting the Conservative Party and popularising the game of badminton. She was secretary of both the local branch of the Primrose League, which brought women into some involvement in Conservative politics, and of the Badminton Club. They had one daughter, Betty, who had been born in 1893. An elder daughter, Margaret, died at Brighton in 1903 at the age of thirteen.

The pleasures of retirement and of family life seem to have satisfied the old warhorse for some years, but in 1912, at the age of fifty, he rejoined the army. Perhaps civilian life began to bore him. Perhaps he sensed the approach of conflict. Whatever the cause, he was appointed to a commission in the Dorset Regiment, in the rank of major. Posted to Dorchester, he served on the administrative staff of the Regimental Depot. And there, on Thursday 23 September 1915, at the age of fifty-three, he died following an attack of pneumonia. Brought back to Tavistock, he was given a full military funeral and was buried in the Plymouth Road Cemetery. Ten years after his death a bronze tablet of commemoration was fixed to the wall of the Clothworkers' Aisle in Tavistock Parish Church.

Major Gallie left only two close relatives. His wife, Ethel, outlived him by almost forty years, and died in Chollacott Nursing Home in 1954. His daughter, Betty, married William David, a captain in the RAMC, in 1918. And Littlecourt? Mrs Gallie continued to live there until the mid 1920s, when she sold it and moved to Glanville Road. A family called Higginson bought it. They were still living there in 1947, when, on one June afternoon, a disastrous fire did great damage, removing the top storey.

ALFRED LETHBRIDGE
Died Saturday 25 September 1915. Aged 21.

Bere Alston War Memorial

Five kilometres north-west of the city of Lens, in the French Department of Pas de Calais, lies the village of Loos-en-Gohelle. A cemetery here holds the graves of over 1700 men who fell at the Battle of Loos. It is situated on the site of some of the fiercest fighting of that battle. A memorial, in the form of a fifteen feet high wall, forming two sides of the cemetery, commemorates, on a series of tablets, a further 20,000 or so men who died in that immediate area between the first day of the battle and the end of the war, and who have no known grave. A central apse holds the Cross of Sacrifice, a feature of all such memorials and cemeteries on the Western Front. One of those commemorated here is Alfred Lethbridge. He died, on the first day of the Battle of Loos, Saturday 25 September 1915, eleven days after his twenty-first birthday.

The allies launched two simultaneous attacks on German positions on the Western Front on that September morning. The British assault, at Loos, coincided with a French offensive at Champagne, to the south. Success was to depend on breakthrough being achieved on the first day. Unfortunately for the allies the Germans were, on both fronts, very well prepared. At Loos the defences were so strong that, even where the front line was breached, a strongly fortified second line, protected by machine-gun posts, proved virtually impregnable. In the event, the British contributed to their own failure. The offensive was preceded by a discharge of chlorine gas, which, because of the windless conditions, either hovered in no man's land or drifted down into the British trenches. This slowed an attack that was also held up by heavy machine gun fire. The following afternoon German machine-gunners had a field day. Half of the 15,000 British troops who took part in an infantry attack were mown down. Three further weeks of sporadic fighting brought little territorial or strategic advantage, and as stalemate finally descended on the sector and the Battle of Loos came to an inconclusive end, British casualties in the battle were seen to have been of the order of 41,000, 16,000 of them dead. Robert Graves recorded, in 'Goodbye to All That', his attempt, at the height of the battle, to obtain information. '"What's happened?" I asked. "Bloody balls-up" was the most detailed answer I could get'. The failures at Loos brought about the resignation of Sir John French and his replacement as Commander in Chief by General Sir Douglas Haig.

One of the units that had its baptism in trench warfare at the Battle of Loos was the 8th Battalion of the Devonshires. Private Alfred Lethbridge No. 10389 joined this, the regiment's service battalion, when war broke out. He and his close friend, George Willey, who lived at Weir Quay, enlisted on the same day. They were to be lost on the same day.

The Lethbridge family had roots in mid-Devon, in that area of small communities between Hatherleigh and Torrington. Alfred was born in the parish of Dolton on 14 September 1894. His father, John, a farm labourer, had been born in the same village, and his mother, Elizabeth, came from nearby Huish. Alfred was one of the younger members of a family that consisted of six boys and one girl. His parents were both in their forties when he arrived and his eldest brother was nineteen. When Alfred reached school age his family, for so long settled in one place, began a series of rapid and bewildering moves. Presumably, John became one of the casualties of the farming depression. Many of the kind of village communities in which families like the Lethbridges had lived for generations lost a third of their population within twenty years, as people were forced to migrate and often to become dependent on temporary employment. For the Lethbridges, the first move appears to have been to Dartmoor, since Alfred began his school career at Postbridge, the family being recorded in the 1901 census as living at nearby Pizwell. By the time he had reached the age of seven they were at Orestocks, and Alfred and his brother William had signed up at Gulworthy School. At some point thereafter the family moved to Hocklake, near Bere Alston, and here they were living when the war began, with Alfred, at the age of nineteen, working as an agricultural labourer on the Bere Peninsular.

Like so many of the fallen, Private Lethbridge of the 8th Devons, has no known grave. He is commemorated on the Loos Memorial, which is close to where he fell at Cite St Elie. He is also honoured nearer home, not only on the monument in Tavistock, but on those erected in the parish where he was living when he went to war. There are four such memorials in Bere Alston and Bere Ferrers, one in each village centre and one in each church. Alfred's name appears on each of them. The Devon County Roll of Honour also associates him with Milton Abbot. This arises from the fact that soon after his death his parents continued their wanderings, settling now at Quither Cottage in that parish. John died in December 1935 at the age of eighty-four. Elizabeth pre-deceased him. She was eighty-one when she died in March 1933.

FRANCIS MAKER
Died Monday 27 September 1915. Aged 22.

Part of Attestation Paper for Francis Maker

On 31 March 1916 the following letter, from a Mrs Mitchell at a London address, appeared in the *Tavistock Gazette*:

> It is now six months since my nephew, Private Frank Maker of the 4th Grenadier Guards, was reported missing. He joined the Guards at the outbreak of the war, and went to France with his battalion in August last. He was missing at Loos on 27th September... A comrade, still in action, writes of my nephew as the best chum he ever had. Another, wounded at Loos, said 'We became great friends. He was always cheerful, and made light of all discomforts. I last saw him as we advanced under heavy fire and shell and shrapnel falling, when he turned to me with a smile and said 'It's getting a bit lively'.

These words, recorded by a dutiful and grieving aunt, were probably the last that Francis Maker uttered. He was lost while taking part, on the third day of the Battle of Loos, in a slow, deliberate, infantry advance across open terrain, which was met by unrelenting German machine gun fire. The casualties were horrific, and the gains nil. One German account described 'the barrels becoming red hot and swimming in oil as they traversed to and fro along the enemy's ranks'. A further sentence from Mrs Mitchell's letter conveyed the scene, with its distinctive mixture of heroism and lunacy: 'His captain, in writing of the attack, said it was the proudest moment of his life, when he saw his men 'just as if on parade in Hyde Park'.' It is not easy now to read such words in the same spirit in which they were either offered or received at the time.

He was always known as Frank. When, on enlistment, he signed the oath of allegience, it was as Francis William Maker. The War Memorial has him as simply 'Maker F'. In fact he was William Francis Maker, born on 23 February 1893. A life-long preference for his second name was something he shared with his father, whose names were Alfred John, and who had been listed in the census, two years earlier, as an eighteen year old plumber's apprentice living with his parents at 10 Madge Lane. In the same count Alfred John's wife-to-be had been entered as a seventeen year old milliner called Kate Boon, the daughter of a naval pensioner whose home was at 19 Dolvin Road. The young couple were married soon after that, and William Francis quickly followed. They lived in the Maker family home in Madge Lane, but the baby was born, not unusually, in his maternal grandmother's home in Dolvin Road. The 1901 census recorded him at the age of eight living in Madge Lane with his paternal grandparents. Meanwhile his brother Harold and sister Gladys, respectively three and one, were living with their mother Kate and their maternal grandmother at 19 Dolvin Road. Alfred John's presence was recorded at neither home.

At some point, and for some reason, Alfred John Maker took his young family to live in London. Frank got a job there as a gents' clothier. He also got a wife. Following his father's practice, he married at twenty, his wife being Edith Annie Coombs. The wedding was at St Marylebone Register Office on 9 December 1913. The young couple set up home in Boston Street, Dorset Square. There were no children.

On 19 October 1914 Frank Maker, gents' clothier, became Private F.W. Maker, 19947, 4th Battalion, Grenadier Guards. He was described at the time of his enlistment at the Marylebone recruiting office as 5′ 8″ high, with a fresh complexion, dark brown hair, and grey eyes, one of which had a brown spot in the iris. The first ten months of his service were in England, but on 15 August 1915 he sailed with his battalion for France and the front. The battlefield of Loos awaited him six weeks later.

The Loos Offensive, launched on 25 September, was the northern arm of a two-pronged allied attack against German positions in French territory. Alfred Lethbridge was a victim of the fighting on the first day of the battle. The third day claimed Francis Maker. Like the great majority of the men who fell at Loos, he has no known grave. His name appears among 20,000 on the Loos Memorial, which was erected close to the scene of some of the bitterest fighting. For the family, the pain of his loss was compounded for some time by the agony of uncertainty. Anxiously awaiting news were wife and parents in London, brother Harold, then in uniform, and the widowed grandmother in Madge Lane, old Mrs Maker, as well as a proud and affectionate aunt. Frank died on 27 September 1915. Notification that he was missing arrived on 30 October. It was to be a further nine months before confirmation was received, by the family, that he was dead. They were months in which it was natural, and perhaps necessary, to cling to a hope, albeit one that was receding by the day, that he had been taken prisoner. The hope was finally extinguished. And, as if that wasn't enough, the folk back home were soon to have to brace themselves for a further blow, the news of Harold's death.

JOHN WESTLAKE
Died Wednesday 13 October 1915. Aged 32.

John Luke Westlake

There was, in the first twelve months or so of the war, a spirit abroad which can be described as an impatience, on the part of many young men, to get to the Front. It was as if they were clamouring for the opportunity to display qualities of courage and fortitude, to taste combat and adventure, and to prove their loyalty and their manhood. Nowhere, perhaps, is this spirit better displayed than in the case of John Westlake. In August 1915, as the war entered its second year, he was a sergeant in the 2nd Battalion of the London Scottish, a unit of the Territorial Army's London Regiment. Twelve months of service at home with this battalion had left him feeling that he wanted some experience of the cutting edge of war. So when the regiment appealed for volunteers to join the 1st Battalion and to go over to France, he was among the first to step forward, even though it meant forfeiting his rank. On 18 August he arrived at Rouen. A month later he was fighting at Loos. And it was to be in this theatre of war that he was to die on 13 October.

The life that ended in the combat that he had sought began thirty-two years earlier at Princetown, where John Luke Westlake was born, the second of four children and the only son of a prison officer. His father, Thomas, and his mother, Elizabeth, both hailed from the parish of Bere Ferrers. Thomas was the son of a farmer, John Westlake, and his wife Jane, whose maiden name was Treliving. Elizabeth, a dressmaker, was the daughter of a Bere Alston carpenter, Samuel Knight, who had married a Mary Dunstone.

John started his education at the local elementary school in Princetown, and then, at the age of thirteen, he entered Tavistock Grammar School. The family was Wesleyan, and his father was a local preacher. As a young man John played a leading part in church life. After leaving school he served an apprenticeship as an ironmonger, living with his employer Edwin Williams in Chapel Street, before joining a Dudley-based firm as a traveller. In August 1914, when he enlisted, he was living in Paddington.

John was thirty-one when he became a soldier. Unmarried, he had lost his mother at the age of fourteen. His father was living in reasonably comfortable retirement in Woburn Terrace, Tavistock, after a career as a warder at Dartmoor Prison. There were thus no obvious family considerations that might have restrained him from seeking more active service. Moreover, he clearly enjoyed army life, and the acquisition of three stripes within three months of enlisting testified to his soldierly qualities. In the circumstances, the decision to accept the invitation to cross the channel was, perhaps, an easy one.

Private Westlake distinguished himself on the first occasion on which he saw action, the first day of the Battle of Loos. The company suffered severe losses on that day, but he came through it unscathed, and his assistance in capturing and bringing in some prisoners was rewarded by promotion to the rank of corporal. After the failure of the initial British thrust, the offensive persisted, albeit in sporadic form, resulting in the gain of a narrow salient two miles deep and the loss of 40,000 British dead and wounded. Corporal Westlake was one of these casualties. According to the regimental records: 'He was killed in action on 13 October 1915, while gallantly leading his men in an attack on the German trenches near Loos, death being instantaneous'. His company commander wrote: 'I find it difficult to tell in what high regard Corporal Westlake was held. His conduct was above all praise. It is such men who add lustre to the fame of the British Army and to the regiment to which they belong'. The officer who directed the operation on the day in question later wrote an account of the events. He described seeking cover in a ditch as they advanced on an enemy trench. They were approaching the Lens road. 'It was five minutes past two in the afternoon. We continued up the ditch to the roadside signpost. The enemy's fire was very brisk and accurate, and on our journey we lost Corporal Westlake and Private Pott, killed, shot through the head'.

In his brief career at the front, John wrote a series of letters to his father. In one, he explained why he was there: 'I rather yearned to see for myself what life all these good fellows were leading, and to share their lot. Then there is the experience, which may be useful, besides the glory of it'. Later, he described his first taste of battle: 'I have had my baptism of fire. I did not receive a scratch and would not have missed the experience, though the sights and the sensational incidents of which I have been an eye witness would give me an opportunity for much writing'. The 'opportunity for much writing' was not to come. The writer of the letters died on the battlefield, and, with no known grave, is commemorated on the Loos Memorial. The recipient of the letters, John's father, died five years later at the age of seventy-five and was laid to rest in the family plot in Plymouth Road.

SAMUEL STACEY
Died Monday 31 January 1916. Aged 31.

H.M. Prison Dartmoor

It might be supposed that, in Tavistock and elsewhere, the great majority of men who joined the army during the First World War enlisted in their own county regiment. The evidence does not support this. For example, if regimental affiliation had been added to each of the names of the soldiers on the Tavistock Memorial, it would be seen that only a quarter of them belonged to the Devonshires. The others were distributed among some thirty other regiments. Nevertheless, the appeal to local loyalties, which a county-based organisation was uniquely able to express, did have its effect. Not that county regiments, as some believed or pretended, were steeped in centuries of British history. They had, in fact, been established as recently as 1871. The Army Reforms of that year had re-organised infantry regiments on a county basis, and provided them with regionally-based headquarters, the clear intention being to tap into currents of local pride and loyalty. But to the mass of recruits who flocked to the colours in the war, the Cheshires, or the Hampshires, or the Devonshires, far from appearing to be fairly recent creations, might as well have had a continuous history since Agincourt. And sometimes they were told that they had. It is not, therefore, surprising to find that, in terms of both enlistment and of casualties, the number of Tavistock men in the Devons far exceeded the number in any other single regiment.

One of the 5787 officers and men of the Devonshire Regiment who died in the war was Samuel John Stacey. He was born at Postbridge on 27 March 1884, and his birth was registered a month later by his father, John Stacey, who had been a miner, but who had later become a warder at the nearby Dartmoor Prison. John had been born at Peter Tavy in 1844. His arrival, together with that of his twin-brother, George, had no doubt resulted in an outburst of unrestrained joy on the part of his parents, who already had five children under the age of eleven. Samuel's mother, Elizabeth, was also one of seven. She had been born at Postbridge in 1845, the fifth child of Mary Rouse and her husband Thomas, a labourer at the nearby Powder Mills.

John Stacey and Elizabeth Rouse were married at Tavistock Register Office on 27 October 1864. Between 1868 and 1884 they had five sons, John, James, Thomas, Walter, and Samuel, and two daughters, Ellen and Annie. The two parents, having both come from seven-child families, thus proceeded to have seven of their own. Samuel, born in 1884, was the youngest. This had also been the name that Elizabeth's parents, the Rouses, had reserved for their youngest. The evidence suggests that Elizabeth died in giving birth to Samuel, and that John senior subsequently married a lady slightly older than himself called Jane, who came from St Cleer.

The Stacey children grew up in the middle of Dartmoor, originally in Postbridge but later in Princetown. They would have attended either the recently-opened church school at the former, or the school built at the latter in 1872 for the children of prison officers. Samuel followed in the footsteps of his father and at least two of his brothers in becoming a miner, and the 1901 census caught him as a seventeen year old tin miner living in the parish of Calstock. At some point, however, he moved away, and he was living in Liverpool in 1915, when he enlisted. By that time his father had died, and his stepmother had moved into Tavistock, and re-settled at No. 2 Bannawell Street, a tenement building.

At the age of thirty, Samuel became a Private, No. 15162, in the 2nd Battalion of the Devonshire Regiment, evidently preferring to return to roots rather than to enlist in a regiment based in the area of his new home. Towards the end of 1915 he found himself in Flanders. The 2nd Battalion had been given Front Line responsibilities in the area of the Lys Valley, to the south of the Ypres Salient. Here, on 31 January 1916, near Neuve Chapelle, in the muddy wasteland that disfigured the border area between France and Belgium, he was killed in action. The date was not identified with any particular action or engagement. Samuel Stacey was just one of the countless number in 'Fred Karno's army, the ragtime infantree' who, through the long drawn-out periods of static trench warfare, fell, day by day, to the grenade, the mortar, the machine gun, or the sniper's rifle.

Bois-Grenier is a small village in the French Department of the Nord. It lies just outside the town of Armentieres, immortalised by the Tommies on account of its 'Mademoiselle' who 'hadn't been kissed for forty years'. The village houses one of the innumerable burial grounds on the Western Front. This one is Y Farm Military Cemetery, and it contains over 800 graves. It was opened in March 1915 to accommodate the remains of those who had died in that particular sector. Samuel Stacey was one of them. Six other members of the Devonshire Regiment also have their graves here. Of the 800 who are commemorated, more than one-third are unidentified.

Samuel's name also appeared, along with twenty-six others, on the original memorial, placed in Tavistock Parish Church on 1st June 1917.

HENRY BARKWILL
Died Thursday 24 February 1916. Aged 29.

THE SOUTH WALES BORDERERS

Within an unbroken wreath of immortelles, a Sphinx resting on a tablet inscribed "Egypt"; on the lower portion of the wreath the burnished letters "SWB". The badge is in silver plate for officers and for other ranks the wreath is in gilding metal and remainder in white metal.

Local sources generally spelt it 'Barkwill'. To the Commonwealth War Graves Commission, and to some other bodies, he was 'Barkwell'. The local registrar who recorded his arrival listed him as Henry John. Army sources and obituarists invariably used only the second name. To his family he was always Jack. This phenomenon was not uncommon. There is no reason to think that it induced an identity crisis, or in any way made life difficult for Henry John Barkwill.

The Barkwills came from what was then, and what to some extent has remained, a rather remote area of scattered villages between Okehampton and Launceston. Henry's father, Robert, had been born in Bratton Clovelly in 1859. Robert's father, Henry's grandfather, died in 1860, leaving five young children, of whom Robert, at one year old, was the youngest. The family had worked on the land for generations, and Robert followed tradition for a time. The 1881 census found him working on the Thrushelton farm of Richard Balman. Soon after that, as the agricultural depression created widespread unemployment, he found a job in the local mines. Growing up in such an isolated community imposed certain inevitable limitations, of which one was the choice of a partner. Robert married Mary Ann Worth, also from Bratton Clovelly. In the 1881 census she had, significantly, been recorded as working as a domestic servant for Thomas Abels, a near-neighbour of Richard Balman in Thushelton. Robert and Mary had four children, Bessie, Jane, Robert, and Henry. Henry, the youngest of the family, was born on 27 May 1886. And then history repeated itself. Before Henry had reached his first birthday his father had died, of pneumonia, at the age of twenty-seven. Henry, as soon as he was able to do so, became an earner. The 1901 census recorded him as an agricultural labourer. Regulations governing children at work, together with the introduction in 1880 of the principle of compulsory education, meant that some of the worst abuses of child labour had been removed. Henry could, however, have been working full-time at thirteen. His wage would have made a vital contribution to the family income. The hardship faced by the family in two successive generations, and particularly by the two young widows, Henry's grandmother and mother, can, in the present age, scarcely be imagined.

By the time of Robert's death, the family had moved to Lamerton, and Mary was to continue thereafter to live in the Tavistock district. In 1893, six years after Robert's death, she married Alfred Waye, a copper miner with roots in Milton Abbot. The 1901 census found Alfred and Mary, with her three youngest children, living at No. 2 Wheal Josiah Cottages, on the Devon Great Consols site. Henry was then fourteen. Soon after that he became a miner and moved away from home as the Great Consols enterprise finally folded. In 1907, when he was twenty-one, he was living in lodgings in South Zeal. On 1 April of that year, at Okehampton Register Office, he married a South Zeal girl called Ethel Wonnacott. She was nineteen, and had been born at Spreyton, the daughter of a shoemaker called James and his wife Elizabeth, nee Endacott. Ethel's first child, Clarence, quickly appeared, but, with a second on the way, Henry lost his job as the bottom finally fell out of the industry that had once made the area so prosperous. The decision was made to move to South Wales, where, it was hoped, his skills and experience would provide him with employment in the coalfields. And so it proved. By 1914 six years in steady work as a collier had helped Henry to raise his young family, which now comprised four children. Fate had, however, not finished with the Barkwills. For the third time the family was to lose its breadwinner before he had reached the age of thirty.

When the war came Henry enlisted at Newport, joining the 1st Battalion of the local regiment, the South Wales Borderers. He spent the first sixteen months of the war, until Christmas 1915, in France, and saw a good deal of front line action, principally at Loos. A month-long furlough in January 1916 brought him to South Zeal, where Ethel had returned with the children to the protection of her parental home. He also visited his mother, still living at Devon Great Consols, and his sister, Mrs Bessie Metters, in her Tavistock home on Trelawny Road. And he was able to offer some comfort to Ethel's sister, whose husband, a member of the Devon Yeomanry, had been a recent casualty. In February, now holding the rank of sergeant, he returned to the front line. On the 24th he was killed in action, near Arras.

Sergeant Barkwill is one of the 35,000 without known graves whose names appear on the Arras Memorial. It is an impressive monument, designed by Sir Edward Lutyens, which features a long west-facing cloister built on Doric columns. The walls carry stone panels on which the names are carved. At home, an 'In Memoriam' notice appeared in the *Tavistock Gazette* on the fourth anniversary of Henry's death. It read: 'In loving memory of Jack Barkwell, killed in France February 24th 1916. Fondly remembered by mother, brothers and sisters, also Godfrey and Lillian'.

WILLIAM GARLAND
Died Thursday 27 April 1916. Aged 16.

Madge Lane, Tavistock, before 1914

William Alfred Garland was not the first Tavistock lad to have set his heart on joining the Royal Navy. Nor was he unique in realising that ambition at the age of fifteen; the tradition of boy sailors was a part of naval history. Young Master Garland does, however, hold two distinctions which are unrecorded on either the memorial in his home town or the tombstone that marks his grave in the Capuccini Naval Cemetery on the island of Malta. He was, at fifteen, the youngest of Tavistock's wartime recruits, and, at sixteen, the youngest of the town's sons to die in the conflict. He was still five months short of his seventeenth birthday when his ship, H.M.S. 'Russell', a 14,000 ton battleship, was mined in the Mediterranean. A Duncan Class vessel, the 'Russell' had been built in 1901, and had operated during the war, successively, in the North Sea and the Channel, before taking up Mediterranean duties based at Malta. On 27 April, while approaching the coast of the island to return to her base after an exercise, she struck a mine, and sank quickly. The nearness of land, and the presence in the area of many small craft, minimised what would otherwise have been a catastrophic loss of life. In the event, there were 625 survivors. William Garland was one of the 124 casualties. His body was recovered from the sea and buried on the island.

    William's short life began on 5 September 1899, when he was born at 14 Madge Lane, Tavistock. His father, Alfred, worked as a grocer's porter. Alfred was the fifth, and last, child born to John, a Thrushelton-born miner, and Mary, his Bridestowe-born wife, who lived at 45 West Bridge Cottages. John was forty-nine and Mary forty-five when Alfred came along to complete the family. By the time the 1891 census was conducted, he was the only one of the children still living at home; he had just, at the age of thirteen, started work. In 1899, when he was twenty, Alfred married Martha Mary Messalla Easterbrook. The Easterbrooks were a large family living at Partridge Ham House on Pixon Lane, and Martha was the youngest of eight children. She was nineteen when she married Alfred at the Bible Christian Chapel in Bannawell Street, one of three chapels that at that time conducted worship within the broad Methodist tradition. William was the elder of two sons of the marriage. The younger son, George, was born nine years later. He was eight years old when William was killed. Through those young eyes the age-gap was a significant one, and George, throughout, saw 'Willie' as the manly hero, a status further enhanced by a heroic death. George was, of course, too young to serve, though not, one might guess, too young to dress in a sailor suit and to try to imitate the bearing and behaviour of his venerated brother.

The father of the family, Alfred, was in his late thirties during the war years, and was therefore eligible for service. He enlisted in January 1917, some seven months after his son's death. His service was exclusively in England. He was on home defence duties on the East Coast, and, mercifully for his family, he survived the war. Thoughts of young men in the forces seeing distant places in Europe and beyond may remind us that many recruits would also, because of the war, see sights in their own country that they would not otherwise have seen. Would Alfred Garland have ever visited, except in uniform, the Fens, or the Yorkshire coast, or London?

William's pre-naval career in Tavistock was, of course, a very short one. For most of his childhood the family home was No. 4 Mount Ford. His earliest school years were spent at the Plymouth Road School, but at the age of ten his parents moved him to Dolvin Road. On leaving school he worked, as an errand boy, successively for two tradesmen in the town, but all his thoughts and ambitions were by now focused on the navy. In July 1915 he joined up, father and son having both given written consent to a contract of service 'for a period of twelve years from the age of eighteen in addition to whatever period may be necessary until he attains that age'. After six months at Devonport, he was drafted to H.M.S. 'Magola', and went to Malta, where he transferred to the 'Russell'.

William's devotional life was obviously very important to him. He would end letters home with 'God be with you till we meet again', and to an aunt he wrote: 'Tell my dear mother that I am living for God and am true to my communion'. He also had an interest in, and a talent for, drawing and design. His mother cherished one of his last drawings, the design of which reflected also the patriotic spirit of the age. Below the flags of the allies were the words :'Come along boys, rally to the flag for freedom. Come along boys, buck up! God save the King!' The *Tavistock Gazette* offered a simple, but moving, tribute: 'He was a lad of whom Tavistock may justly feel proud, as one who feared God, honoured his King, and sacrificed his life for his country'.

CECIL MERRIFIELD
Died Wednesday 31 May 1916. Aged 22.

Cecil Edmond Merrifield

By the Summer of 1916 the Great War had degenerated into a contest of attrition. On the Western Front the armies of both sides slugged it out across a line of trenches that stretched from the North Sea to the Swiss border, both sides hoping that victory would come through the sheer exhaustion of the enemy. Meanwhile the losses mounted. As yet, naval power had played little significant part in the conflict, and this caused some surprise, particularly in view of the public hysteria that had accompanied the pre-war competition between Britain and Germany over the building of new battleships. The fact was that the German Fleet had been largely confined to its North Sea ports by the close attentions of the numerically superior British fleet. Any attempt on the German side to break the general war deadlock by a decisive naval victory, of the same significance as the British victory at Trafalgar over a century before, would involve great risk. Admiral Scheer, who was appointed Commander-in-Chief of the Fleet at the beginning of 1916, argued that the risk should be taken, and in May he took it. The German High Seas Fleet sailed out of Wilhelmshaven. On the 31st it engaged the British Grand Fleet at Jutland.

Cecil Edmond York Merrifield was a seaman gunner aboard one of the ships that went down at the Battle of Jutland. He came from an old Tavistock family. His grandfather and great grandfather, both of whom had been called John, had lived and worked in the town, as cordwainer and mason respectively, and there was a family home on Trelawny Road. Cecil's father was Charles Merrifield. He had been born in Tavistock in 1864 and had served an apprenticeship with John Carter, the founder of the Creber's grocery dynasty, before joining the army. Charles was an effective soldier, and came out as a sergeant-major in the 8th Hussars. He then, in 1906, became proprietor of the Queen's Head Hotel in Bodmin, and it was while he was there that he received news of the death of his son. His versatile career ended with a period, from early 1917, in which he was an Inspector of Army Canteens. Based at Salisbury, he died there in February 1919, at the age of fifty-five.

Charles Merrifield had two sons who were born during his long period of service as a cavalry N.C.O. in the army of late Victorian England. Both were destined to become casualties of the Great War. The elder one, born in 1891, was called Charles after his father, with the second name, Willoughby, adding an extra touch of refinement. Cecil, the younger son, entered the world with an even louder flourish as Cecil Edmond York, the last name, perhaps, being a dutiful nod towards Prince George, who had recently been created Duke of York. Given the interest in naval affairs shown by the Duke, later to be King George V, it was to prove an appropriate choice. Cecil was born on 10 September 1893 in India. A fair number of his early years, during his father's military career, were spent in the Trelawny Road home with his grandparents and three uncles and aunts. In his early teens he began to share with his newly-settled father a new life in Bodmin. Two weeks after his sixteenth birthday he presented himself at Devonport, 5' 1" tall and straight out of school, for enlistment in the Navy.

Admiral Scheer's master plan in May 1916 was to eliminate British naval superiority by enticing enemy ships into individual, self-destructive, actions. His detailed plans, however, lacked the surprise element, since the British had long since been able to decipher the German codes. The two fleets met off the Danish coast, with a total of 250 ships involved, including battleships and their escorting cruisers and destroyers. Twenty-five admirals were present, as the battle got under way at four o clock on the afternoon of Wednesday 31 May. Twelve hours later, what remained of the German fleet was back in Wilhelmshaven. The German Commanders and their Government were quick to claim the battle as a victory, and they pointed to the casualty figures as evidence. In tonnage terms the British had lost 111,980, and the Germans 62,233. The corresponding figures for loss of life were 6945 and 2921. On the basis of the 'index of attrition', Germany had won. And yet the German fleet was now back in harbour, never to re-appear. Paradoxically, a 'losing battle' had confirmed British naval supremacy. The Germans were now driven to adopt towards the conflict at sea the same emphasis on the long-term wearing-down of the enemy as had already become the main feature of the land campaign. It was to be the age of the U-boat.

Cecil Merrifield, Leading Seaman R.N. No. J/5602, was aboard H.M.S. 'Defence' when she succumbed to enemy fire and sank soon after six o'clock on the evening of 31 May at Jutland Bank. Of the two local commemorations, he has a place on the Tavistock Memorial, while on the Plymouth Naval Monument his name appears together with those of two other Tavistock victims of the battle, Robert Wilson, who went down with him on the same ship, and John Yard. Cecil is commemorated also on the two War Memorials at Bodmin.

ROBERT WILSON
Died Wednesday 31 May 1916. Aged 33.

H.M.S. 'Defence'

The 1891 census listed seven members of a family named Wilson as living at No. 3 Lumburn Cottages. These houses were in the western part of the parish of Tavistock, in the Lumburn Valley between the town and Gulworthy. The inhabitants would tend to look towards Gulworthy for some of their requirements. Here was an inn, the Harvest Home. And here, since 1854, there had been both a church and a school. The head of the household at Number 3 was George Wilson, aged forty-four, a farm labourer, who had been born at Stratton in North Cornwall. His wife was one year older. She had been born Jane Colwill at Whitsand, close to Stratton. Living with them were their four children. Mary, aged nineteen, had been born at Bratton Clovelly. Then came Rosa, twelve, and Robert, eight, both of whom had been born at Bridestowe. Florence, the youngest, was three years old, and had been born in the parish of Milton Abbot. The family, of modest size for that period, was fairly typical of working class families in rural areas at that time in that, during a period of agricultural depression, there was a readiness, indeed a necessity on the part of many, to move home to find employment.

    Robert was the only son in the family, his brother John, two years his senior, having not survived. Young Robert's birth is recorded as having taken place at Buddlebrook in the parish of Bridestowe on 5 September 1882. When, on 10 October 1898, he became Stoker 2nd Class Robert Henry Wilson No. 290128, he was thus sixteen years and one month old. He claimed, in time-honoured fashion, that he was eighteen, and, presumably to render futile any search by the naval authorities to discover whether he was telling the truth, he told them that he had been born at Newton Abbot. His previous occupation was listed as that of a labourer. He was described at the time of his enlistment as 5' 5" high, with light brown hair, hazel eyes, and a sallow complexion. Rising through the ranks, he became a Leading Stoker in 1908. In 1910, his twelve year term completed, he re-enlisted, having, since his initial enrolment, grown two inches and developed blue eyes and a fresh complexion. He was thirty-one, and still in the service, when the war came. By that time his father had died, following a distressing decline, in the County Asylum at Exminster in 1912, at the age of sixty-five. His mother, Jane, survived to the age of seventy, her last years at her home at Colcharton Cottages having been brightened by listening to stories of some of her only son's wartime exploits. Her death, in April 1916, was the occasion for Robert's last home leave. He stayed then in his mother's old home, with his youngest sister, Florence, who had performed the duty, or penance, that, by tradition, fell to the youngest daughter of the family, of staying in the family home to care for ageing parents. Within days of his mother's funeral, Robert was back aboard his ship, and preparing for what, in the event, was to be her last mission.

H.M.S. 'Defence', on which both Leading Seaman Cecil Merrifield and Leading Stoker Robert Wilson served, was a Minotaur Class cruiser of 14,600 tons. Built in 1907, she had been re-commissioned at Devonport in 1913, at which point Leading Stoker Wilson joined her. 'Defence' was the Flagship of the Rear-Admiral Commanding the First Cruiser Squadron, Sir Robert Arbuthnot, a man who had a reputation in the service for being a disciplinarian. Arbuthnot's conduct at the Battle of Jutland reveals something of the impatience that had developed on both sides during months of cat-and-mouse activity. There was a mutual desire to come to grips with the enemy and to produce a decisive result. In the event, it was to be the only occasion during the war when the two battle fleets engaged in European waters. As the Grand Fleet deployed for action at Jutland, Arbuthnot was required to move to a position in the rear of the line, since armoured cruisers like 'Defence' were thought to be too vulnerable to operate in the battle line. In passing down the side of the fleet, he spurned the disengaged side, which would have been the safe route, in favour of the engaged flank, which gave him the opportunity to have a go at the enemy. Four Dreadnoughts opened fire on the 'Defence'. Within five minutes she blew up in a massive explosion. There were no survivors. Casualties numbered 907.

Robert Wilson's name appears on the War Memorials at both Tavistock and Gulworthy, as well as on the Naval Memorial at Plymouth. The latter includes 725 names of casualties of the 'Defence'. Leading Stoker Wilson's name also features on the family grave in Gulworthy Churchyard. Below the names of his parents, George and Jane, there appear the words 'Robert H Wilson, only son, died in the Jutland Battle, May 31st 1916, aged 33'. In this way the family could affirm that even a wandering seaman whose bones lie far away retains an unbreakable link with the soil of his native land.

JOHN YARD
Died Wednesday 31 May 1916. Aged 34.

H.M.S. 'Indefatigable'

One can imagine the kind of jokes that might have circulated among the wedding guests. They had gathered on a Saturday afternoon in September 1910 in Tavistock's fourteenth-century Parish Church. On one side of the aisle sat the Yards, on the other the Foots. John Yard was marrying Mabel Foot.

John Henry Yard was twenty-nine when he married Mabel. He was an Able Seaman, and had been in the Royal Navy for eight years. Born on 12 July 1881, he was the son of William Yard, who was working at the time as a smith at the iron foundry in Parkwood. The blacksmith's trade was one with which the Yard family had been associated for many years. John's mother was Annie, who came from a Tavistock family called Woolridge. Over a period of twenty years William and Annie, in their Dolvin Road home, raised a family of seven sons and two daughters. John came third in order. The 1901 census gave the family's address as Hills Court, Dolvin Road.

John's naval enlistment came at Devonport in July 1902. He was twenty-one, and had been working as a labourer. Joining as a bugler, he was described in his enlistment profile as being 5' 1" high, with blue eyes, brown hair, a fresh complexion, and a tattoo of a pierced heart on his left wrist. It was at about that period that the family moved into a house in College Avenue. William, having lost his job at the foundry when it closed in 1891, had become a steamroller driver, a job he was to do for twenty-four years. He also developed a reputation as a potato grower. It was reported of him in one particular year that 'he lifted a stalk of six "Up-to-Date" potatoes weighing over seven pounds, the largest tuber turning the scale at thirty-three ounces'. The first of his sons to see active service was William junior, the eldest son, who fought in the South African War. Later, during the Great War, three others of the total of seven brothers were to join the colours. Russell and Henry both joined the Devons in 1914 and served in India and Egypt. Charles, the youngest of the family, enlisted in 1917 as a bugler in the Oxford and Bucks Light Infantry and was wounded at the Second Battle of the Marne. Throughout these difficult times the family home continued to be No. 4 College Avenue. Here Annie died at the age of sixty-two in February 1922. William enjoyed the remaining years of a contented life in the home of his daughter, just a few doors away at 23 College Avenue. And here, in January 1931, having grown his last potato, he died, at the age of seventy-three.

John's marriage to Mabel brought together two local families. Mabel had been born in 1886 in one of the cottages at Two Bridges, in the Wilminstone area, in the north-eastern reaches of Tavistock Parish. Her father, James Foot, was a miner, and her mother, Jessie, formerly Miss Martin, had worked as a kitchen maid at Kelly College before her marriage to James in 1881. Mabel and John, the bride and groom, entered their addresses as '21 Trelawny Cottages' and 'H.M.S. Leviathan', respectively. The young couple moved into a Fitzford Cottage, No. 36, which remained their married home. Here a daughter called Nellie was born in July 1912. She died of meningitis at the age of two.

In July 1914, as the twelve year period of his enlistment drew to its close, John decided that he would volunteer to renew his service. He therefore continued, with the rank of Seaman Gunner, an association with H.M.S. 'Indefatigable' that had begun in May 1912 and was destined to end four years later with the deaths of both man and ship.

At the Battle of Jutland, Sir David Beatty's battle cruiser fleet consisted of six ships. Three of them were sunk in the battle. The 'Indefatigable' was one of them. Built at Devonport in 1909 at a cost of £1,500,000, she was a battle cruiser of 18,750 tons. As one of the smaller and less well protected ships, she was at the rear of the battle cruiser line when the battle opened. Within minutes she had become engaged in a duel with her German opposite number. This tactic of reducing the battle to a series of one-to-one shoot-outs lay at the heart of the German Commander-in-Chief's strategy for the day. Two shells fell on 'Indefatigable's' upper deck, causing a magazine to explode. As she pulled out of line, sinking by the stern, she was hit again on the forecastle, and there followed an explosion accompanied by 'a vast column of smoke arising to the sky'. Sir David Beatty, commanding the battle cruisers, turned to Lord Chatfield as they both watched these mishaps, and said 'There seems to be something wrong with our bloody ships today'. The 'Indefatigable' was totally destroyed. A German destroyer picked up the only two survivors. Casualties numbered 1022. Of that number, 790 have their names recorded on the Memorial on Plymouth Hoe. John Yard is among them.

Nine years after John's death, Mabel married a mason's labourer called Francis Paige. The remaining forty-seven years of her life were spent with her second husband at 6 Mill Hill Cottages, where she died in 1972 at the age of eighty-five.

ALFRED COOMBE
Died Tuesday 13 June 1916. Aged 31.

Alfred John Coombe

The discovery that, on a First World War Memorial in a small westcountry town, five per cent of the names are of Canadian soldiers, might, at first, occasion some surprise. But this is Tavistock. And Tavistock had, for some years before the war, been one of those centres from which, because of dire economic conditions, there had been a steady haemorrhage of population, particularly of young men. Favoured destinations were the old colonies. And, for a variety of reasons, Canada offered particularly attractive prospects to would-be emigrants from the southwest. The story of that westward flow of population, and its effects on communities at both ends of the process, has yet to be written. Among the interesting questions that such a study might confront would be: Why did so many young pre-war emigrants, having successfully made the adjustment to the New World, volunteer to return to Europe to fight in the interests of a country that, they may well have felt, had denied to them the personal opportunities that they had in the past sought? The six migrants commemorated on the Tavistock monument constituted only a small proportion of this incoming wave, which, while not of the same order as the outgoing tide that had preceded it, was nevertheless of some significance.

Alfred John Coombe was born in Tavistock on 16 August 1884. Eight years later, in 1892, his mother, who had been born Elizabeth Barkell, married for the second time. Her new husband was William Coombe, aged thirty-six, the same age as Elizabeth. William was a shoemaker, who lived with his widowed mother at 29

Exeter Street, Tavistock. Elizabeth arranged for Alfred to adopt the name of his new stepfather; he was to retain it throughout his life. The evidence provided at the wedding, in 1892, indicated that Elizabeth had earlier been married to a miner named Kennedy, and that Alfred was a child of this marriage. Elizabeth had, in fact, married John Kennedy in October 1877, but he died in the late 1880s, leaving her with six children, all of whom had been born between 1877 and 1888. Elizabeth was described, in the record of the second marriage, as a tailoress living in Gunnislake, the daughter, and the widow, of miners.

The Coombes were a well-established working-class family in Tavistock. In the middle of the nineteenth century their home was in Paull's Buildings, where William was born in 1856, the son of a labourer. They later moved to Exeter Street. William's career as a shoemaker took him through long phases as apprentice and journeyman before, in late middle age, he became his own master. He lived with his parents until, at the age of thirty-six, he could afford a wife and home of his own. In these respects he was typical of so many small-town artisans of the period. Perhaps, however, few of his contemporaries would have been prepared to take on the responsibilities that he assumed through his marriage. There were six children, their ages varying from fifteen to four. There were to be, in addition, two fresh arrivals in John and Emily. By 1901 William was, at the age of forty-five, back where he began, in Paull's Buildings.

Of the six children whom William 'inherited', three of the boys were to pre-decease their stepfather. The two other stepsons moved away to London, while the stepdaughter married and settled locally. The youngest two of the eight followed contrasting routes, John emigrating to Canada while Emily stayed in Tavistock. Alfred John was, in seniority, the fourth of the stepsons. He did not follow his stepfather's calling. After leaving Dolvin Road School, he worked for a time as a barman at the Newmarket Hotel in Duke Street, and became as popular a figure there as he did on Saturday afternoons at Torlands, playing for Tavistock Football Club. He was also a member of the local Volunteers. He emigrated shortly before the war, settling in Toronto and getting a job as a railway conductor.

Alfred Coombe's enlistment took place at Niagara on 11 August 1915, a few days before his thirty-first birthday. He joined the 58th Battalion of the Central Ontario Regiment, with the Regimental Number 452041 and the rank of corporal. The army documents of the time describe him as 5′ 6″ tall, and as having dark hair, a dark complexion, and blue eyes. He sailed from Halifax on 22 November, arrived in England on 2 December, and embarked for France on 20 February. Four months later he was killed at Ypres. He has no known grave. His name appears, among the thousands, on the Menin Gate Memorial at Ypres.

Towards the end of July 1916, Mrs Elizabeth Coombe, then living at 36 Brook Street, received a letter from the Canadian Defence Ministry expressing sympathy on the death of her son, Corporal Alfred Coombe, who was described as 'a worthy citizen and a heroic soldier'. He was said to have 'done his duty fearlessly and well and given his life for the cause of liberty and the upbuilding of the empire'. Elizabeth was to outlive her son by only three years. She died at the age of sixty-three in 1919. William lived a further ten years, dying at Whitham Park at the age of seventy-three in 1929.

JAMES HARRIS
Died Wednesday 28 June 1916. Aged 34.

R.F.A. Snipers

The main theatres of war between 1914 and 1918, such as the Ypres Salient, the Somme, and Gallipoli, are well known, and their names resonate through history. There were, on the other hand, some campaigns of the First World War that were conducted in the most obscure settings and in the most unlikely places. They received little publicity, it seems, at the time, and have attracted little attention since. One such was the expedition to Iraq. The military campaign there in 2003 revived interest in an area which, in the early nineteenth century, was known to Europeans as Mesopotamia.

In 1914 knowledge of Mesopotamia in British Government circles, as among the wider public, was limited. The area was part of the sprawling Turkish Empire, and Turkey's entry into the war, in October 1914, as an ally of Germany, was the justification for Britain to send an expeditionary force of Indian-based troops. There was also the question of oil. The first objective of this force, the occupation of the port of Basra, was achieved without much difficulty. Thereafter, progress north along the Rivers Tigris and Euphrates was delayed and hampered by a combination of factors, particularly related to the lack of adequate specialised shipping and the failure to appreciate the value of gathering local knowledge.

The ultimate objective of the operation was to enter Baghdad. Strategically important en route was the town of Kut, 200 miles down-river on the Tigris, and in September 1915 it was reached and occupied. Thereafter, stern Turkish resistance and a chronic lack of supplies spelt disaster for the expeditionary force. Reinforcements arrived at Kut, both men and materials, but the supply of both was late, haphazard, and inadequate. Heavy fighting began in January, and a siege ensued. On 29 April 1916 General Townshend surrendered the town to the Turks. Some 12,000 prisoners were taken. Of the British troops, the survival-rate of those who were interned was 30%. Among those who died was James Harris.

Driver James Harris, Number 49282, 63rd Battery, Royal Field Artillery, had enlisted in 1907, at the age of twenty-five. He had previously worked as a carpenter. His address at that time was given as 10 King Street, Tavistock, although for some reason he appears to have enlisted at Tiverton. He had been born on 4 December 1881 at the family home, Bears in Broadwoodwidger, a parish of wooded valleys, old farmsteads, and captivating views of Dartmoor. Both his parents were Devonians. His father, Samuel Stanbury Harris was a farm labourer who hailed from St. Giles-in-the-Heath, near Launceston, and who had been born to John and Thomasine Harris at Boxes Shop, in St. Giles in 1856. James's mother, Elizabeth, formerly Miss Bailey, was a native of Black Torrington. She married Samuel in 1881, when she was twenty-nine and he was twenty-five. Within two years they were joined in their Broadwoodwidger home first by William and then by James. The 1891 census found the family, now augmented by the arrival of Mary in 1884 and Ann in 1888, living at 2 Church Park Cottages, Whitchurch. Here Elizabeth died in December 1903 of intestinal disease, at the age of fifty-two. Samuel continued to live there until, towards the end of his life, as his health deteriorated, he went to live with one of his daughters whose home was in King Street. Here he died of cerebral thrombosis in August 1924, at the age of sixty-nine.

There is, unfortunately, no evidence on which to base any account of James's nine years in the service or of the circumstances that led to his being in Mesopotamia. Either he was a member of the original expeditionary force, or he joined it later, possibly as part of the hastily assembled relieving forces that arrived at Kut from either India or France. Nor do we know anything, in specific detail, of the conditions in which he was held as a prisoner of war over the period between his capture and his death. The general view of historians has been that, even by the standards of the regime of the Ottoman Empire, the conditions, in which the 12,000 who were captured at Kut were kept, touched the lowest levels of both cruelty and incompetence. It is significant that the Turks long held out against requests to allow observers from neutral countries to inspect their prisoner-of-war camps, and the mortality figures speak for themselves. James's internment lasted for just sixty days.

When Baghdad fell into British hands in March 1917, a war cemetery was laid out near the city's North Gate. When the war ended it was extended to include 2975 graves that had hitherto been scattered among graveyards throughout the city and the area. Driver Harris's body was one of those brought at that time to Baghdad (North Gate) War Cemetery. The 75,000 square yards provide final resting places for Muslim and Hindu, as well as British, casualties. They had participated in a military diversion which, like many other campaigns in that war, had turned out to be costly and ill-judged, but which had also produced an abundance of heroism and sacrifice. One of the few comforts that helped to sustain the relatives of the fallen in the years that followed was the realisation that, however distant or remote, the graves or memorials of men like Driver Harris were being tended with care.

ERNEST DAVEY
Died Saturday 1 July 1916. Aged 36.

Higher Maudlin Street, Barnstaple, in 2001

Saturday 1 July 1916 was the worst day in the history of the British Army. It was the first day of the Battle of the Somme. On the morning of that day, 100,000 British soldiers, massed along a fourteen mile front, left their trenches to cross No Man's Land. By the end of the day, 20,000 of them were dead and a further 40,000 lay wounded. No significant gains had been made.

The Devonshire Regiment featured prominently in the heroic, albeit catastrophic, events of that day. Ernest Davey, a corporal in the 2nd Battalion, was one of those who died in action. He was thirty-six years old at the time of his death, having been born on 3 January 1880. His roots lay in North Devon. His father, Charles Richard Cann Davey, a mason, had been born at Hartland in 1845. Charles had, in 1873, married Sarah Pomeroy Kelly, who had been born at Marwood in 1846, the daughter of a yeoman farmer called John Kelly. The couple had settled in Barnstaple, where Ernest was born. He was the second son, three years younger than his elder brother Wilfred. A third brother, the resoundingly named Walter Ricardo Kelly Davey, was to follow in 1889. Meanwhile two girls were born and christened Florence and Beatrice, names that had been given to the eldest two daughters, who had died in childhood.

Ernest's entries in the census returns for 1891 and 1901 list him as schoolboy and carriage examiner respectively, on both occasions living with his family in Higher Maudlin Street in Barnstaple, where he had been born. The date of his enlistment is not known, although his place of residence at the time was given as Exeter. The enlistment took place at Tavistock, but his connection with the town beyond that has still to be established. It must be presumed that he lived in Tavistock for some time between his youth in Barnstaple and his middle age in Exeter. It is possible that the Mrs Davey listed in 1916 as living at No. 6 King Street was his widowed mother. If so, she was presumably the person responsible for seeing that Ernest's name was included on the first version of the Parish Church Memorial, erected in June 1917.

The Battle of the Somme was, according to General Haig who planned it, and to the British authorities who supported it, to be the turning point of the war. The infantry assault was preceded by a fierce and prolonged artillery bombardment which lasted for a week, consumed a million shells, and was unprecedented in its scale and persistence. It was assumed that nothing could have survived such an assault. All that was needed to finish the job was a final pounding at dawn on 1st July together with the explosion of several mines under German positions. The infantry would then be able to walk, in an orderly and unhurried fashion, over No Man's Land and to capture, without opposition, the enemy's former positions. The 8th Division, of which the 2nd Devons formed a part, was given the specific objective of occupying the enemy trenches and then sweeping on to take the village of Ovillers. The reality of the day was to destroy these ambitions and to mock these carefully-laid plans and these hopes. Burdened by baggage (each man carried sixty-six pounds of equipment) the troops found themselves crossing terrain which had been made more difficult by the effects of the bombardment. Moreover, the Germans, it was now discovered, had not only not vacated their positions, but had indeed strengthened and deepened their defences. They now had time to position their machine guns and to methodically mow down the approaching waves of men who came walking or stumbling towards them. The 2nd Battalion's War Diary for this fateful day includes the following: 'Immediately our troops advanced the enemy opened a terrific machine gun fire from the front and from both flanks, which mowed down our troops. This fire did not deter our men from continuing to advance, but only a very few reached the German lines alive. Some of these managed to effect an entry into the German lines, where they put up a determined fight against enormous odds and were soon killed'. For Corporal Davey, we must assume, the Battle of the Somme had lasted for but a few minutes.

The day that produced this carnage was a bright summer day of blue skies and high temperatures. There had, however, been a lot of wet weather over the preceding week, and the battlefield became churned and swampy and covered with mud-filled shell holes and craters. Into these fell the bodies of many of the casualties. Of the British soldiers who died on the Somme in 1916, either on the first day or at later phases of a battle that was to last for five months, half have no known graves. These men, some 73,000, whose bodies remained unrecovered or unidentified, are commemorated on the Thiepval Memorial. Designed by Edward Lutyens and unveiled in 1932, this impressive monument occupies a key site on the Somme battlefield. A high proportion of the names recorded there are of those who fell on the first day, and these include Ernest Davey.

J. DAVEY
Died Wednesday 5 July 1916? Aged ?

A feature of the Devonshire Regiment Cemetery near Mametz

The name Davey, with or without the 'e', is far from uncommon in Devon. In 1916 there were five families bearing the name who lived in Tavistock, at 60 Bannawell Street, 18 Dolvin Road, 6 King Street, 37 Exeter Street, and 20 Trelawny Road. In addition there were two families at Chillaton and at Milton Abbot, and one each at addresses at Gunnislake, Lewdown, and Thrushelton. It has not proved possible to link the name of J. Davey, which appears on the Memorial, with any of these families. The net was cast more widely, since there is clear evidence that in the case of some of the names, the connection with the town is neither natal nor residential. The other Davey warrior, Ernest, for example, was a North Devon man for whom it has proved impossible to establish a link with Tavistock beyond the fact that the young man enlisted there. The search for J. Davey has produced nothing conclusive in spite of the broadening of the focus and the widening of the enquiry. No relationship with his commemorated namesake has been discovered. All other leads have failed to cast any light on his possible identity.

Two Exeter-housed sources contain references to a Lance Corporal John Davey of the Second Battalion of the Devonshire Regiment. An unattributed manuscript in the County Records Office which lists the Tavistock men who served in the Great War has him as enlisting on 2 November 1914 and dying on the Somme on 5 July 1916. The Devon County Roll of Honour has no enlistment date, but gives a date of death of 2 November 1914. It is likely that the second source was, in this instance, based on the first, and that a mistake was made in the transcription of the dates. Whether the information, limited as it is, is accurate, must remain in doubt, in view of the lack of corroborative evidence. If, however, Davey did serve in the Devons, and did die on the Somme, then he shares to this day, with the other Devonians who fell, a special place of remembrance on the old battlefield. Here, near the town of Mametz, is a small cemetery holding the remains of 163 men. They were all in the Devonshire Regiment, and they all died on the first day of the battle. The mass grave in which they lie buried was an old trench. The working party, having completed the task of filling this trench with the bodies of their comrades, marked the site with a small wooden notice. It bore the words: 'The Devonshires held this trench. The Devonshires hold it still'. This place, commemorating directly a few of the fallen, seems, in a very evocative way, to be honouring, and marking the sacrifice of, a whole regiment, indeed of a whole county.

The obscurity that surrounds J. Davey, in terms of both origins and fate, is frustrating. It is, however, in one sense, helpful, as a reminder that the carnage was on such a scale that for thousands of warriors the phrase 'known only unto God' seemed to be the only one that was appropriate. This might be the opportunity, therefore, to recall the moment when those words entered the national consciousness. It was Thursday 11 November 1920, the second anniversary of the armistice. The setting was Westminster Abbey. The occasion was the burial of the Unknown Soldier. The Manchester Guardian's Francis Perrot reported the event:

> We heard, from outside, a band, rolling out the Chopin march, the weeping ghost of a tune. Drums rolled and trumpets shrilled. Bells pealed louder. Then, down the lane of khaki and naval blue and hospital blue, the guardsmen carried the coffin. On it lay the man's steel helmet and a laurel wreath. The soldiers set it down over the grave. The King stood at the foot, facing west. As we were singing 'Lead kindly light', the guardsmen lowered the soldier into the grave. The Dean handed the King a silver shell in which was soil brought from France. The King cast it upon the coffin. Last of all, in the secular key of warning, Kipling's cry against 'the frantic boast, the foolish word' rang through the church. From the east came a reiterated roll of drums, then the clear call of the reveille, a cheerful challenge carrying us on to the life that must be lived in action. The King's wreath lay at the head of the grave. It was over. The Unknown Warrior lay there wrapped in his purple. There was a pause, and the cathedral bells alone rang silverly high in the air. Soon the throng of dignitaries, statesmen, soldiers, and sailors who had followed the King went by, casting each a look into the grave as they passed. Then the women left their seats and began that long file past of the bereaved that was to last all through the day. West End and East End, all was one in this democracy of memory. The rich woman and the poor, for all the open grave meant exactly the same thing. A woman plucked a white chrysanthemum from a bunch she carried and threw it into the tomb. This example was quickly followed, and soon the purple carpet was thickly scattered with flowers white and red.

FRANCIS COLLACOTT
Died Saturday 8 July 1916. Aged 23.

Francis James Collacott

The Battle of the Somme in 1916 began with an enormous bang on 1 July and ended in stalemate on 18 November. Each day of the battle British casualties, dead and wounded, numbered, on average, 3000. The total number for the whole battle was 419,000. If figures for allied and enemy losses are added the sum tops the million. On 18 November the front lines of the contending forces were very near where they had been on 1 July.

Francis Collacott lost his life on the eighth day of the battle. During the period of a little more than a year when he had been at the Front he had been wounded four times. His luck ran out while he was on duty on a sector of the line near the village of Bray-sur-Somme, five miles south-east of Albert. Along with his colleagues in the 25th Siege Battery of the Royal Garrison Artillery he was involved in a twelve day stint of firing in support of battle operations. On a Saturday afternoon, when, if he had been at home, he would no doubt have been playing cricket, he was hit by a high explosive shell. He died instantaneously.

The Collacotts have, for over a century, been among the best-known of Tavistock dynasties. They have long been associated with the trade of carpentry and with Dolvin Road. The 1881 census recorded John Collacott, a thirty-six year old carpenter, as living at 10 Dolvin Road with his thirty-four year old wife Susan, whose maiden name was Cook, and their children, William eleven, James nine, Edith seven, and John four. All the members of the family had been born in Tavistock. Ten years on, and the census enumerator found that No. 10 had two additional residents in Beatrice, seven years old, and a six month old baby called Ethel. The older children now had jobs. William and John had become carpenters like their father. James, the second son, was a coach painter. In the early 1890s James married Amy Owen, from Plymouth. They set up home at Green Hill Cottages, which nestled near the foot of the steep climb from Mount Tavy Road up to the Sports Field at Torlands and beyond to Whitchurch Down. In 1893, as the arrival of their first child became imminent, Amy returned to her mother's home for the confinement. Francis James Collacott was thus born in Plymouth. The date was Tuesday 4 July 1893.

Francis was the oldest of the five children of James and Amy. He was followed, in order, by Jack, Elsie, Winifred, and Edith. They were still young when they moved from their Green Hill Cottage into the family home at 10 Dolvin Road. Here, in 1903, their father, James, died at the age of thirty-one. Francis was at that time ten years old, and was a pupil at the Dolvin Road School. When he left school he got a job as a messenger at the Tavistock Post Office. After his mother's re-marriage, to Daniel Sargent, who was in the Royal Navy, the family moved to Plymouth. Their new home was 6 Trelawny Avenue in St Budeaux. It was at this address that Mrs Amy Sargent was to receive the fateful telegram telling her that her eldest son, a Gunner in the Royal Garrison Artillery, had been killed on the Somme.

The regimental chaplain wrote a letter to Mrs Sargent that was dated July 9th, the day following Francis's death. Its final passage read:

He was buried by me this afternoon in a little cemetery behind the firing lines, a large number of his sorrowing comrades attending the funeral. His grave has been numbered by a wooden cross erected by his mates. He has made the great sacrifice and has laid down his life for us all, and no man can do more than he has done. He has received his reward, and I believe that in afterdays you will feel proud to think you were able to give so great and living a gift to your country in her hour of need.

The 'little cemetery', to which the chaplain referred was Bronfay Farm Military Cemetery. The farm had been pressed into service as a Dressing Station, and here a burial ground, first opened by the French, was used over a period of eighteen months to provide graves for British troops, particularly those who had, like Francis, fallen in that area or died at that station.

The Plymouth blitz during the Second World War brought the Sargents back to Tavistock. Their retirement home was 13 Dolvin Road, very close to the house in which Amy had brought up her family. Daniel died there in 1951. Amy spent her final years just along the street, at No. 2, close to Abbey Bridge, where her second son, Jack, was carrying on the family tradition as a carpenter. She died there in 1954, at the age of seventy-nine, in the house that was to remain the Collacott family home for the rest of the century.

As young brothers with shared interests, Francis and Jack had been very close. Fate, it seemed, decreed that one should die in a foreign field while the other should lead a long, honoured life in his native town and play his part in the continuing story of a respected local family.

FRANCIS HARVEY
Died Wednesday 26 July 1916. Aged 22.

Thiepval Memorial

Thomas Henry Cranch was the Registrar of Marriages. His office was at No. 1 Bedford Place, facing the Vicarage across Plymouth Road. Here, on 22 April 1878, John Arthur Harvey married Mary Ellen Brock. John was a miner who had been born on Christmas Eve 1856 at Foundry Cottages, Parkwood Road, Tavistock, but who now lived at Westbridge Cottages. He had been in the mines since leaving school. The 1871 census had described him, at the age of fourteen, as a 'mine boy'. At the same time his elder sister, Elizabeth, who was nineteen, was said to be a 'mine woman'. John's mother, who had been born Ann Pike, was, at the time of her son's wedding, a widow. John's father, after whom he had been named, had been, in turn, farm worker and miner. Young John's new wife, Mary Ellen, was a twenty year old domestic servant, who had been born in Shebbear, but whose family had later moved to the parish of Calstock, where her father, James Brock, worked as a labourer. John and Mary Ellen began their married life at 3 Ralph's Court, where their eldest son John was born in 1879. Soon after that they emigrated to Australia, where a second son, Horace, was born in 1887. On their return, in the early 1890s, they lived at 49 Westbridge Cottages, where three more sons appeared, Francis, Albert, and William. Since family sources give Francis as the fourth of six children, it is possible that another child was born in Australia, who may not have returned home with the rest of the family. Francis, or Frank as he was universally known, was born on 23 July 1894.

When Francis was nine years old his mother died of cancer at the age of forty-five. His father subsequently re-married. John's second wife, Lucy, died in April 1920 at the age of fifty-five, having survived her husband by three days. At that point the Westbridge Cottage that had been the family home through the whole of Francis's life passed into other hands.

Francis enlisted at Devonport in February 1914. He was nineteen years old, and became Number 9597, a Private in the 1st Battalion of the Devonshire Regiment. He followed two brothers into the services. Both Albert and William had joined the Royal Navy, and both were to survive the war. Francis had been a soldier for six months when war came. He was soon to find himself in France.

The British Army that fought on the Somme in 1916 was composed of three different elements. There was the Standing Army with its relatively small professional body of volunteer regulars. Secondly, there were the Territorials, who in 1914 carried out their contractual obligation to assume full-time service. And thirdly there were the new wartime recruits who responded to the unprecedented national campaigns, and enlisted in the mass organisation known as Kitchener's Army. The first of these groups made up ten divisions, each of some 18,000 men, that fought in the battle. The 5th Division was divided into three infantry brigades, one of which was the 95th Brigade. And the 95th, in turn, was made up of four battalions. One of these was the 1st Battalion of the Devonshires. As the battle developed, the 5th Division, in mid July, was operating on a sector of the front near the village of Longueval, in an area where the principal features surrounding the village were Mametz Wood, High Wood, and Delville Wood. Fierce, prolonged fighting was to go on in this area as the British mounted, over a four month period, a succession of largely ineffective attacks.

The 1st Battalion of the Devons were called into the front line on 23 July to replace a mixture of units. They had had a period in reserve positions, though they had been within shelling range. Now they were given a twofold task of consolidating the position and rescuing the numerous wounded who were lying out in front of the trenches. Enemy shelling made this latter exercise a hazardous one. The battalion spent three strenuous days on these duties. They then withdrew to a support position, but not before they had sustained 100 casualties. One of them was Private Harvey.

The bitterness of the fighting on the Somme throughout the last half of 1916, and the huge losses sustained in return for marginal gains, led the authorities to intensify the search for a new weapon that might revolutionise the battlefield. The mounted cavalry charge against High Wood, that took place in July, did not provide the answer. But the arrival, in September, of the first tanks, was a different matter. On 26 September the capture of Thiepval was helped, it was said 'by the appearance of three tanks'. The war had, nonetheless, half its course still to run.

Of the British soldiers who died on the Somme in 1916 during the five months of the battle, half have no known graves. These men are commemorated on the Thiepval Memorial, one of the great landmark memorials of the Western Front. Here are the names of members of every regiment in the British Army, of every rank, and of every age from fourteen. Among them is that of Francis Harvey.

THOMAS CHENHALL
Died Monday 31 July 1916. Aged 22.

Gravestones of Thomas and James Chenhall in Baghdad

In Victorian and Edwardian England, much more than in more recent times, children were given traditional family names. It was as if each family had a limited pool of acceptable names, the main criterion for inclusion of a name being its recent use by a close relative. The Chenhall family was a case in point. The two brothers who were to die within nine days of each other in the Summer of 1916 were Thomas and James. Their father was Thomas. His father was called James.

James, the grandfather of the two brothers, hailed from Bere Alston. Between 1857 and 1864 he was running a watchmaking business in Plymouth. The 1861 census lists him as living at 20 Drake Street, Plymouth, and as having seven children. In 1864 he moved his business, and his family, to 24 West Street in Tavistock. From the early 1880s he shared the premises with his eldest son, inevitably also called James, who established one of the pioneer photography businesses in the town.

The sixth of the seven children of James senior was Thomas, and he had been born in Plymouth in 1855. He served a seven year apprenticeship as a cycle and sewing-machine engineer with the Bristol firm of Snell, Hale, and Company. He then worked for seven years in Tavistock, at Pearce's iron foundry at Parkwood. Presumably during that period he lived in the family home, although the 1881 census found him lodging in Plymouth with a widow called Lucy Northey. This was the year in which he opened his own cycle and sewing machine engineering and sales business at 20 West Street, Tavistock, just a few doors away from his father's emporium. The business at No. 24 continued until after the turn of the century, by which time Thomas had moved from No. 20 to No. 21.

Emily Virginia Lambert was born at West Bradenham, in the middle of rural Norfolk, in 1862. She became a governess/companion, such as one meets in many a Victorian novel. In 1881 she was living in London, with a family called Everett. Soon after that she moved to Tavistock to become the companion of Lady Hamilton, who was living at Mount Tavy House. The plausible story, which there is no reason to doubt, is that someone in the household alerted Thomas Chenhall one morning that the sewing machine needed repair. Thomas went up to the house, and there he met Emily Lambert. They were married in 1884, in Plymouth, when Thomas was twenty-nine and Emily was twenty-two, and began their married life where they were destined to complete it, at 21 West Street, Tavistock. The year after the wedding saw the arrival of a daughter, called after her mother, and born, as was so often the case with a first-born, at the home of the maternal grandmother. The rest of the family, James, Lilian, Thomas, John, and Lucy, were born, in that order, at 21 West Street.

Thomas Chenhall, the fourth child and second son of Thomas and Emily, was born on 4 January 1894. He attended the National School in Dolvin Road until the age of thirteen, and followed this with two years at Tavistock Grammar School. In 1909 he left to take an engineering job. He is remembered during this period as an excellent soccer player, playing for the town club. His decision to enlist, in November 1910, interrupted both career and football. He had decided that he wanted to try to catch up with his brother James, who had been in the army for six years. Successful in persuading the recruitment agency that he was eighteen (he was really sixteen) he joined the 1st/5th Battalion, Devonshire Regiment. The early part of the war found him in India, and from there he was drafted to Mesopotamia, where he was attached to the 2nd Battalion of the Dorsets, to take part in the campaign to deprive the Turks of their control of the lands of the Tigris and Euphrates. He was reported as having been wounded in September 1915. Pushing north up the Tigris towards Baghdad, the British force met strong resistance at Kut, where, on 29 April 1916 the Turks took 12,000 prisoners. Among them were three Tavistock men. James Harris died after sixty days of captivity. The two others were the Chenhall brothers, Thomas and James. Seventeen months after the beginning of their internment, the *Tavistock Gazette* reported that their father had 'received from the *Central News* a very fine photograph of prisoners at Kut. In the group his two sons are plainly discernible. Mr Chenhall hopes, therefore, that both his sons are alive, but he cannot find out the date when the photograph was taken'. Mr Chenhall's hopes were soon to be cruelly dashed. He finally got the news that Thomas had died, in enemy hands, on 31 July 1916, and that James had died, in similar circumstances, nine days later. Neither parent really recovered from this double-blow. Emily, the mother, was to die within four years, and Thomas, the father, within six.

The two brothers, both born above the shop at 21 West Street, Tavistock, lie together in death. Their graves are side by side in Row B of the Baghdad North Gate War Cemetery.

JAMES CHENHALL
Died Tuesday 8 August 1916. Aged 29.

The 5th Devons march out of Whitchurch

It is impossible to imagine the grief of a bereaved parent. For many mothers and fathers of young men who fell in the First World War the sense of loss was compounded by the anxiety and the uncertainty that had preceded it. In many cases the interval between a report that someone was missing or captured, and an announcement that he was dead, was agonisingly long. For the Chenhalls the experience must have been excruciating. Two of their three sons, James and Thomas, had been taken prisoner by the Turks at Kut in Mesopotamia in April 1916. For twelve months there was no news. Then, in April 1917, a message came from the British Red Cross Society that they had been informed by the Red Crescent Society that James, the elder of the two brothers, had died in the previous August of malaria at a place called Baghtche. There followed a letter of sympathy from James's Commanding Officer, Colonel Hawker, who wrote: 'We are all fond and proud of your sons.' The parents, naturally, clung to the hope that the news of James might be unreliable, and they were comforted also by the fact that no similar message had been received about Thomas. And then, in August 1917, there arrived at the family home from a news agency a photograph of some of the Kut prisoners, in which the faces of both sons could be clearly distinguished. Hopes again soared, this time to be finally dashed as confirmation was finally received that both men had died in a Turkish prison camp, Thomas on 31 July 1916, and James nine days later. Even then there remained the agony of hearing that the one remaining son, John, had been severely wounded in action in Palestine, in November 1917. Mercifully, John survived both his wounds and the war. But the comment in the *Tavistock Gazette* on the death of Mrs Chenhall, soon after the end of the war, at the age of fifty-eight, was surely justified: 'Her death was largely due to grief at the decease of two of their sons while prisoners-of-war in the hands of the Turks'. Her husband died just two years later, in April 1922, at the age of sixty-seven. They were both buried in the Plymouth Road cemetery.

James Chenhall was the second in a family of six children. His father, Thomas, had launched a business at 21 West Street, selling and repairing cycles and sewing machines. Thomas had married Emily Virginia Lambert. Their eldest child, also named Emily Virginia, was born in Norfolk, the pregnant wife having retreated to her mother's home for the first delivery. Thereafter, starting with James, the children arrived at regular intervals at 21 West Street, in the home above the shop. Lilian came after James, and was, in turn, followed by Thomas, John, and Lucy.

James was born on 1 November 1886. He was a scholar at the National, or Church of England, School in Dolvin Road, and then at Tavistock Grammar School, at that time recently-reconstituted, newly-housed, and enjoying the early years of the mastership of J.J. Alexander. As a teenager he played a good deal of sport, and was also a solo tenor in the Parish Church Choir. He worked for a time at the Tavistock Foundry, learning his trade as a turner and fitter, as his father had done thirty years before. And then, at the age of eighteen, he enlisted. He became a sergeant in the 1st/5th Battalion of the Devonshires. His regimental number was 91.

The 5th Battalion sailed for India in October 1914. By the time the war ended this, the Territorial Battalion of the County Regiment, had alone contributed eight names to the Tavistock Roll of Honour. Increasingly, with Turkey's entry into the war, the India-based forces were used in campaigns against Turkey's Middle East empire. So it was that Thomas and James Chenhall were lost in Mesopotamia, and that the fighting in Palestine claimed Charles Bickle, Thomas Edwards, William Hellier, and Charles Spooner. The last two casualties, Alfred Pendry and Robert Roberts, died in France in the last summer of the war, after the 5th had been moved back to Europe to stem the latest, and as it turned out the last, German thrust on the Western Front. Among local men the Battalion's toll had indeed been a heavy one.

Sergeant Chenhall was evidently an effective soldier. In his first few months in India he had made a strong impression, and in July 1915, as the *Tavistock Gazette* put it, he was 'selected, out of 59 sergeants, as the sergeant of 25 picked Devons to go to Egypt.' This small group formed an element of the expeditionary force which aimed to push north through Mesopotamia, along the Rivers Tigris and Euphrates, with the ultimate objective of taking Baghdad. Strong Turkish resistance was encountered in November 1915, and James was wounded in fierce fighting. Five months later the strategically important town of Kut fell to the Turks, and some 12,000 British troops surrendered. Both James and his brother Thomas were interned in prisoner-of-war camps. James died in captivity, reportedly of malaria, on 8 August 1916. He lies buried in Baghdad (North Gate) War Cemetery, alongside his brother Thomas, who died nine days earlier.

CHARLES PHILP
Died Friday 11 August 1916. Aged 32.

Unveiling of the Whitchurch Memorial

The town of Albert in northern France was, throughout the war, never far away from some of the fiercest combat. One of the most potent symbols of the conflict was the figure, atop the church of Notre-Dame, of the Virgin holding aloft the child Jesus. In January 1915 a German shell had struck the Golden Madonna. The figure did not fall, but assumed a crazy horizontal tilt: a demented totem overlooking an unhinged world. Visible for miles, it could be clearly seen from Bouzincourt, a village two miles to the north-west. Here, throughout 1916, as the Battle of the Somme raged, the British established a Field Ambulance Station, just a few miles from where their front-line troops were straining every nerve to drive the Germans back from the gates of Albert. It was a convenient place to bury your dead, both those that had been carted back on the field ambulances and those killed in action and carried back from the line, just down the road. In one of these categories came Charles Richard Philp. Surrounded by a rubble wall, the Bouzincourt Communal Cemetery Extension provides a final resting-place for him, and for some 600 other 1914-18 war casualties. To the army he was Private C.R. Philp, No. M2/053193, 328th Mechanical Transport Company, Army Service Corps. To the folk in his home town he was 'Char' Philp, son of Mary and John Philp of 1 Church Park Cottages, Whitchurch, and brother of Jack, Susy, Emm, and Will. He was a few days short of his thirty-third birthday when he died.

Charles's roots in the local community were deep. His grandfather, John, had been born in the town in 1830. The 1861 census recorded John as living in

Bannawell Street, and earning a living as both a baker and a labourer in a chemist's shop. His versatility did not end there. He and his wife Susanna, nee Southcombe, who was also a native of Tavistock and was four years older than her husband, had already, by 1861, had seven children, the oldest being fourteen. John, the father, was then aged thirty. He was dead before he was forty.

John's eldest son was the fourth child. He was called after his father, and was born in 1852, when John senior had reached the ripe old age of twenty-two. Young John carried on the family tradition by marrying, at an early age, a woman older than himself. In July 1873 the twenty year old mine labourer from Bannawell Street married twenty-three year old Mary Geist, the daughter of William Geist, a labourer, and his wife Charlotte. The Geists were at that time living at 2 Bedford Place. Two years earlier the census had found them at Bowrish. John and Mary (surely the most common pair of names for marriage partners in the nineteenth century) were married at Tavistock Register Office. They proceeded to have five children, three sons and two daughters. John, a modest mine labourer at the time of his wedding, soon after became a gardener, and by the time of his death, he had become a 'retired farmer'. His last residence was 5 Marshall's Cottages, one of the charity homes established in 1890 under the will of a publisher called John Marshall. The cottages were a short step along the Whitchurch Road from Church Park Cottages, where John and Mary had brought up their family. It was, surely, appropriate that a couple who had spent so much of their lives in Whitchurch should finally be laid to rest in the grounds of its Parish Church. John died at the age of seventy, and was buried there in August 1923. Mary followed him into the family plot when she died in 1935, aged eighty-five.

Charles Richard was one of the three sons of John and Mary, and he shared his parents' sense of place and feeling of belonging. He was born on 30 September 1883 at Derby Cottage in the parish of Sampford Spiney, but the family soon after moved to Church Park Cottages, close to Whitchurch village centre, which remained Charles's home base for the rest of his life.

It was at Taplow in Buckinghamshire, for some reason as yet unexplained, that Charles enlisted and became a private in the Service Corps. He could drive, and it was, perhaps, natural that he should join one of the Corps' Mechanical Transport Companies. He may have been driving one of the field ambulances when he met his death near Bouzincourt on Friday 11 August 1916. Two battles were going on in the area at that period, with the British and German armies contesting fiercely for both Pozieres Ridge and Delville Wood, and it is probable that Private Philp lost his life in one of these actions. It was a stormy day, and there was thick mist in the morning.

Charles Philp is commemorated back home on the parish monuments of both Tavistock and Whitchurch. But perhaps the memorial that he would have cherished most appeared as a short 'In Memoriam' notice in the *Tavistock Gazette* on the first anniversary of his death. It read:

Charles Richard, son of John and Mary Philp, killed in action in France August 11th 1916. Char, brother of John, Sus, Em, Will. 'One of the best'.

REES MARTIN
Died Monday 4 September 1916. Aged 28.

Headstone in Delville Wood Cemetery, France

Rees Martin and Fred Warren must, one thinks, have been close friends. They were the same age. They both enlisted at Tavistock and became privates in the same battalion of the Devonshire Regiment. And they fell, at the same engagement on the Somme, within two days of each other. In death they were parted. Rees lies in Delville Wood Cemetery. Fred has no known grave.

Rees Martin was born on 15 September 1887 at Higher Grinacombe in the parish of Broadwoodwidger. His father, John, was a farm labourer. His mother had been Mary Jane Branch before her marriage. After the birth of Rees, the sixth child, the family moved to Beckwell Farm at Milton Abbot, where a seventh child was born. Young Rees made the natural, almost automatic, decision to follow his father onto the land, and, at thirteen, he was living and working at Park Farm, Milton Abbot. He later got a job with John Fuge Alford, who was at that time farming at Taviton. Rees lived in one of the cottages on the farm. In another lived a fellow farm labourer called George Giles. George had a teenage daughter. On 3 January 1912 at Tavistock Parish Church twenty-four year old Rees Martin married nineteen year old Edith Emma Giles. On 19 March 1913 Doris was born, at Lower Pennington, Whitchurch. Many years later Doris, in her eighties, recollected that she had not, as a child, got to know her father's family. 'They lived out of town', she recalled, 'and except for my grandmother visiting us on a couple of occasions we had practically no connection with them'. Edith's mother, originally Emma Miles, and her father, George, were both Whitchurch people.

Rees and Edith were resettled at 40 Bannawell Street by the time their second child, Edward, arrived, in January 1914. Hilda followed in December 1915, one month after Rees had enlisted. Edna was born in February 1917, five months after her father had died. Soon after that Edith moved her young family – four of them below the age of five – from the top of Bannawell Street, No. 40, to the bottom, No. 5.

The great drama of the Battle of the Somme extended throughout almost all the second half of 1916. It was to be the British contribution to the turning of the tide, a major and sustained offensive which would relentlessly push the Germans back. What developed, after the failure of the initial thrust, was a series of engagements along a front of twenty miles or so, in which villages, woods, ridges, and other strategic points, were disputed and fought over, in some cases changing hands a number of times. A case in point was the village of Ginchy. Here, Rees Martin's life was to be one of thousands laid down in pursuit of the possession of a small settlement that, except for a brief period in 1916, has rested throughout history in blissful obscurity.

Rees enlisted in Tavistock on 15 November 1915. He joined the 9th Battalion of the Devonshire Regiment, and was soon in France. The following summer was spent on the Somme. His battalion, along with the 8th Devons and two battalions from the Border Regiment and the Gordons, made up the 20th Brigade of the 7th Division. The task that was given to this division in early September was to capture and secure the village of Ginchy, which stood on a high plain, occupying a forward position in the German defence line. On 3 September, a day of low cloud and showers, the first objective, the occupation of the village, was achieved, but by nightfall the Germans had counter-attacked behind a heavy artillery onslaught, and had won it back. On the following day, 4 September, a fresh attack was made, with the 9th Devons spearheading the assault. The village was strongly held, but the Devons managed to enter it. They were, however, unable to consolidate their position, and were beaten off and forced to withdraw after fierce fighting. Heavy casualties left the strength of the battalion at no more than 400 of all ranks. Among those who had been killed was Private Martin No. 20839. His body was retrieved two days later, the day on which the 9th Devons, including Rees's old friend Fred Warren, once more threw themselves at Ginchy.

The Martin children were too young to understand what had happened, or to have any clear recollection of their father. They grew up in their Bannawell Street home and began the process of shaping their own lives. All three girls were married within twelve months of each other, two of them on the same day. Doris married Herbert Dashper, a carter, in 1935. Hilda and Edna shared a day in January 1936 to marry, respectively, William Cox, a builder, and Albert Price, an electrician. Meanwhile their mother, Edith, lived to the age of eighty-two, dying in 1976.

When Rees Martin died the Great War had entered its third year. No one at the outset had contemplated the possibility of a modern war of this duration. And yet, in September 1916, the war had run only half its course. And if only the people of Tavistock had been able at that time to look into the future they would have glimpsed with horror the prospect that more than two-thirds of the deaths were yet to come.

FREDERICK WARREN
Died Wednesday 6 September 1916. Aged 28.

Frederick Samuel Heath Warren

One of the visitors to the front during the Battle of the Somme in the late summer of 1916 was the member of the government who was to become Prime Minister in December of that year. David Lloyd George, in describing this visit in his memoirs, published after the war, was scathing about the military thinking behind the conduct of the battle. He wrote:

> The whole mind of the western strategists was concentrated on one or other of the hamlets along the Somme. They exaggerated the effect of every slight advance, and worked themselves into a belief that the Germans were so pulverised by these attacks that they had not the men, the guns, nor the spirit to fight anywhere much longer. They were only waiting, with hand cupped to ear, for the crack which would signify the final break of the German barrier.

The fate of the 9th Battalion of the Devonshire Regiment at Ginchy may be taken as a good illustration of Lloyd George's claims. In the first week of September 1916 the village of Ginchy had come into focus as a prime goal of the next phase of the great advance that it was thought would so change the fortunes of the war as to bring about a speedy victory. Ginchy occupied a key position on a high plain, and its capture and occupation was, it was considered, a major objective. The village was strongly fortified and, rather like a golf hole protected by bunkers, it was surrounded by trenches, known to the British as Porter Trench, Stout Trench, and Beer Trench.

Responsibility for capturing Ginchy lay with the 20th Brigade of the 7th Division. Of the four battalions that made up the Brigade, one was the 9th Devons. On 3rd September, and again on the 4th, the objective was reached, but the gains were lost in effective counter-attacks. The 9th Battalion sustained heavy losses, including Tavistock's Private Martin. On 6 September, an overcast day, the remains of the Battalion was called up to renew the assault, and during the afternoon the village was taken again, though casualties were heavy, the 9th losing a quarter of its remaining strength. German machine guns had done their work, but also, as a warrant officer of the 9th reported to his headquarters, some of the bloodshed was caused by 'our own guns firing short'. Private Warren, No. 17076, lost his life on that day. He has no known grave. His name is on the Thiepval Monument.

What remained of the 9th Battalion fell back, exhausted, and for the next three days other units moved in as the pendulum continued to swing and the casualty figures to rise. On the 9th the village was captured, and attention could be diverted to the next hamlet. The 9th Battalion, nicknamed the '9th London and Lancs' because it had attracted a considerable number of recruits from outside Devon, had paid a heavy price.

Frederick Samuel Heath Warren was twenty-eight years old when he died. The life that ended at Ginchy began on 27 May 1888 at 17 Brook Street, Tavistock. He was the eldest child of William Henry and Elizabeth Jane, who had been married three years earlier. At the time of the marriage, William had been listed as a twenty-one year old miner from Bannawell Street, the son of Robert Warren, also a miner. Elizabeth was aged twenty, a domestic servant, living and working at Bella Vista, the Kilworthy Hill home of John Goldsworthy. She had been born in Calstock, and was the daughter of a greengrocer called Samuel Heath. Frederick's birth, in 1888, was followed by that of Charles in 1890, and a daughter, Edith, followed. The young family lived at 21 Exeter Street, where they were joined by William's mother and his sister. They later moved to 55 Westbridge Cottages, where William died, of heart disease, in 1908, at the age of forty-four. In 1911, when the Duke of Bedford sold most of his Tavistock properties, Elizabeth, who had been paying 1s 9d per week rent for her cottage, bought it for £100. There she was to spend the thirty-five years of her widowhood, and there she was to die in December 1943, at the age of seventy-five.

Frederick's first job was that of a greengrocer's errand boy. When his father died, he was working as a postman. He had also become involved in the work of the Salvation Army which, at that time, was still a comparatively new feature of the town's religious landscape, having become established on Kilworthy Hill in 1882. Frederick played cornet in the Salvation Army Band, which was then the best, and the liveliest, band in town. He was not to be forgotten by his colleagues. Among the wreaths that adorned the Memorial on the day of its dedication was one 'from comrades of the Salvation Army'.

Frederick enlisted at Tavistock on 2 March 1916 as his fellow-townsman and exact contemporary Rees Martin had done three months earlier. The two men fell fighting in the same unit, within two days of each other. Frederick died on 6 September 1916. Since his body was not recovered, the authorities were able only to report him as missing. For his widowed mother at Westbridge it meant a further two months of uncertainty before there arrived, in mid November, the news that she had been dreading.

HENRY WEAVER
Died Friday 8 September 1916. Aged 33.

Henry James Weaver

A few miles east of Taunton lies the small Somerset village of Curry Rivel. It was here that Henry James Weaver was born on 3 October 1882. His parents were called William Henry and Jane. William, generally known as Harry, was a shoemaker, who had been born in 1848 and was to live into his nineties. Jane, who hailed from Nuneaton in Warwickshire, was, according to the 1901 census, employed as a collar worker. Henry was one of four children, two boys and two girls, brought up in the family home in Curry Rivel. A rural working-class upbringing in that period may have had its compensations, but it certainly restricted opportunity and ambition. Few avenues would have opened up to young Henry beyond the one that he pursued, an elementary education at the village school and a job as a labourer. He did, however, break loose to the extent of finding himself, at the age of eighteen, living in Bristol and working as a mason's labourer. It remained true that, for him, and for his generation, the war interrupted a pattern of life that was predictable and, perhaps, pre-ordained. It must have been the case that, to many of these young men, such an abrupt change offered a heady mixture of challenge enhanced by the newness of the setting, of excitement heightened by risk, and of exhilaration sharpened by danger. To others, perhaps, the prospects were pitched at a more modest level; to them the war did, at least, bring a welcome break in the otherwise relentless routine of working class life. Whether Henry Weaver shared any of these feelings when he enlisted at Weymouth in March 1916 we do not know. Domestic factors must, however, have offered some restraint. Henry had recently become a married man, and, even more recently, had learned that his wife was pregnant.

Florence Smale, who married Henry Weaver at St Andrew's Church, Curry Rivel, on 12 December 1915, came from Tavistock. She had been born at Heathfield in January 1888, the third in a family of ten children. Her father, William Henry Smale, had appeared in the 1881 census as a fifteen year old farm hand employed by Richard Wevill. At the time of Florence's birth he was described as a railway labourer, but three years later the 1891 census listed him again as a 'farm servant'. His fast-growing family was now located at No. 2 Mana Butts. His wife, Florence's mother, was Grace, nee Martin. She was nine years older than her husband. Both she and William were Devonians, he having been born at Sheepwash and she at Bradford. For someone of Florence's class and background the future was pre-determined to the same extent as if she had been a boy. She went into domestic service. In 1901, at the age of thirteen, she was living and working at Hatherleigh, her parents having recently moved from Tavistock to Okehampton. It was while working for a family in Curry Rivel during the early part of the war that she met, and married, Henry Weaver. She was twenty-seven; he was thirty-two.

Henry enlisted in the Oxfordshire and Buckinghamshire Light Infantry, joining the 1st/2nd Battalion and becoming No. 4732. In the early weeks of his training he gained qualifications for marksmanship, and was picked out as a specialist bomb thrower. After four months he was sent to France for operations in the area of the River Lys, to the south of Ypres. Periods of front-line duty alternated with spells behind the line in which there could be recuperation, re-training, or supply duties. It is thought that what happened on 8 September was that, during a training exercise, a hand grenade went off in a soldier's hand, killing the man himself and two of his comrades who were close by him. One of these was Henry Weaver. The three men were buried in the town of Merville, in the Communal Cemetery Extension, which had been opened in the previous month, and which was used by the nearby British hospital.

When Henry left for France in August 1916, Florence was in the later stages of her pregnancy. She decided to have the baby in Tavistock, where her parents had now re-settled at 22 Ford Street. There, on 18 September, she gave birth to a daughter, whom she called Phyllis, a name that Henry was known to favour. She did not know that her husband had died ten days before. It is believed that the news reached Tavistock either just before or just after the birth, but was not given to Florence until the child was ten days old.

Florence died of meningitis at the age of thirty-three, less than five years after the death of her husband. Phyllis was brought up first by her grandparents, and then by an aunt and uncle, Edith and Jack Martin. In 1938, at the age of twenty-one, she married a baker called William Geake. On 26 October 1999 Mrs Phyllis Geake fulfilled a lifelong ambition when, together with five members of her family, she visited her father's grave at Merville. The plot was originally marked by a wooden cross, which recorded Henry as having been accidentally killed. The permanent War Graves Commission headstone reads: 'In loving memory of my dear husband, from his sorrowing wife and child'.

FREDERICK MAKER
Died Thursday 28 September 1916. Aged 45.

Frederick Maker in stable yard at Ebrington Hall

The name 'Maker' appears four times on the Tavistock War Memorial. The men honoured are two pairs of brothers. Frank and Harold lived in London, but belonged to Tavistock on grounds of both birth and family bonds. Similar ties applied in the cases of Frederick and Henry, who were born into a Tavistock family, but moved away to further their careers. As far as Frederick was concerned, the journey's end, unlikely as it seems, was revealed in the entry on the original memorial in the Parish Church. It read: 'Frederick Maker, Ebrington, Gloucs. 28-9-16.'

Frederick's paternal grandfather, James, was a carpenter. In 1851 he was living at No. 49 Bannawell Street with his wife Mary and their three children. The middle child, John, was then sixteen, and was in the middle of an apprenticeship. In the mid 1870s, John, now in his forties, went into business as a builder and carpenter, originally with his younger brother Henry, and later on his own. By this time he had married, and set up home at 57 Bannawell Street, a few doors away from the house in which he had been brought up. His wife's maiden name was Bilkey. Her first name, Thomasine, proved too much for some officials, who recorded her, at various times such as weddings and census days, as Tamsin, Tamzine, or even Tansar. She had been born in Newlyn, and was a year older than John. The couple had seven children over a period of twenty years, and celebrated the imminent arrival of the seventh by moving a few doors down the hill to 63 Bannawell Street. Meanwhile, John's business prospered and outgrew its original Abbey Mead premises. In the early 1880s the business and domestic addresses both moved to No. 1 Canal Road, where trade and family remained until a final move to Ford Street in the late 1890s.

The seven children of John and Thomasine arrived at well-spaced intervals over a period of twenty years, from Mary in 1861, through Richard, William, Frederick, John, and Florence, to Henry in 1881. Frederick, who arrived halfway through this period, was born on 19 June 1871 and reared in Bannawell Street. A belated baptism, a week before his third birthday, may suggest a parental intention that he should attend the Church School in Dolvin Road. The 1891 census found him, at the age of nineteen, still living in the family home, which by now had moved to Canal Road, and which had been depleted by the departure of Mary, William, and John. Frederick was listed at that time as an assistant to a horse trainer. The horse theme was to run through the rest of his life.

In 1897, at Plympton, Frederick married Elizabeth Mary Walke, who had been born at Holbeton. She was the daughter of a Holbeton couple, Philip and Charlotte Walke. Frederick and Elizabeth's first child, Florence, was born in 1898, to be followed two years later by Frederick. At some point Frederick senior began working, as a groom, for a Mr M.A. Sands, and when Mr Sands moved to Ebrington in Gloucestershire in 1907, Frederick went with him. His employer settled at Ebrington Manor, a distinguished country house belonging to the Fortescue family. Frederick moved into a house near the entrance to the estate, which suited his position as a trusted retainer and was substantial enough to house the growing number of Makers. Leslie, Gordon, and Flora were born in Ebrington, bringing the number of children to five.

Mr Sands, fulfilling one of the duties normally associated with a country squire in that period, became an officer in the local Territorial Force in 1909. When war came he quickly found himself on foreign service with the Royal Gloucestershire Hussars. Frederick Maker was at his side as his batman and groom. They were at Gallipoli in 1915, attached, for a time, to the Worcestershire Yeomanry, but by the end of the year they were back with their regiment at its base in Egypt. It was there that Trooper Maker was medically discharged. He returned home, where he died within six weeks of his return. His tombstone in Ebrington churchyard records, under the insignia of the Hussars, that he died 'from disease contracted in the service of his country'.

Frederick's parents did not live to experience the grief of his death. They had shared their final years together in retirement in a house in Ralph's Court, close to the last site of John's building business. Here, John died in February 1912 at the age of seventy-five, and Thomasine three years later at the age of seventy-nine. They were spared also the loss of a second son. Henry, the youngest of the family, was to die in September 1918, within weeks of the armistice.

Frederick's widow Elizabeth died in Ebrington in 1945 and was buried with her husband. Of the children, Florence and Gordon also lived out their lives in the village. Frederick and Leslie found their futures in Scotland and in Windsor respectively. Flora, who remained a spinster, died in retirement in Mickleton.

Meanwhile, Mr Sands, having returned from his wartime experiences, announced in 1919 that, his hunting days being over, he and his wife would shortly be retiring to France. In 1920 Ebrington welcomed its new squire, Hugh Fortescue.

WILLIAM DAVY
Died Thursday 26 October 1916. Aged 42.

Grave in Salonika Lembet Road Cemetery, Greece

In a war which is remembered for claiming the lives of so many men in their teens and twenties, William Henry Davy, a middle-aged casualty, was something of an exception. He was forty when the war began, and forty-two when he died, at Salonika, in October 1916. This Greek town, now known as Thessalonika, lies at the head of the gulf that shares its name. Its Military Cemetery, on the northern outskirts of the town, holds the graves of servicemen from Britain, France, Serbia, Italy, and Russia. In the British section, which was in use from November 1915 to October 1918, can be found Grave Number 634, that of Private Davy, No. 13394, 17th Veterinary Hospital, Army Veterinary Corps.

William was born at No. 10 Exeter Street, Tavistock, on 5 May 1874. His parents both had roots in the rural area to the north of the town. His father, John, had been born in Lifton, the fourth of six children of a mason called William and his wife Maria, whose maiden name was Buckingham. John had become a carpenter. In 1873, at the age of thirty-four, he married a widow called Grace Dingle, who was six years older than himself. Grace, the daughter of a Coryton miner called John Worth, had a nine year old daughter named Caroline. The 1881 census recorded the family as consisting of John and Grace, with Caroline Dingle, now working as a general servant, and William, a six year old schoolboy, together with a sister named Bertha. By 1891 the family is still at No. 10 Exeter Street, but there is no longer any sign of either Caroline or Bertha. William, now sixteen, is described as a groom. In another part of the same census return the members of the Burgoyne household, living at No. 12 Millhill Cottages, are listed. The enumerator noted that William and Jane Burgoyne were being visited, on the day in question, by Edith, described as a twenty year old general servant. Edith was, in fact, a daughter who was calling in on her ageing parents. Her father and mother had been, respectively, fifty and forty-four at the time of her birth. At some point over the next few years Edith met William Davy. They were married at Tavistock Register Office on 26 March 1901. William, described as a coachman, was twenty-seven. Edith, whose father, a former miner, had died five years earlier, was twenty-nine. William had followed his father's example in marrying an older woman. The couple's first home was in Devonport, at 12 Home Park. They later moved to Mill Hill, where they occupied a cottage, Number 14, which was two doors away from the Burgoyne family home. Edith was still living at No. 14 in the late 1920s.

William's history following his marriage is far from clear. He enlisted at Woolwich, his experience as a groom leading him to join the Veterinary Corps. A continuing major wartime role for the horse had been clearly anticipated by the pre-war government when, in its contingency planning for the opening phase of a European war, it had insisted that a scheme should be drawn up to requisition 120,000 horses within two weeks. The huge demand for horses, driven by the high casualty rates, made it essential to have a significant veterinary component in every theatre of war.

The war in the Balkans was, to some extent, a sideshow, in comparison with the titanic struggles that were going on on both the Western and the Eastern Fronts. It was, nevertheless, of significance, partly because it drew off substantial men and resources from other theatres. The Balkans had, for more than a century, been an area over which the Powers of Europe had vied and jostled for territory and influence. Now, in wartime, the two power blocs competed to establish and nurture client states in the region. From the Anglo-French standpoint, a friendly Serbia needed to be protected against a hostile Bulgaria and against the potential might of the empires of Austria, Germany, and Turkey. Greece, neutral but appearing to lean towards the Anglo-French position, invited the allies to establish a base at the port of Salonika which would act as some kind of guarantee to the otherwise beleaguered Serbs. Troops began to arrive in the Autumn of 1915, some of the first being transferred from the ill-fated expedition to Gallipoli. Thereafter the size of the base grew until it came to occupy 200 square miles and to house eight divisions, with their huge supplies of arms, naval support and necessary transport, including horses and their attendant veterinary services. For the three years that Salonika remained the base for operations in the area, the principal enemy of the Anglo-French forces proved to be, not the Bulgarians and their supporters, but malaria. Battle casualties were of the order of 20,000. Hospital cases over the same period, among the 1 million men who took part in the campaign, numbered 1.3 millions. At the time when William Davy died, in late 1916, over 500,000 men were based at Salonika, making up the so-called 'Army of the East'. The overcrowding, the marshy setting, and the humidity, meant that fewer than 100,000 were fit for combat. It may be assumed that Private Davy was one of the many thousands who fell to the malaria that rampaged through the settlement.

JOE PLUMMER
Died Monday 20 November 1916. Aged 53.

No. 65 West Street, Tavistock, in 2002

Mr Plummer was a genuine Joe, not an abbreviated Joseph. He was born near the Devon-Cornwall border, at Hingston Down in the parish of Stoke Climsland on 28 October 1863. His mother had been Jane Lean before her marriage. His father, William Plummer, was a miner who worked in that area between Gunnislake and Callington in which there are more than eighty known mines, and in which, between 1850 and 1880, some 150,000 tons of copper ore was brought to the surface. It may be that William and Jane were the couple discovered by the 1881 census at St Marylebone, in London. He, then aged forty-five, was recorded as having been born in Oxford, and she, aged forty-three, was said to be a native of Chatham in Kent. It appears that, in moving to London, they had left Joe behind in the westcountry. The young man was apprenticed to a carpenter called William Laundry, in the Cornish village of Menheniot, nestling in the south-eastern corner of the county, between Liskeard and St. Germans. Joe lived in with the family, along with two other apprentices who were brothers named Payne, and who were of a similar age to himself. The Laundry home, Pengover Cottage, was, at the time of the 1881 census, accommodating the three teenage boys together with the Laundry parents and their seven children. The whereabout of Joe's elder brothers is unknown. It is assumed that he had at least two, because he was described, at the time of his marriage, as 'the youngest son of William Plummer'.

The details of Joe's naval career have yet to emerge, and the influences that led him in that direction remain unclear. Two factors in his early life may have significance. One was having a mother who came from Chatham, one of the great historic homes of the Royal Navy. The other was the fact that he spent much of his youth close to the Tamar, and to the port of Plymouth. He was to be described at the time of his death as a pensioned shipwright, Royal Navy. At the time of his wedding he was a shipwright aboard H.M.S. 'Ganges' at Falmouth. This was in October 1891, when, at the age of twenty-seven, he married Annie Higman at Charles Parish Church in Plymouth. Annie, who was three years younger than her husband, was the fourth daughter of Thomas Higman, a farmer. She had been living for some time in Treville Street, in Plymouth, presumably in service, but she still felt that she belonged to Menheniot. She and Joe had got to know each other living in the same small village community, and the wedding announcement described them as 'both of Menheniot Parish'.

H.M.S. 'Ganges' had been established as a training ship for boy entrants into the Royal Navy in 1865, and had been hulked and anchored at Falmouth since then. She was a teak-built eighty-four gunner. The reputation that she acquired was that of an institution with rigid rules and austere conditions. A high proportion of the young recruits were from broken homes, orphanages, and borstals, and it was considered necessary to enforce a regime that was harsh, disciplined, and punitive. Joe, as a seasoned and experienced shipwright, was a staff member. It may be that he remained in that post until 1903, the year in which the 'Ganges' abandoned her old home and became a shore-based establishment on the Shotley Peninsular.

In 1911 Joe Plummer, then described as 'of Liskeard', bought No. 65 West Street, Tavistock, and began an association with the town that was to be curtailed by his death five years later. The occasion of the purchase was the sale of most of the Duke of Bedford's properties in the area, an event made necessary, according to the Duke, because of his difficulty in meeting mounting tax bills. The sale raised over half a million pounds. Mr Plummer's contribution to easing the plight of the Duke was £280. The house, on the north side of the street and close to the foot of Rocky Hill, had previously been tenanted by a Miss Seager.

Joe had turned fifty by the time that the First World War broke out. It must be assumed that he was recalled as a reservist, and that he served in some capacity, presumably related to the work he had done in his old job on 'Ganges'. His subsequent discharge could have been on grounds of either age or health.

Joe Plummer died of heart disease at his West Street home on 20 November 1916. He was fifty-three. His wife Annie, who continued to live at No. 65 after Joe's death, succumbed to carcinoma of the uterus on 9 October 1918 at the age of fifty-four. Both deaths were registered by a daughter. Both burials took place at the Plymouth Road Cemetery, where the plot is accompanied by inscriptions commemorating 'My dear father Joe Plummer', and 'My dear mother Annie Plummer'. Joe's name also appeared on the Ancient Order of Foresters Memorial that hung for a time in the Town Hall. One of the many floral wreaths that surrounded the foot of the War Memorial on the day of its dedication was in the name of G. Plummer.

THEODORE MARTIN
Died Friday 24 November 1916. Aged 24.

Tavistock Hospital in 1900

In the quiet and secluded churchyard at Gulworthy the Martin family occupies its family plot. The first commemoration is 'In loving memory of Thomas Dingle, the beloved husband of Bessie Martin, who died at Morwellham, March 9th 1903, aged 39 years'. There follows: 'Also Bessie Martin, who died 15 August 1946, aged 82 years'. And then are listed their four children, Wesley Dingle, Theodore, Thomas Dingle, and Ivy. They died in, respectively, 1915, 1916, 1956, and 1983. They belonged to a Morwellham family. Thomas senior was living there and working as a mine labourer when, in 1890, he married Bessie Willis. They had both been born in 1863. Bessie was a Gunnislake girl, whose father, Charles Willis, was a mine labourer, and whose mother had been born Sarah Shepherd. Thomas was a second generation Morwellham-based copper miner, whose father, Solomon, had married Sarah Dingle, a circumstance from which derived the practice in succeeding generations of freely using 'Dingle' as either a first or a second name.

The eldest of the four children of Thomas and Bessie, Ivy, was born in Gunnislake, during a short period following the marriage when the couple were living there, in a house in King Street. The other three were born after a move across the River Tamar in 1892. All four were brought up in Morwellham. It was inevitable that in such a small, isolated, community they should spend a lot of time together as family members. In particular, the two eldest sons, Theodore and Wesley Dingle, born within sixteen months of each other, came to share a range of interests and ambitions, which led them from the same school, in Dolvin Road, Tavistock, to the same employment as cab drivers, to membership of the local Battery of the Royal Field Artillery of the Territorial Army, and ultimately to a similar fate.

Theodore was the eldest of the three sons. Born on 20 August 1892, he was ten years old when his father died in a mining accident, which was, in the coroner's judgment, 'caused by the negligence of another'. Soon after that the family moved into Tavistock, re-settling at No. 9 Dolvin Road. For the children this move brought the advantage of living in the same road as their school. For Theodore and Wesley, when they began their working lives, it meant that they were closer to their employment as drivers for Backwell's and Truscott's respectively. These were the two principal 'conveyance agencies' in the town, who traditionally operated coaches and omnibuses on local routes. Backwell's, Theodore's employers, were particularly well known for their regular services between the LSWR station and the Bedford Hotel, and for their excursions to such Dartmoor beauty spots as Two Bridges and Burrator. As the Internal Combustion Engine began to replace the Horse, they were to concern themselves increasingly with motor cars, offering hire facilities and taxi services. Theodore's experience as a driver in civilian life was to prove useful in his military career.

It was after the outbreak of war that the paths of the two brothers diverged. They had both been members of the local Battery, and had enlisted together, along with their other colleagues, on 4 August, at the Battery Headquarters at Crelake. But while, after initial training, Wesley went off with the majority of the unit to India, there to fall a victim to malaria in August 1915, Theodore joined the 28th Division Ammunitions Column of the Royal Field Artillery, and went to France. As No. 1187 Driver T. Martin, he saw service at Ypres. At some point he contracted an illness, which led the authorities to discharge him on health grounds, to grant him a pension, and to send him home. He came back to his home town, and for a time was able to resume his old calling as a cab driver. In November 1916, however, his condition rapidly deteriorated, and on the 24th he died in Tavistock Hospital. The record gave, as the cause of death, exhaustion, and cellulitis, a form of inflammation of the body tissues characterised by fever, pain, and swelling of the affected area. The *Tavistock Gazette* reported that he had died 'from an illness contracted at the front'. On the day of the funeral a service was conducted in the family home in Dolvin Road by the Rev. Robert Tebb, the Methodist Minister. The cortege then left for Gulworthy, where Theodore was to be buried alongside his father. The chief mourners were his mother, his brother Thomas, and his sister Ivy. For his mother, who had been widowed at thirty-nine, this was the second time, in successive years, that she had had to endure the agony of a lost son. Wesley had died in India in August 1915. But he had been buried in faraway Bengal, and the prospect of ever visiting Barrackpore cannot have crossed her mind. It may have been the smallest crumb of comfort that Theodore's grave was nearby, and could be visited and tended frequently. It was to be many years before Bessie was to join her husband and son in the family plot at Gulworthy. By the time she died, at the age of eighty-two, a Second World War had been fought and won, and had garnered its own harvest of casualties.

PHILIP PALMER
Died Friday 24 November 1916. Aged 32.

Commemoration at Tyne Cot

Philip William Palmer was born at 9 Queen Street in the parish of Stoke Damerel, in Plymouth, on 26 July 1884. His father, Allen Sambels Palmer, worked as an upholsterer, but died when Philip was young, and the boy was brought up by his widowed mother, whose name is variously given as Louisa or Lucy, and who had been born in Tavistock in 1855, the daughter of an engineer called James Bawden. She had been working as a dressmaker when she married Allen Palmer in July 1872. Like so many young men in Plymouth at that time, and indeed in later periods over the next century, Philip found that the natural place to turn to for a job was Devonport Dockyard, which was by far the biggest employer of labour in the area. Philip began work as a labourer in the Dockyard, just a few minutes walk away from his home. At the age of thirty he married a near-neighbour, Mabel Lillian Potter. The marriage took place at the Devonport Register Office on 6 March 1915. Philip was five years older than his bride. They both, at that time, lived in their family homes in James Street, Devonport, a working class area in the Mount Wise district of the city. Mabel was the daughter of James Potter, a naval pensioner. She had been born, in the parish of Stoke Damerel, in 1889, and was the eldest child in a large family.

The Devonshire Regiment, which Philip joined, had a history going back to 1685. It was raised at that time to combat the threat of an armed rising on behalf of the Duke of Monmouth. The 11th Regiment of Foot, as it was originally known, had its depot at Bristol, but recruited throughout the counties of the westcountry. During the eighteenth century it was employed to carry out the basic duties of an infantry regiment, in containing outbreaks of civil disorder at home or in Ireland, and in participating in the continental wars in which Britain occasionally became involved. The nineteenth century saw, in addition to the long French Wars, a series of colonial conflicts, culminating in the Boer War. The response to the latter emergency was to increase the strength of the regiment from two battalions to five. By the time of the 1918 armistice this number had increased to sixteen.

Philip Palmer enlisted at Devonport as Private No. 25741 in the 1st Battalion of the Devonshire Regiment. The Battalion had landed in France on 21 August 1914. Thereafter, the men of the 1st were almost continually occupied on one or other of the principal epicentres of the British Army's efforts on the Western

Front, Flanders and the Somme, winning honours, earning a reputation for steadfast devotion to duty, and justifying the famous motto of the regiment: 'Semper Fidelis'.

The Battalion had spent a good deal of 1916 on the Somme, where it had sustained heavy casualties. A summer of struggle and slaughter now gave way to an autumn in which both sides, exhausted by their efforts and weakened by their losses, looked to a period in which they could recover their strength and re-assess their strategy in the light of the inconclusive battle that had now produced stalemate. In the first week of October the Battalion, after a short break, was given responsibility for a section of the front centred on Cuinchy and Neuve Chapelle. Those who had joined the Battalion at the beginning of the war found themselves on familiar terrain. They had been here, in the same place, doing the same job, two years earlier. Here, on Christmas Eve 1914, George Tyrrell had become the first Tavistock-based member of the Battalion to die in the war. Now his successors faced a further six months stint, which was to occupy the third winter of the war. These months proved to be relatively quiet on long stretches of the front. The victors, in that winter, were the conditions. The whole of the frontage had become a marshland, with, in many places, the line being held by detached posts, islands in a sea of mud and water. The efforts to bale or pump water out of the trenches, where such efforts were effective, required huge investments of manpower, which left little time or inclination for the business of killing or being killed. It was, of course, to be a temporary pause in the slaughter. The 1st Devons, over the six months, lost 250 men to hospitalised sickness and sustained 150 casualties in the sporadic fighting. Of the latter, twenty-two were killed. They included Private Palmer, killed in action on 24 November 1916.

A burial ground very close to where Philip Palmer was killed was the Gorre British and Indian Cemetery, and here he found his final resting place. The ground occupied a corner of the estate of a chateau on the edge of the village of Gorre, near the Belgian border. The chateau had been occupied in the early days of the war by troops, who had laid out the cemetery to be used for the burial of those who died while holding that particular sector of the line. It came eventually to hold the graves of over 900 casualties. The village of Gorre, two miles east of Beuvry, was, in spite of its closeness to the front line, never taken by the Germans.

ERNEST FRIEND
Died Sunday 26 November 1916. Aged 23.

Transloy: November 1916

On 1 July 1916 Ernest Davey became the first Tavistock casualty of the Battle of the Somme. Almost five months later, on 26 November, Ernest Friend became the last. The great battle had ended one week earlier, when the allies abandoned an offensive which, it had been hoped, would lead to speedy victory in the war, but which, notwithstanding some remarkable bravery and a few minor territorial gains, had degenerated into an attritional stalemate in which the fields of the Somme turned brown with churned mud and red with spilt blood. The only satisfaction that could be drawn was the knowledge that, by diverting so much enemy attention to the Somme, the British Army had given a breathing space to the French Army, holding the line to the south. The French had come under intense pressure, and it was feared that the fortress of Verdun might fall, with catastrophic results. The Battle of the Somme did, at least, reduce that pressure, and in so doing it contributed to the protection of Verdun and to the capacity of the French Army to maintain the war effort at a high level. But the cost to the British Army was high: 2955 casualties for each of the 142 days of the battle. Private Friend was wounded in one of the last engagements of the Somme Battle, one of the last sub-plots in the great tragic drama. He died of his wounds.

Ernest Willie Friend enlisted in the Royal Army Medical Corps, and became attached to the 6th Divisional Signal Company of the Royal Engineers. The Company was heavily involved in October 1916 in the battle for the Transloy Ridges, an engagement that went on for eighteen days, on twelve of which persistent rain turned the whole area into a sea of mud. The battle began on 1 October, on the old Roman road that runs as straight as an arrow from Bapaume south-west to Albert. The British Fourth Army under Sir Henry Rawlinson attacked the German lines and gained its immediate objectives. Thereafter, the prize was the occupation of the Transloy Ridges, to the south of Bapaume. Fortunes swayed over the course of the eighteen days, as neither side was able to press home advantages they might have gained. Finally, on 18 October, the whole enterprise came to an end as combatants sank into a sea of clinging, liquid mud. The battle had, in essentials, been a microcosm of much that characterised the whole Western Front conflict. At some point during the engagement Private Friend, attending to his medical duties, sustained wounds which resulted in his being moved behind the lines to Bethune, where there was a hospital and a casualty clearing station. Here, on 26 November, he died. He lies buried in Bethune Town Cemetery. The burial ground covers an area of 8475 square metres, and contains the graves of some 3000 casualties of World War One.

Northlew is a large rural parish to the north of Okehampton, in which, according to an old saying, 'the devil died of the cold', on account of the winds blowing uninterruptedly across the central Devon plateau. Here, in 1851, at Harper's Hill, lived James Friend, a farm labourer, his wife Anna, nee Dennis, and their four children. The youngest child, six months old, was named Charles. He became an ostler, moved into Tavistock to take a job at one of the town's hotels. Since he lived in West Street, it is probable that he was plying his trade at one of the two inns in that street, in the employ of either John Down at the Cornish Arms or Mary Northway at the Queens Head Hotel. In February 1873, at Tavistock Register Office, Charles married Mary Jane Abell. The new Mrs Friend was at that time lodging in Duke Street, but she had been born in Hatherleigh, the daughter of a cordwainer called Henry Abell and his wife Mary. The young couple set up home at No. 8 Ford Street. Henry, the oldest child, was born in 1875 under his grandmother's eye at Hatherleigh. The three who followed were all born in Tavistock, Charles in 1880, Florence in 1888, and Ernest in 1893. There was enough room in the Ford Street cottage to accommodate also a lodger.

Ernest, familiarly Willie, was the baby of the family, and was born on 7 February 1893. He lost both his parents before reaching his teen years. His father, Charles, died of heart disease on 9 December 1900, at the age of fifty. Mary Jane, his mother, was fifty-three when she died on 8 August 1905. It was decided that Ernest should go to live with his eldest brother, Henry, who, at the time of Mary Jane's death was thirty years old and living in Leeds. The young twelve year old moved north and re-settled in Henry's home, 48 Beverley Street, in the Hunslet district of Leeds. Here he finished off his schooling, entered adult life, and, when the war came, enlisted as No. 12004 Private Ernest Willie Friend. A Yorkshireman, perhaps, at least by adoption. But, as his family understood when they asked for his name to be included on the local memorial, he was a Tavistock lad, and his native town should not, and would not, forget him.

GEORGE HILL
Died Thursday 4 January 1917. Aged 33.

Beaumont Hamel: January 1917. The mounds represent the village

George Henry Hill was a Cornishman. He was born in Northgate Street, Launceston, on 23 April 1883. The birth was registered by George's mother, who before her marriage had been Sarah Ann Jones. Unable to sign her name, Sarah Ann had, on that occasion, made her mark. She was thirty-eight at the time of the birth, having been born in Launceston in 1845. The marriage to Henry Hill, a fellow-resident who worked as a mason's labourer, had taken place recently. Henry thereafter appears to have not been on the scene for very long, and he is certainly absent from the family setting in 1901. In that year the census describes Sarah as earning a living as a self-employed charwoman and sharing a two-roomed dwelling with her seventeen year old son, George, described as a grocer's storeman.

George Hill married Mabel Wooldridge on 18 September 1907, when he was twenty-four and she was eighteen. George was still living in his native town, in a house in Tower Street, and the wedding took place at Launceston Register Office. His bride was a domestic servant who had been born in Launceston in 1889, but who had been living and working in Virginstowe prior to becoming Mrs Hill. She was the daughter of a labourer called John Wooldridge. George and Mabel later moved into Tavistock, renting accommodation at No. 57 West Street, a house that in 1911, in the Duke of Bedford's sale, changed ownership, for £120, from the Duke to Mr George Williams. George Hill worked as a mason's labourer, as his father had at a similar age. He also got a part-time job at the Constitutional Club, which had opened at the foot of Drake Road in 1896. One of the main interests of Edred Marshall, the club's founder and first president, was billiards. He employed George as a billiard marker. The young man became a popular figure with club members, and the extra money from this second job proved very helpful when four children, of whom two were called William and Sidney, arrived in quick succession. They were to be too young, at the time of their father's death, to retain any clear memory of him.

George enlisted at Tavistock soon after the outbreak of war. He joined the 9th Battalion of the Devonshire Regiment as a Private, Number 25793. Whatever the reasons for his decision to respond to the pressures to join up, money cannot have featured among them. A Private earned one shilling (5p) a day. The acquisition of a stripe brought an extra threepence (1p). Officers, of course, fared differently. A lieutenant, a captain, and a colonel, would enjoy, respectively, daily rewards of 7/6 (37p), 12/6 (62p), and 23/- (115p). But such riches were out of the reach of young men like George Hill.

Towards the end of 1916 the 9th Battalion was doing duty at the Front, with responsibility for a section of the line in the area of Beaumont Hamel, which had been so fiercely fought over in the Somme Battle. On New Year's Day 1917 two officers of the Battalion, on a reconnaisance walk towards an advanced post, found German troops in possession. Later in the day, having collected some bombers, they made an effort to re-capture the post, but the combined effect of thigh-high mud and steady machine gun fire forced them to withdraw and postpone the attempt. The following evening the Battalion was relieved, and moved out. However, in order to benefit from their experience, fifty men who knew the terrain in detail were left behind and were given the task of recovering the post in question. Casualties were expected. On 4 January the chosen fifty went into action, rushing and capturing the target and taking nine prisoners. The exercise was, however, at a cost of fifteen casualties. Of the five who were killed, one was George Hill. Such skirmishes were typical of the kind of activity that took place along the Western Front. Officers who made the decisions had to get used to making calculations which involved assessments of potential gains as against probable losses, the gains being measured in yards and the losses in lives. In the exercise in which George Hill lost his life the casualty-rate was 30%. One wonders whether this price was considered, in retrospect, to have been a reasonable one, and how it might have compared with the mornings's predictions. It might also be fair to ask about the psychological effects on those whose duty it was to make such judgements. Of the effects on the ordinary Tommies, who simply did as they were told, there is perhaps no need to ask.

Private Hill lies buried at Gorre, a small village in the Pas de Calais department of Northern France, in a cemetery which was established in a corner of the grounds of a chateau near the village, and which is shared by some 900 British and Indian casualties of the war. The ground remained in British hands throughout the war, but its closeness to the front line made it a convenient final resting-place for those who had died in that sector.

George Hill spent the thirty-one years of his prewar life in the two neighbouring towns of Launceston and Tavistock. He is, appropriately, commemorated on both War Memorials.

FREDERICK GAWMAN
Died Tuesday 30 January 1917. Aged 31.

Frederick Gawman

Saturday 11 November 1939 was a sombre day. The sense of loss and the remembrance of sacrifice, the characteristic features of the previous twenty-one annual commemorations of the 1918 armistice, were now heightened by the fact that the country was once more at war. Many people in Tavistock noted also that the day brought the death of one of the town's older citizens. In the Ford Street house where she had lived for many years, Mary Jane Gawman died at the age of eighty-six. She was one of the longest local survivors of that group who had borne so much of the grief and burden of the First World War, the bereaved mothers.

Mary Jane had been born in Back Street, Tavistock, on New Year's Eve 1852. Her father, Nicholas Hynes, was a mason, and her mother, formerly Miss Pike, was called Elizabeth. When she was eighteen, Mary was married, at Tavistock Parish Church, to a local boy called Samuel Henry Gawman. He was also eighteen, and was the son of a shoemaker called Thomas Gawman. Young Samuel was a tailor. He was to pursue that career, but also to do a long spell as an able seaman that earned him the rank of Chief Petty Officer and a naval pension. Like his wife, he was to have a long life; he died in 1940 at the age of eighty-seven.

Samuel and Mary Jane had two daughters and four sons, one of whom was Frederick George, born on 20 May 1885. Samuel's job meant that the family tended to move around quite a lot, and Frederick was born while they were living at Exmouth. One result of this pattern was that, in order to provide the children with some domestic stability, they were housed for long periods with the Hynes grandparents at No. 10 Fitzford Cottages. When, eventually, Samuel retired, and exchanged a wandering life for the delights of a Ford Street garden, the family at last acquired a permanent base. Before then, Frederick had enjoyed the interesting childhood experience of growing up in close company with itinerant parents, a clutch of siblings, grandparents in their fifties, two aunts, and two cousins.

One of the most prominent businessmen in Tavistock at the turn of the century was the builder William Henry Higman. Frederick Gawman served his apprenticeship with him as a joiner. It was during this period that the Gawman parents settled in No. 6 Ford Street, his father's seafaring days having come to an end. Samuel bought the house in the Duke of Bedford's sale in 1911. In a final act of ducal generosity, sitting tenants were offered preferential deals. Samuel bought his house for £151. In the same year Frederick married Jessie, and they moved in just along the road, at No 13. Jessie, seven years older than her husband, was the daughter of a Lamerton couple called Henry and Elizabeth Williams. Henry was a GWR platelayer.

Like his father, Frederick Gawman was an itinerant worker. He was in Saltash when he enlisted on 31 August 1916. Conscription had been introduced for single men between the ages of eighteen and forty-one at the beginning of the year, and had been extended in the Summer to include married men. Frederick joined up during this period when the voluntary principle was being superseded by the compulsory one. He joined the Duke of Cornwall's Light Infantry. He was recorded as being 5′ 8″ tall, significantly the average height of recruits at that time. After a couple of days at Bodmin, the time needed for medical examinations, documentation, and the issue of the basic kit, Private Gawman No. 34251 was posted to the 3rd Battalion for three months training at Freshwater Camp on the Isle of Wight. Then, in December 1916, he was ready for duty at the Front, and found himself, by Christmas, with the 6th Battalion in the Arras area.

The Battalion War Diary for 30 January, which records Frederick's death, conveys very well a typical day of attritional warfare, between major engagements, on the Western Front:

> Enemy active. From 7 a.m. to 10 a.m. with trench mortars and 77mm shells blowing in part of the support line between Hetsas and Holborn Streets and the front line in trenches 34 and 35. Shrapnel also fell behind the support line near Hamilton Street. The enemy also fired several rifle grenades about 2.30 a.m. These fell on the front line near H41 Trench. The enemy was very active with trench mortars on the Left Company Sector between 7 a.m. and 9 a.m. These fell on the front line. The night was quiet. Casualties: 1 Killed, 1 Wounded.

The '1 Killed' was Frederick Gawman. He was buried in the Faubourg D'Amiens Cemetery in the town of Arras. The site contains over 2500 First World War commemorations.

Frederick and Jessie had one child, a daughter, who was six when her father died. Soon after the end of the war, mother and child moved from Ford Street to Parkwood Road, where Jessie died in 1950. The daughter was called Hilda. In 1938 she married a greengrocer called Charles Frost. As the century drew to a close, Hilda Frost was in good health, and was still living at Parkwood, in one of the most distinctive houses in that interesting area of the town.

HENRY PENGELLY
Died Thursday 1 February 1917. Aged 23.

Headstone in Assevillers Cemetery, France

On 9 February 1917 the *Tavistock Gazette* carried the following report:

> Information was received yesterday by Mr H Pengelly of No 1 Taviton Cottages that his son Harry had been killed at the front. He was a promising young man. Much sympathy will be felt for the parents in their bereavement.

A few days later another letter was received at the same house, addressed this time to Mrs Pengelly. It had been sent by Harry's Commanding Officer, and was dated 3 February. It read:

> I am very sorry to have to tell you that your boy was accidentally killed the night before last. He was sleeping in a dug-out with five other men and a fall of earth took place which buried him and two others. They were got out as quickly as possible, and a stretcher-bearer applied artificial respiration. I arrived to find one of my officers already there, and shortly after the medical officer came. He gave an injection of alcohol but it was to no avail, and he gave it as his opinion that Pengelly died from some internal injury received from the great weight of earth, and not from suffocation. I know this will be a great blow to you. It has been a great loss to me, for he was a very promising NCO. He was liked by his men. He handled them well, and I had my eye on him for further promotion. His death was practically instantaneous, and he was properly buried by the chaplain in the presence of his officers and comrades. You must realise that your boy has died for his

country every bit as much as though he had been struck by a bullet in the front line. I sincerely trust that you will take this fact to your comfort in your great sorrow.

The 'proper burial' to which the officer referred almost certainly took place at the Plantation Cemetery, which lay close to the River Somme and between the villages of Cappy and Herbecourt, near the place where the accident occurred. This was a French military burial-ground occupying a large orchard. Henry Pengelly was the only British soldier to be buried there. After the armistice the practice was followed of concentrating graves in fewer, larger, more accessible cemeteries. Henry's grave was moved about three miles to the New British Cemetery in the village of Assevillers. He is one of some 800 casualties who are commemorated there.

Henry had enlisted, at Tavistock, in March 1915, at the age of twenty-one. The 1st/8th Battalion of the Worcestershire Regiment, that he joined, was a Territorial Battalion. It is not clear what connection he might have had with Worcestershire, as all his roots appear to have been in Devon. His father, also called Henry, was a farm worker who had been born in Whitchurch parish in 1857, and who, on the eve of his marriage, was working for a local farmer called Glanville. Henry senior married Caroline, a Plymouth girl whose father, William Brown, was a solicitor's clerk. She was living in Sampford Spiney in 1881 and working as a domestic servant. In a period when domestic service accounted for a quarter of the employment in the local area, and farming and mining together made up another quarter, it was hardly surprising that liaisons were common between young servant girls and young farm workers or copper miners. The only unusual feature of this particular relationship was their ages. Henry was thirty-five and Caroline twenty-eight when they were married, on 5 June 1893, at the Congregational Church in Duke Street. This building was twenty years old at the time; its impressive spire-topped presence was to remain a feature of the town centre landscape until its demolition in 1960. On 29 December 1893 Henry Pengelly junior was born at Moorshop. The 1901 census recorded him as having been joined by a sister, Beatrice, born in 1895, and a brother, Alfred, then eight months old. Reginald was to follow. The two successive family homes of the Pengellys were Moorshop and Taviton. Within a mile of each other, they both occupied small satellite settlements to the north-east of Tavistock, and within the parish of Whitchurch.

Private Henry Pengelly, later Lance Corporal, No 20705, arrived in France with his Battalion on 31 March 1915, following a short period of initial training. It was almost two years later that he was killed. On 28 January 1917 the Battalion moved up by train from its billets behind the line to Cerisy, on the banks of the Somme, where it remained in reserve for three days. Then, on 1 February, it took over trenches in an area one mile west of Herbecourt. No fighting was reported on the following two days. Henry's accident was one of those incidents which will inevitably happen from time to time, given the conditions that prevailed.

Henry's mother survived her son by only three months. Caroline Pengelly died on 28 May 1917 of hemiplegia and exhaustion, at the age of fifty-two. Her death was registered by her husband, Henry senior, who, like many of his class and generation, remained illiterate, and certified his wife's passing with a mark rather than a signature. Henry himself died in July 1921 at the age of sixty-three.

WILLIAM PARSONS
Died Sunday 11 February 1917. Aged 30.

Grave in Karasouli Military Cemetery, Greece

The native or adopted sons of Tavistock whose sacrifices are recorded on the town's Memorial are buried, or commemorated, in scores of different locations. Some lie near their homes. Many occupy plots in the hundreds of cemeteries, or feature on the many monuments, that mark so poignantly the killing fields of the Western Front. Others lie in more remote and unlikely settings, in the Balkans, the Middle East, or India, their wide dispersal a testimony to the fact that this was, in reality as well as in name, a World War. One of the more obscure sites is the Karasouli Military Cemetery in Northern Greece, some thirty-five miles north of the Aegean port of Thessalonika and close to the borders of both Serbia and Bulgaria. Here lies Private William Parsons, No 17127, of the 10th Battalion, the Devonshire Regiment, and of Brook Street, Tavistock.

William Samuel Parsons was born on 15 August 1886. His father, William Henry, and his grandfather, John, had both worked as copper miners. John had married Mary Northey, and they had had three children, of whom William Henry, the youngest, had been born in 1858. The family lived at Mill Hill. William Henry began a career in the mines because to do so was a natural, almost an automatic, course for a miner's son to follow. There was also, in spite of rapidly gathering economic clouds, an unwillingness to contemplate the possibility of the decline of the industry. The shocks soon followed, and within a few years copper mining in the area had practically disappeared. The whole process was to be replicated in the case of coal, in other parts of the country, a century later.

By the time the redundancies began to multiply, in the last quarter of the nineteenth century, William Henry had, at the age of twenty, married Mary Ann Waldron. Mary was twenty-three and lived in Trelawny Road. She was the daughter of Samuel Waldron, who was first a sawyer and then a painter, and of Jane, whose maiden name was Worth. William Henry and Mary Ann set up home at No. 21 West Street, and children began to appear, the first of whom were John in 1880 and Hettie in 1882. By the time number three was on the way William Henry had left the ailing copper industry and had managed to launch a greengrocery business at 17 Market Street. And here, in August 1886, William junior was born. His father's enterprise, alas, was short-lived. Within a short time the family, which continued to increase, had moved to Bannawell Street, but had lost the father. William senior had decided to take his mining experience and his business enterprise to South Africa. The 1891 census records, for 55 Bannawell Street, a household led by Mary Parsons, a miner's wife whose husband had 'gone to the Cape', and containing, with the recent addition of Florence and Maud, five children between the ages of eleven and one. It appears that no more was seen of their father, and the 1901 census described Mary as a widow. At that time her household included all five children, three of them now in work, together with Harry Doidge, the recently bereaved widower of Mary's sister, and his one year old daughter. There was space also for a lodger. The family subsequently moved from Bannawell Street to 28 Brook Street.

Young William was baptised in Tavistock Parish Church in September 1886. The holding of a joint ceremony involving also his elder sister Hettie provides another example of the practice, not uncommon, of christening a family's children in batches rather than individually, so long as those held in the queue remained healthy. William started school at the age of four. At fourteen he was apprenticed to a butcher, John Palmer of 41 Brook Street. It is not clear whether he completed this training, but he had certainly, before the war broke out, exchanged butchering for driving. He became an employee of Thomas Truscott, who ran a considerable, and expanding, business from a site near Vigo Bridge, providing a variety of transport needs from Dartmoor tours to funerals. This was what young William was doing when he enlisted, at Plymouth, and joined the 10th Battalion, the Devonshire Regiment.

The 10th Devons formed part of the huge build-up of Anglo-French forces at the Greek port of Salonika (now Thessalonika). Here, from Autumn 1915 onwards, an army was assembled to support the Serbian ally and confront the Bulgarian foe, and to resist the presence in the Balkans of Germany, Austria, and Turkey. In part, the Bulgarian Campaign echoed the struggle in France in that it became an attritional tussle of which trench warfare was the main feature. By October 1916 the Battalion had taken its place as part of the allied front line at a point opposite a Bulgarian-held ridge called Petit Couronne. There it remained for six months. During that time, occasional raids were made to test the strength of the defenders of the ridge. The most formidable of these raids occurred on 11 February, having been postponed for two days because of a blizzard. A force of 600 men were involved. There was stern fighting, and the Devons suffered 25% casualties. Among the dead was Private Parsons.

JOHN SYMONS
Died Monday 12 February 1917. Aged 26.

Morwellham Cottages

The small church of St Paul, Gulworthy, built in 1854 to serve the rapidly growing population in the western part of the parish of Tavistock, was the scene of a wedding on Sunday 14 January 1917. For working class families, many of whose members worked six days a week and could not afford to lose a day's pay, Sunday was the best day on which to hold such occasions. And the guests on that day were members and friends of two local working class families. Lilian Pethick was being given away by her father, a woodranger whose home, at The Rock, was within a stone's throw of the church. The groom was John Symons. He was a carrier from Morwellham, but his recent career had been as a member of the Royal Flying Corps, in which he was an Air Mechanic. After the wedding he returned, with his new bride, to the Yorkshire village of Brantingham, near the Humberside air station where he was based. The marriage had a life of four weeks. On Monday 12 February John Symons died of cerebro-spiral meningitis in the 1st Eastern Central Hospital at Cambridge.

It may be assumed that everyone knew everyone else in that small world of Tamarside communities that had its natural focus on the church and school at Gulworthy. Certainly the Pethicks and the Symonses who gathered on that January afternoon were well-known families. Lillian's father was John and her mother's maiden name was Elizabeth Budge. John Pethick was a woodranger, and the family lived at The Rock, where Lillian was born in 1893. John Symons was a Morwellham boy, having been born there on 28 January 1891. He and Lillian could have been childhood sweethearts. They would certainly have known each other from an early age, and they almost certainly attended the same school.

John Symons was the youngest in a family of six children, having been preceded, in order, by Edith, Mary, Gilbert, William, and Emma. The mother, who, like so many of her counterparts in that generation, spent more than half her life in the full-time activity of producing, nurturing, and raising her children, was Mary Ann, who had lived in Morwellham all her life. She had been born in 1854, the daughter of a labourer at the quay called Richard Smale and his wife Mary. As to the identity of her husband, the father of John and the other five Symons children, there have been some problems, relating not so much to the spelling of the surname, although the number of variations on that theme can lead to confusion, but to the fact that Mr Symons did not often use his first name. His real name, James, appears in the 1891 census report, and again on his tombstone. In the face of the census enumerator and of God the truth had to be told. At all other times he is referred to as Richard. This applies to documents relating to his son's birth, education, marriage, and death, to other official information, and to press notices and reports. We may assume that the name Richard is the one that he, and his family, wanted to be used. He was the son of a labourer called Richard and his wife Jane, nee Bath. Richard junior married Mary Smale in 1874. Like so many of his contemporaries, he lived his whole life within one sharply defined area. Born at Newton, he raised his family in a cottage in Morwellham and died in Canal Cottage, overlooking the village. For most of his working life he was a miner. In his forties he turned instead to a little market gardening, but not in time to arrest the advance of the strain of phthisis, common in miners, that killed him in 1906 at the age of fifty-three. John, who was fifteen at that time, had left school. He had originally attended the small village school in Morwellham, but its numbers were now dwindling as the port declined (the school was to close in 1908), and in 1901, at the age of ten, John moved on to Gulworthy School. The details of the job that he later took as a carrier have not emerged. Nor have the circumstances in which he enlisted in the Royal Flying Corps. During his service the Corps remained very much an auxiliary arm of the military, its function not clearly assessed and its potential as yet unglimpsed. At the time of John's death it consisted of 41 squadrons and some 700 machines. One year later things had changed. At the beginning of 1918 the R.F.C. had 4000 combat aircraft and employed 114,000. It had gone some way towards shedding its image as the Cinderella Service.

When John died on 12 February 1917 his family decided that his funeral should be at the place he still considered home. He was buried in the churchyard at Gulworthy, close to his father. Six weeks later the plot received another member of the family. John's mother, Mary Ann, succumbed to pneumonia and died at the age of sixty-two. In the same week as her funeral, a child was born at 16 Morwellham Cottages, to Lillian Symons. The young widow called her infant son after his father. His name was John Symons.

GEORGE ROOKE
Died Sunday 18 February 1917. Aged 19.

Merrivale in 1900

British soldiers had their own names for many of the places that they got to know between 1914 and 1918. In some cases it came down to using memories of home to provide real or ironical labels. Thus a British Tommy might from his position look out at Stirling Castle, Inverness Copse, Clapham Junction, and Surbiton Villas. At other times the French or Flemish place-name was slightly anglicised. Many new arrivals in France found themselves at the re-training camp at Etaples. It inevitably became Eat Apples. When they arrived in Flanders the habit was ingrained and the temptation irresistible. Ypres quickly became Wipers. Ten miles away, to the south of Ypres, is Ploegsteert. The British called it Plug Street. Here there is a British war cemetery with 353 graves. Not all the dead here belonged to the London Rifle Brigade, after whom the ground was named. One, for instance, was a Lance Corporal in the 8th Battalion, the South Lancashire Regiment. He was George Henry Rooke, and he came from Merrivale.

One of the cliches of the First World War is that there was scarcely a community in the land, however small, that was untouched by the losses. Merrivale Bridge is an example. Here, on the eve of the war, were a few cottages, a row of twelve dwellings to house quarrymen and their families, a school, a chapel, and what Crossing in his 1912 'Guide to Dartmoor' described as 'a roadside house of entertainment called the Dartmoor Inn'. The community owed its existence to the quarry. Merrivale granite had a nationwide reputation. The quarry had opened in 1876, and, in the early years of the twentieth century, it gave employment to 150 men. One of these was John Henry Rooke.

John Rooke was born in 1873, and became a stone mason, like his father James. The family settled at Merrivale in the early years of the life of the quarry, and young John got to know Ada Clarke, who lived just a few doors away along

Walkham Terrace. Ada, who had been born in Aldershot, was the daughter of an army pensioner called William Clarke. She was the same age as John, and they both must have been among the children, forty or so at any one time, who attended the school, set near the small cluster of houses, which served the community until the opening of the Foggintor School in 1915.

John and Ada were married at Tavistock Register Office on 19 October 1895. They were both twenty-two. George, their first-born, arrived on 18 November 1897. He was baptised at Whitchurch, in which parish Merrivale lay. Three other children followed, Dorothy, William, and Percy. Their parents, as they got older, began to assume an unofficial position within the community of some authority. Ada's slightly haughty style earned her the soubriquet 'Lady John', while her role as midwife to the community, albeit unqualified, was much valued. She and John were to lose two of their children prematurely, George at nineteen in the war, and Percy at twenty in a road accident in Tavistock.

Young George Rooke enlisted at Camelford at the age of eighteen. He joined the 8th Battalion of the Prince of Wales Volunteers, otherwise the South Lancashire Regiment. Towards the end of 1915 the Battalion, which was part of the 75th Brigade, arrived in France for service in the area of Armentieres. They were joined by other units in the Brigade, including the 2nd Battalion of their own Regiment, which was made up principally of battle-scarred veterans of the original expeditionary force. Over the next two years the two battalions, the new recruits of the 8th and the veterans of the 2nd, relieved each other in the front line.

The Regimental History records the circumstances in which Lance Corporal Rooke met his death.

> On the 18th February the 8th Battalion carried out a large raid against the German trenches south-east of Ploegsteert. The raid was conducted with the greatest determination and gallantry, although it failed in its main object owing to the vigilance of the enemy. Its leader and four men were killed, and thirty-three other ranks were wounded, together with two officers.

The 'vigilance of the enemy' amounted chiefly to alertness in ensuring that the defensive wire was not cut. The War Diary of the Unit adds some disquieting detail about the artillery bombardment that accompanied the raid. The firing was intense between 11 p.m. and midnight, and the enemy responded with heavy shelling and machine gun fire.

> A considerable number of our shells were 'shorts' and several 'prematures', causing a number of casualties among our men. Unfortunately, the raid failed. Very dark night with heavy mist'.

George Rooke lies buried in a cemetery at Ploegsteert, close to where he fell. He is commemorated also on the Memorials of the parishes of both Tavistock and Whitchurch, as well as in the Book of Remembrance lodged in St. Elphin's Parish Church in Warrington. His father and mother, who died in 1949 and 1966 respectively, are buried at Whitchurch. For some years they had inserted 'In Memoriam' notices in the *Tavistock Gazette* on the anniversary of George's death. The first of these, in February 1918 had an additional sentence: 'Also fondly remembered by his dear friend Doris (Swindon)'.

FREDERICK ATTEWILL
Died Wednesday 28 February 1917. Aged 37.

Elizabeth Attewill's gift

The Church Plate that is used for sacramental purposes in Tavistock Parish Church includes a silver bowl, which holds communion wafers. It is inscribed: 'In proud and loving memory of David Attewill, 2nd Royal Fusiliers, killed in action Feb 28 1917. Aged 37 years. "Faithful unto Death".' The donor was Sgt Attewill's widow, Elizabeth Violet, who lived at No 21 Exeter Street. When he died they had been married for eight years. Elizabeth was left with two small children, Eleanor, aged five, and Annie, who was three. The fact that the plight of this young family was, at that time, being replicated many times locally and countless times nationally, did not alter the cruel reality that every case was unique to those involved. Mrs Attewill had to come to terms with her grief and loss at the same time that she was facing the economic realities of bringing up two children. In her case there was an additional responsibility that she felt she had to discharge. A short part of what had anyway been a brief married life had been passed in Tavistock. Here, before the war, they had shared the happiness of having two children. What more natural, on Elizabeth's part, than to present the town with a practical gift that would serve as a constant reminder of his personal sacrifice? Hence, the silver bowl.

   Frederick David Attewill had his roots some distance away from Tavistock. He was born on the Channel Island of Alderney on 4 June 1879. His family and friends, as the inscription on the bowl testifies, invariably used the second name. The surname, in which the 'i' sometimes gives way to a second 'e', is common in

Devon and Somerset. Young Frederick was born into an army family with long associations with the Royal Fusiliers. His father, William, was an army pensioner who was the Ordnance Foreman at Fort George on the island of Guernsey. His mother was, before her marriage, Anne Ryder Walk. Frederick was the third son. There were to be nine altogether plus a daughter. All nine brothers joined the army at an early age. All but one enlisted in the family regiment, the Royal Fusiliers. One of the family was decorated for bravery at Mons, one was taken prisoner, and another fell at Loos. Yet another was wounded in the same attack in which Frederick was killed.

After attending the Garrison School on Alderney, young Frederick Attewill took the earliest opportunity to enlist. This occurred on 15 January 1894, when he was fourteen years and seven months old. He was, at that time, 5′ tall and weighed 6½ stones. His trade was entered as that of 'musician', and his first rank was that of Drummer Boy. He gained experience of combat in the Boer War, and served throughout that war, from 1899 to 1902, coming out of it with the Queen's Medal with five clasps and the King's Medal with two clasps. Back home, he was appointed Corporal in 1903, Sergeant in 1904, and Drum Major of the 1st Battalion in 1905. Three years later, while stationed with his unit on Salisbury Plain, he married Elizabeth Violet Sleeman. The wedding took place at South Tidworth on 3 June 1908. Elizabeth was the eldest daughter of Henry Albert Sleeman, an instructor at Parkhurst Prison on the Isle of Wight, who had recently returned, with his family, to Tavistock, where he had lived as a young man. For Frederick Attewill, now approaching the end of his military career, the prospect opened up of Tavistock becoming the first permanent home he had had since his childhood on Alderney. In 1912 he was discharged, at his own request, after serving eighteen years. He had just completed a spell of service in Dublin, where his first daughter had been born.

Within two years Frederick was back in the colours, re-enlisting on the outbreak of war, at the age of thirty-five, and joining the 8th Battalion of his old regiment. He arrived in France on 31 May 1915. On 2 March 1916 he was wounded at the notorious Hohenzollern Redoubt, on the Loos Battlefield. Invalided home, he returned to France five months later, and never saw England again. On 28 February 1917, in the Sailly sector of the Somme region of the front line, he died in an attack on enemy trenches. The Battalion Daily Report described an attack being launched at 5.30 on that morning. German trenches were occupied and many prisoners taken, but the new positions came under heavy bombardment and persistent sniper fire from high ground above the trenches. An enemy counter-attack led to stubborn fighting and to heavy casualties, and the day ended with minimal territorial gains. 'During the night', concluded the Report, 'the line was reorganised'.

Frederick had been awarded the Long Service and Good Conduct Medal. The regimental chaplain, in his letter to the widow, quoted the Commanding Officer as referring to the 'generations of Attewills in the Royal Fusiliers', and as saying that 'your husband has well maintained the high tradition set by his family'. He was buried in one of the many ad hoc Somme burial grounds. At the armistice a number of these were concentrated into the Sailly-Saillisel British Cemetery. There he lies.

FRANCIS SKINNER
Died Monday 9 April 1917. Aged 21.

The Skinner family business, 25 West Street, Tavistock; 1908

There can today be no more hauntingly evocative site on any European battlefield than Vimy Ridge. Here are preserved trenches and tunnels that aid the imagination in the reconstruction of events. And here also is one of the great war monuments, the Canadian National Memorial. For Canadians the name 'Vimy Ridge' has the same resonance as Verdun has for the French or Gallipoli for the Australians, in that it kindles images of comradely heroism, patriotic ardour, and youthful sacrifice. The ridge itself constituted one of the strongest defensive positions in northern France, and had been held by the Germans since October 1914. It formed a part of the front known as the Arras Sector. General Haig called it 'an important tactical feature, possession of which I considered necessary'. In March 1916 the British took over that sector from the French, who had lost some 130,000 men in repeated efforts, throughout 1915, to take the Ridge. There followed twelve months of preparation, during which time the Canadians arrived in the sector, following their punishing ordeal on the Somme. They were to spearhead the assault on Vimy Ridge, scheduled for 9 April 1917. The attack began, in driving sleet, at 5.30 on that morning, and all four Canadian divisions were involved. Within five days Vimy Ridge was in allied hands, but at a cost, to the Canadians, of 14,000 casualties. One of those who were killed on the first day of the assault was Private Francis Reginald Skinner, No 184042, of the 31st Battalion, Alberta Regiment of the Canadian Infantry. He was twenty-one years old.

The road that took young Francis Skinner to Vimy Ridge began on 21 July 1895, when he was born in Tavistock, at 25 West Street, above his father's butcher's shop. The business had been operating since the 1840s, under three successive generations of Skinners. It was, at the time, one of eight butchers' shops in the town. Hugh William Skinner, Francis's father, had been born in 1860, and had taken over the family business from his father, John, who had done well enough to buy Down House and to employ eight people on his farm. In 1891 Hugh married Emma Wills, who had been born in St Dominic, where her father was an innkeeper. Hugh and Emma had four children. Of the three sons, one, William, died at the age of six. The daughter was called Emma, and the two surviving sons were Henry and Francis.

Francis was baptised in Tavistock Parish Church on 12 August 1895. His education began at a small private school which was then being run on Spring Hill by a well-known public figure in the town called William Winney. In May 1904, at the age of eight, Francis signed on at the Tavistock Grammar School, at that time, and for long after, under the headmastership of J.J. Alexander. The decision was premature, and from 1905 to 1908 he attended, first the Oxford Street Council School in Plymouth, and then the Stoke Public School in Devonport. Re-admitted to Tavistock Grammar School in 1908, he left in the following year at the age of fourteen. At some point in the next two or three years both he and his elder brother Henry took the same step as a number of their generation, and came to terms with their restlessness and ambition by emigrating to Canada. The brothers both settled in Calgary, Alberta. Francis got a job as a clerk and married a local girl called Alga Sarah.

Francis enlisted at Calgary on 14 June 1915. He was described as 5′ 6″ high and weighing 140 lbs, with a dark complexion, black hair, and brown eyes. There are two interesting points about the documents of attestation that he signed on that day. One was that he originally entered his next-of-kin as his brother Henry. In a subsequent amendment he crossed this out to substitute the name of his wife, Alga Skinner. The inference would be that enlistment and marriage came in that order. Further on into the form he gave a date of birth that suggested his age as twenty-one, whereas in reality he was still short of his twentieth birthday. This may have been done to improve his chances of a swift transfer to Europe. In the event his ship arrived in Liverpool from Halifax on 8 June 1916. One month later he attended his father's funeral in Tavistock. The two sons, affectionately known as Harry and Frank, both attended in uniform, Henry having enlisted and travelled to Europe before his younger brother.

Francis's war began when he arrived in France on 28 August 1916, and ended on 9 April in the following year at Vimy Ridge. He lies buried at Nine Elms Military Cemetery in the village of Thelus, close to the town of Arras. Alongside him are many comrades from both his native country and his adopted land. His wife and his mother, both widowed within a year, began to rebuild their lives. Alga remarried, and became Mrs Woolley of Albert Park, Calgary. Emma moved to the Victoria Hotel, Paignton, and lived into her eighties before joining her husband and other Skinners in the family plot in Plymouth Road.

MAX TEGLIO
Died Wednesday 11 April 1917. Aged 21.

Max Teglio

There may have been some special, personal, factors that caused Guglielmo Teglio to leave Italy in the 1880s and seek a new life in England. Or it may simply be that he was one of the half a million Italians a year who emigrated from the recently-united kingdom during that period because of the harsh social and economic conditions that prevailed for so many people. Something about his hopes and ambitions may be deduced from the fact that his journey began in one port and ended in another. This appears to be confirmed by his appearance, in the 1891 census, as a fish merchant. He had been born in Genoa in 1860. He was now, at the age of thirty, living at No. 4 Citadel Terrace, Plymouth. Hammond's Plymouth Directory, published in 1893, lists him at the same address, describing him as 'Cooper in the Great Western Docks and Fish Curer at Commercial Wharf'. Other members of the family may have made the journey with him or joined him subsequently; by 1896 the fish curing business on Commercial Wharf had become the concern of 'Teglio Bros'. By this time William had married Jane Paddon, of Plymouth. Their son, Max, was born in 1895. A daughter, Nora, followed in the next year.

The business did very well, and the Teglio family prospered. Like the great majority of immigrant families who gained middle class comforts and status within a generation, they were concerned, above all, to assimilate, and to behave in the way expected of an indigenous family of comparable wealth and standing in the commercial or professional world. Mr Teglio had, early on, become William

Charles. He now moved his family to Buckland Monachorum, and was later to buy a house in Tavistock's select Down Road, called Athol House. The 1901 census made no mention of fish; the family business now was wine. And, when his son was old enough, he would go to a public school.

Young Max Teglio was born on 10 September 1895 at the family's original home in Citadel Terrace. The Teglios moved to Athol House shortly after Max became a pupil at Kelly College. The school that he joined in 1907 was thirty years old. Built as a result of a bequest of Admiral Kelly, and occupying a hillside terrace overlooking the Tavy valley, it had just increased its numbers by adding a second house. It now had eighty-three boys and nine masters. Max was to spend five years there, playing for the school in his final years at both cricket and rugby. He left at the age of sixteen, and began a career as a chartered accountant.

At the age of nineteen, and with the war in its eighth month, Max enlisted. It was March 1915, and he was to serve for eighteen months in the ranks. Four of those months were spent with the British Expeditionary Force in France as a Private in the Royal Fusiliers. In the Summer of 1916, after attending an Officers' Training Course in Scotland, he applied for a commission 'in any infantry regiment', supplying references from the Chaplain of Kelly College and an officer in the Devonshire Regiment. The application was successful, and in August 1916 he joined the Devons as a 2nd Lieutenant. Army records describe him at this time, as he approached his twenty-first birthday, as 5′ 11″ tall, with a fair complexion, brown hair, and grey eyes. He occasionally wore glasses.

In December 1916 the young subaltern was posted to Mesopotamia, where he was attached to the 9th Battalion, the Worcestershire Regiment. He arrived on 17 January 1917. The long drawn-out campaign against the Turks in this theatre was then just about to reach a crucial point as British forces prepared to attack Baghdad. The city was taken on 11 March. Sixteen days later, Max wrote a letter to his old school. He began: 'As you see, I am attached to the 9th Worcesters. I came here just in time to see the fun'. He then went on to describe the scenes that he had witnessed in Baghdad: 'The inhabitants in general were awfully pleased to see us. The town had been looted and everybody had hidden their merchandise so that at first we could get nothing, but after two or three days the shops began to open up and trade was quite brisk. The weather here at present is fairly warm'. He then added his name to those who were pressing for 'the founding of a scholarship for the sons of Old Kelleins who have fallen on service'. And he concluded: 'The flies are driving me mad. I hope that I have not said anything to which the censor will object'. By the time the letter arrived at Kelly, Lieutenant Teglio was in his grave.

On 11 April the 9th Worcesters were advancing, in support of the 9th Royal Warwicks, against Turkish positions at Kowar Reach, about fifty miles north of Baghdad. Max's CO described the end:

He was shot through the heart and died almost at once and without pain. We were not able to bury his body until after dark that night, when the Padre and I went over to the trench in which his body lay, and there the Padre said the Burial Service.

He now lies buried at the North Gate War Cemetery in Baghdad.

HAROLD MAKER
Died Saturday 21 April 1917. Aged 19.

Peronne in 1917

Harold John Maker was born at 17 King Street, Tavistock on 21 December 1897. His parents, Alfred John and Kate, were both born in Tavistock. All four grandparents were, on the other hand, originally village folk who had joined the popular migration that led to the depopulation of so many small rural communities. On the Maker side of the family, grandfather William, a slate quarry worker, and grandmother Annie, nee Williams, both hailed from Lifton. On the Boon side, Thomas, a naval pensioner and hotel waiter, came from Rattery, near Totnes, while his wife Elizabeth, originally Miss Frayn, had been born in Egloskerry, between Launceston and Camelford. The Makers moved to Tavistock in the early 1870s, and their son, Alfred John, was born in 1873 at No 10 Madge Lane. At about the same time the Boons arrived in Tavistock, via Stonehouse, settling first at West Bridge and then at No 19 Dolvin Road. Their second daughter, Kate, was born in 1874. Alfred John Maker was an only child. Kate Boon was the second of four children. Alfred John became a plumber. Kate became a milliner. And, while they were both still in their teens, they became man and wife. For some time they shared the Makers' family home in Madge Lane. Their first child, William Francis, Frank to relatives and friends, was born in February 1893. Harold was the younger son. By the time he was born, almost five years after Frank, the family had moved to King Street. Little is known of the early years. The Makers were Wesleyans, and it is probable that, for that reason, the two boys attended the Plymouth Road School. A sister, Gladys, was born in 1899. The 1901 census records her and her brother Harold living with their mother Kate and their maternal grandmother, Elizabeth Boon, at 19 Dolvin Road. Meanwhile, older brother Frank, now eight, shared 10 Madge Lane with the paternal grandparents. Father Alfred John was not reported as being present at either residence.

It is not clear when, or why, Alfred John (like his elder son, he preferred his second name) took his young family to London, or whether he continued there to practice his trade as a plumber. They had re-settled by 1914, when they were living in Dorset Square. Frank, who had married a London girl, joined the Grenadier Guards when the war came. Harold was only sixteen at that time, and was still only seventeen when he and his parents learned of the disappearance, subsequently confirmed as the loss, of Frank on the battlefield of Loos. In the following year, 1916, Harold enlisted at the age of eighteen, turning up at the same enrolling centre at Marylebone at which his brother had taken the shilling two years earlier. The feelings of his parents, now living in Balham, can only be imagined as their remaining son, within a short time of joining the colours, was swept off to service on the Western Front.

Harold joined the 1st/4th Battalion of the Oxfordshire and Buckinghamshire Light Infantry. He left for France in October 1916, but was sent home shortly before Christmas suffering from trench foot. This was a fungal infection, caused by the cold, wet and insanitary conditions that prevailed in the trenches, and feared particularly because of the risk of gangrene. Elementary preventive measures, such as regular foot inspections, seem to have been largely neglected on both sides. In February 1917 Harold rejoined his regiment on the Somme. Here the Battle of Arras was fought in April. Seen as the centrepiece of the allies' offensive strategy in the early part of 1917, the attack was launched on 8 April. Following a familiar pattern, it began with a heavy bombardment, which heralded an infantry offensive. Some modest territorial gains were made, at considerable cost. The campaign later degenerated into a pointless slogging stalemate accompanied by a long period of cold weather with rain and sleet which reduced the battlefield to a sea of clinging mud, in some places more than ankle deep. In the middle of this, Private H.J. Maker, No. 17537, received wounds from which, on 21 April, he died.

The town of Peronne is on the River Somme, some thirty miles east of Amiens. It was in German hands between September 1914 and March 1917. When it was liberated, an extension was made to the Communal Cemetery, and here, by the time the armistice had been signed, had been buried 177 British and Australian casualties of the fighting that had been taking place in the immediate area. Harold Maker was one of the 177. In the months that followed, the Extension Area, which measured 5535 square metres, became the site of a number of re-burials. In the heat of battle small plots had been hastily pressed into service as burial places. In some cases they held only one or two graves. After the armistice, in a procedure replicated at various points along the Western Front, these scattered burials became concentrated in larger, more accessible cemeteries that could more easily be maintained and more readily visited. Thus it was that the original 177 occupants of the Peronne Communal Cemetery Extension were joined by a further 1400 or so of their fallen comrades.

WILFRED LEWIS
Died Sunday 29 April 1917. Aged 20.

Wilfred Reginald Austen Lewis

In the last half of the nineteenth century, Exeter Street was one of the most populous streets in Tavistock. In 1891, for example, its forty inhabited dwellings housed 104 households and 342 people. It was a street in which there were high levels of multi-occupancy and of large families. The boys who grew up there in the years either side of 1900 were the young men of the First World War generation. Survivors of that generation, who remember the Street in its pre-1914 days, recall that there was scarcely a house that did not give at least one son to the war. Number 4 was just one example. Here lived the Lewis family.

A certain amount of mobility was a common, and accepted, feature of working class life in West Devon in the late nineteenth century. It was quite normal for a miner, a labourer, or a farm worker, to move himself, and his family if he had one, as often as was necessary to respond either to job opportunities or to the need for fresh accommodation. But such moves were, in most cases, confined within geographical bounds, the limits of which were imposed by a network of personal and family ties, and by the narrowness of the horizons that prevailed for many people, in both their ordinary lives and their imaginations, and which the railways were only just beginning to widen. Take Alfred Lewis. Born at Heathfield in 1872, much of his early boyhood was spent at No 1 Kilworthy Cottages, while most of his teenage years saw him living at 35 Fitzford Cottages, his family having moved across town. His marriage in 1895 to Thirza Williams brought him to 17 Brook Street, and later to what proved to be the permanent home, No. 4 Exeter Street.

Alfred Lewis had been born, the third of four children, when his parents were both in their forties. His father George was a farm labourer, and his mother Mary was originally Miss Geake. Alfred secured a steady job with the GWR as a railway packer. Fond of cycling and shooting, he was often to be seen crossing the town astride a bicycle with a gun under his arm. He was twenty-three and Thirza twenty-four when they were married at Tavistock Register Office in May 1895. Thirza was the sixth of ten children, whose births, potential and actual, pre-occupied their mother Betsy, and presumably also their father James, for twenty years. Like the young Lewises, they marked the arrival of their teenage years by becoming labourers, miners, and domestic workers. Thirza got a job as a cook at Moor View, Glanville Road. She lodged at Fitzford, and it was there that she met Alfred.

Wilfred Reginald Austen, known in the family as Reggie, was the first of the children born to Alfred and Thirza. He arrived on 4 April 1897. A pupil at the Church School in Dolvin Road, he left in 1910 and went to work for W.E. Baker's, the well-known town-centre ironmongery business. By that time the family had grown, with the additions of Percy, Doreen, Harry, Kathleen, and Cecil. Only the two eldest boys were to be old enough to serve in the war. Wilfred enlisted at Tavistock on 11 April 1916, describing himself at that time as a smith's mate. He joined the 1st/7th Battalion of the Middlesex Regiment, otherwise the Duke of Cambridge's Own. In France he became a specialist signaller. Percy, who enlisted in July 1918, survived the hostilities, and served in the Army of Occupation after the Armistice.

On 16 March 1917 the *Tavistock Gazette* reported that Alfred Lewis had received a letter from his eldest son Wilfred, serving in the Arras sector of the front line in France. He had been slightly wounded in the back and shoulders by shrapnel, but 'he writes in a cheerful strain, and hopes that he will soon be right again'. Two months later the news arrived that he had been killed during the battle of Arleux when their trench was heavily shelled. The letter from the CO ended: 'He was buried close to the village where he fell. A cross has been erected over his grave. He was a brave lad, and liked by everyone'. Some time later Wilfred's mother was informed that his body had been moved to a more permanent setting at Wancourt, about five miles from Arras. Wilfred Lewis, No. 202465, lies buried in the British Cemetery there.

The first anniversary of Private Lewis's death produced, in the *Tavistock Gazette*, an 'In Memoriam' entry in which some of the passion and anger of bereavement came to the surface. It recalled 'Reggie, slain in France. A cruel blow!' It then listed three cousins who had been killed, and concluded:

Loved too well, lost too soon, through the selfishness of others.
When wilt thou save the people, O God of Mercy, when?
Not kings and lords but nations, not thrones and crowns but men.
God save the people.

It was signed 'T. Lewis'. Here was surely a mother's pen.

Thirza Lewis died in 1953 at the age of eighty-two. Alfred thereupon moved to Westbury to live with one of his daughters. He died there in 1958, at the age of eighty-five.

JOHN WATTS
Died Thursday 3 May 1917. Aged 28.

War Memorial in Easton Parish Church, Suffolk

The Battle of Arras was planned as the centrepiece of an all-out British attack on established German defensive positions in the Spring of 1917. The assault was made along a thirty-mile front north and south of the town of Arras, and was launched on 9 April. Between then and the end of May, using a variety of methods including mines, gas shells, aircraft, the few available tanks, and even a cavalry charge, every effort was made to punch decisive holes through a well-prepared defensive screen. With the single exception of the capture of Vimy Ridge, these efforts proved to be unsuccessful, and the cost, in terms of British casualties, was of the order of 150,000. The infant Royal Flying Corps, in a month that was to be remembered as 'Bloody April', lost 151 aircraft and 316 aircrew. By the end of that month it became apparent that little more could be expected in the way of strategic or territorial gains, and that the troops involved had become exhausted. Nevertheless the attacks continued. On 3 May there began a two-week period of stern engagement and heavy losses near Bullecourt. One of the many casualties on the first day of this bloody and relentless contest was John Watts.

The name of John Watts (and of his namesake, a private in the Northamptonshire Regiment who died on the same day) is among the 35,000 names inscribed on the Arras Memorial. Those commemorated at this particular site have no known graves. The monument stands in the Faubourg-d'Amiens Cemetery in the town of Arras. The Commonwealth War Graves Commission offers the following description:

The design, by Sir Edward Lutyens, consists of a cloister, 25 feet high and 380 feet long, built up on Doric columns and faces west. In the broader part of the site the colonnade returns to form a recessed and open court, terminated by an apse. The names of the casalties are carved on stone panels fixed to the cloister walls.

John Watts was an eldest son, and was called after his father. John senior had been born in London in 1853. Susan Duke, who married John senior and gave birth to John junior, was a native of Ashwater, between Launceston and Holsworthy and close to the border with Cornwall. Here she had been born in 1859. Both families, Watts and Duke, were of farm labouring stock. The itinerant life, which it appears John and Susan were accustomed to before their marriage, continued after it. As the size of their family grew, John sought fresh jobs that would pay a little more and help him to meet the growing family expenses. Daughters Elizabeth and Emma were born at Holsworthy in 1880 and at Lewdown in 1887. When their eldest son, John, appeared, on 2 October 1888 they were living at Alder Quarry, in the parish of Thrushelton, between Launceston and Okehampton. His father was working there as a lime quarrier. James and Isaac, when they came along in 1891 and 1894, were born in, respectively, Calstock and Tavistock. The longest period of stability that the family had experienced began when John senior got a job as a forester in the Tamar Valley, and the Wattses settled in Morwellham. This village, with a long history as a major river port, had by now become a largely forgotten backwater.

Growing up in Morwellham at the turn of the century must have been an interesting, but in some ways a limiting, experience for such children as those of the Watts family. There were five of them, but Emma, the second daughter, died in 1907. The three boys no doubt felt the need to spread their wings, particularly since economic depression and joblessness had taken a firm grip of their home area. They were all to seek pastures new. James, the middle son, went to sea. John and Isaac, the oldest and youngest, migrated to other parts of the country, where they settled and married. All three were caught up in the war, on active service. None of them survived it.

It is not clear whether John junior made his decision to enlist before or after the death of his younger brother. James had succumbed to kidney disease on board his ship in October 1914. John's preference was for the army rather than the navy. He was living at Easton in Suffolk when he joined up, and the enlistment took place at Wickham Market. Easton is a village lying close to the Suffolk coast, between the towns of Ipswich and Aldeburgh. Initially in the 25th Battalion, the Middlesex Regiment, he was later attached to the 9th Battalion of the Royal Fusiliers. The obituary in the local press revealed that he was married by referring to his widow as 'Julia, of Whitecroft, Gloucs'. This was almost certainly a misreading of Whitecliffe, a village on the edge of the Forest of Dean.

With the death of John Watts junior, at the age of twenty-eight, on 3 May 1917, John and Susan lost the third of their five children. Isaac, the youngest, was the only son left. At the time of his brother John's death he was with his battalion in Flanders. The Battle of Passchendaele was about to begin.

WILLIAM RAYMONT
Died Sunday 6 May 1917. Aged 26.

Headstone in Vlamertinghe Military Cemetery, Belgium

In English communities in the nineteenth century it was the norm for children reared in working class homes to adopt, almost without question, the same limited set of expectations as their parents, when it came to matters like education and jobs. There were, however, always, in every generation, a significant number of exceptions. In the late nineteenth and early twentieth centuries the institution that, throughout England, was mainly instrumental in widening the horizons of the bright working class boy was the local grammar school. A combination of educational opportunity and parental determination could often change the fortunes of an individual, or a family. Tavistock furnishes a number of examples. The Raymont family is one.

Simeon Raymont was another victim of erratic recording, in that he, and some of his descendants, emerged sometimes, according to an official hand, as Simon, and sometimes as Raymond. He was born at Winkleigh in 1825. In about 1850 he married Tavistock-born Elizabeth Martin, and they set up home in Taylor Square. Simeon was a blacksmith. Two of his seven children, Harry and John, followed their father and became smiths. Simeon junior went into the grocery business. Two others, Jethro and Elizabeth, went to work for a local draper. The other two, Thomas and Charles, became pupil-teachers, the term given to older children, in their teens, who were serving, in effect, teacher apprenticeships in elementary schools, after which, subject to success in an examination, they could proceed to a training college and gain professional qualification. Thomas later became a university lecturer, a Professor of Education, and the author of several learned books.

Simeon junior, the eldest of the Taylor Square family, was still living in the family home in 1881, by which time it had moved a few yards away, to 10 King Street. Ten years on, and the 1891 census enumerator found Simeon senior, still smithing, with Elizabeth and four of the children, now living at 30 Bannawell Street. But Simeon junior had by now fled the nest. On 14 October 1884, at the Wesleyan Church in Tavistock, he married Julia Clifton, the daughter of John Clifton, a Bannawell Street butcher, and his wife Maria, nee Peard. The young couple set up home at No. 6 Abbey Mead. Simeon's career in the grocery business had prospered, and he was now a partner in the firm of Williams and Raymont, grocers and wine merchants, who operated at 12 West Street. In mid-life he changed direction, went to South Africa for a time, and then returned to Tavistock to run, very effectively, the W.H. Smith bookstall at the LSWR station. A man of many parts, he then managed to fit in a spell with the auctioneers Ward and Chowen, a term on the Urban District Council, and an intense commitment to both the Methodist Church and the Bowling Club. He died in 1940 at the age of eighty-one.

Simeon and Julia had five children, Maud, Ethel, William, Charles, and Doris. William was born on 14 July 1890 at 6 Abbey Mead. He was given, as a second name, his mother's maiden name, Clifton. A pupil at the Grammar School, which was at that time a novel feature of the town landscape on its Plymouth Road site, he left at the age of sixteen to follow in the footsteps of two of his uncles, and become a pupil-teacher at the Council School just 200 yards down the road. He then went on, at the age of eighteen, to Bristol University. Having gained a degree in Mathematics he joined the teaching staff of the King Henry VIII Grammar School at Abergavenny. It seemed that a long, happy scholastic career stretched ahead of him. And then came the war.

The 3rd Battalion of the Monmouthshire Regiment, a unit of the Territorial Force, was formed in early 1915, with its headquarters at Abergavenny. The young schoolmaster joined it, and was commissioned. He subsequently underwent a course of training at the School of Musketry, and went to the Front with his battalion in September 1916. He found himself at Vlamertinghe, about three miles west of the town of Ypres, and occupying a reserve position from which units in the front line of the Ypres Salient could be relieved. The circumstances of his death, on 6 May 1917, are not recorded, other than the fact that he was hit by a stray shell. He was buried at Vlamertinghe Military Cemetery, which holds over 1000 graves, and which, according to the Commonwealth War Graves Commission, 'is remarkable for the very high proportion of graves of Territorial units'.

Lieut. William Clifton Raymont was twenty-six when he was killed. Like all the casualties of the war, he died before his time. War was not, of course, particularly in that period, the only carrier-off of the young. William's youngest sister Kathleen, for example, died of croup at the age of three. But most of the Raymont family lived long fulfilling lives. Brother Charles served through the war and lived to the age of eighty-three. Father and mother had long retirements at their last home, 'Redferns' on Plymouth Road, before dying at eighty-one and eighty-five respectively. Paterfamilias Simeon, the old Bannawell Street blacksmith, would no doubt have been proud of them all.

WILLIAM JAGO
Died Monday 7 May 1917. Aged 32.

Stanley and Amy Jago. Children L to R – Roy, Kathleen (Cissy), Alan

For Lance Corporal William Stanley Jago, if not for the country, the war was at an end. It was 23 March 1916. He was being formally discharged, as his official papers sonorously put it, 'in consequence of the termination of his period of engagement, after serving 10 years and 232 days with the colours, and 2 years and 149 days in the Army Reserve'. He was now thirty-one years old, and he could look back with pride and satisfaction on a military career that had begun on 10 March 1903, when he originally enlisted at Exeter at the age of eighteen.

On both sides of his family, William Jago had deep local roots. His father, the splendidly named William Henry Pennington Jago, came from Taylor Square. He had married Emma Osborne, the daughter of a copper miner called Andrew and his wife Mary Ann, who lived at Westbridge. Emma was a dressmaker. W.H.P. had already begun the long period in the employ of Messrs Dennis, the West Street furnishers, that was to cover the remaining forty-five years of his life. The young couple were married at Tavistock Wesleyan Chapel in 1883, and lived at 9 Chapel Street and later at 4 Pym Street. William Stanley was born on 26 June 1884. He was to be joined by Harold, who was to be widely remembered as the organist at the Abbey Chapel, and then by Hilda, later to become Mrs Slocombe.

William Stanley Jago did not follow his father into cabinet making. Nor did he persist with the baking trade, which he entered after leaving school, or with the blacksmith's apprenticeship that followed. Instead, it was the army. William was described at the time of his enlistment as 5′ 5½″ tall, with a fresh compexion, hazel eyes, and dark brown hair. A Tavistock boy, he had been born, educated, and employed in his native town and had attended the local Wesleyan Church. This was the young man who was now to serve for nine years before his transfer to the reserve. During those nine years, two of which were spent abroad, he impressed his superiors as 'a thoroughly sober and reliable soldier', whose conduct was 'exemplary'. Apart from the range of general duties required of him, he had been effective in certain specialist roles, such as telephone operator, church orderly, and officers' servant. Alongside these duties, he had taken on, within two years of enlistment, the responsibilities of married life. He married Amy, a domestic nursemaid who was the youngest daughter of John and Emma Couch of 2 Paisy Cottages in the parish of Whitchurch. Here it was that William and Amy began their married life, but they later moved around a good deal, as an army career required, living for a time at Tidworth Camp, as well as having successive homes in Exeter Street in Tavistock. They had five children. Stanley, born prematurely in August 1906, lived for only two days. There followed Edward, known as Roy, Kathleen, Cissie to everyone, and Alan. Edwin, the youngest child, known as Ted, was born in 1917, eighteen days before his father died.

In March 1912 William became a reservist, to be required again in the colours only in a time of national emergency. Under the terms of his contract he rejoined his old regiment, the Devons, when war was declared in August 1914, and was in France before the end of the month, earning the Mons Star. On 18 October 1914 he was wounded in the left thigh, and was brought back to England, to be nursed at Torquay Hospital. In 1915 he served at Gallipoli, before returning to the Western Front, where he was again wounded. He spent the last months of his term of service in France, returning home in March 1916. The final discharge, the farewells to old comrades, the return to civilian life; all were now accomplished. It only remained to get a job. He applied for a post as a warder at Dartmoor Prison. His daughter-in-law, Lillian Jago, recalled what happened next. The reply to his letter of application took a long time to come. William finally ran out of patience, and decided he would be of more use back in France. Early one morning he left to re-enlist. He never returned. That same morning the post brought a letter offering him the prison job.

A letter home from William to Amy, written on Christmas Day 1916, has survived. He was now with the 9th Battalion in a reserve position. He had had his Christmas lunch of 'bully, biscuits, and a drop of tea', and was ready for another night 'sleeping in a barn with no blankets'. Four months later he was in the front line, and was wounded at Bullecourt. While going back to have the wound dressed, he was hit by shrapnel for a second time, this time fatally. He was buried close to where he fell at Achiet-le-Grand.

Amy died in 1961 at the age of seventy-four. Ted, whose birth had followed so quickly on his father's death, eventually became mayor of his native town. In 1976 he died while on a visit to negotiate a twinning agreement between Tavistock and the German town of Celle.

ROBERT BROOKS
Died Thursday 7 June 1917. Aged 25.

The Menin Gate Memorial in the 1920s

Just after three o'clock on the morning of Thursday 7 June 1917 a large number of people in London were woken by the sound of an explosion. The source was 150 miles away, at a place called Messines, just south-east of Ypres. The Germans had held this spot, a strategically important ridge, since the early weeks of the war. The noise was the combined effect of the detonation by the British of 600 tons of explosive in nineteen mines, painstakingly dug during the previous six months. The tunnels totalled half-a-mile in length under the German lines. The explosion, when it came, followed the usual protracted period of intense bombardment. The blast may have disturbed the sleep of some Londoners. At Messines it killed 10,000 men.

The early morning bang was the prelude to a carefully prepared British plan to take Messines Ridge. It was followed by the application of a novel technique of using artillery fire in support of infantry movement by advancing the barrage step-by-step, so that at any stage it was just ahead of the infantry advance. This, the idea of the 'creeping barrage', needed to be precise in its execution if it was not to risk what was later to be termed 'friendly fire'. On this occasion it worked well. By mid afternoon all the principal objectives of the operation had been reached. The British authorities could congratulate themselves on a successful exercise. There was, of course, a price to be paid in terms of casualties, and, on the British side, they numbered some 17,000. Among the dead was Lance Corporal Robert Brooks of the Machine Gun Corps.

Lance Corporal Brooks's war began when he enlisted at Camberwell in the middle of 1916. He was then twenty-four years old, and was living in Lambeth. He joined the Nottinghamshire and Derbyshire Regiment, otherwise known as the Sherwood Foresters, a regiment that gloried in the nickname 'The Old Stubborns'. He quickly earned a stripe, before transferring, in early 1917, to the Machine Gun Corps. Thereafter, he served with the 122nd Brigade Machine Gun Company, completing his training with them at Grantham before being sent to their base depot at Camiers. From here individuals were drafted as required to replace men who had been lost. The 41st Division, of which the Company formed a part, had seen action in the battles of the Somme throughout the last half of 1916, and remained in the area during the first half of 1917, taking part in the preparation and execution of such engagements as the Battle of Messines. Under Brigadier General F.W. Towsey, it played a leading part in the events of 7 June.

The success achieved at Messines on 7 June, and the following days, by the Second Army, was a triumph for its commander, General Sir Hubert Plumer, for whom this represented the culmination of twelve months of preparation. This single engagement did not, however, prove decisive. The Battle of Messines was the prelude to a long series of contests stretching over five months, which reached a horrific climax at Passchendaele, and which are usually taken collectively to constitute the Third Battle of Ypres.

Ralph's Court, off Ford Street, is a byeway of character with a name of obscure origin. Here, at an address sometimes designated as No. 1 Ford Street, Robert Brooks was born on 1 October 1891. He was the fifth child in the family, having been preceded by William, John, Maud, and Emily. He was to be followed by James, who was born in 1896, at about the same time that the family was moving into one of the recently-built houses in College Avenue. Robert's father, who was thirty-six when he celebrated the arrival of the third of his four sons, was John Budge Brooks, a journeyman stonemason. John had lived all his life in Ford Street, and, by becoming a stonemason, had followed in the footsteps of both his father and his elder brother. John's wife, Robert's mother, was two years younger than her husband, and had been born Matilda Parsons Medland in the Cornish parish of Stoke Climsland. John died of pernicious anaemia in March 1913, at the age of fifty-seven. Robert registered his father's death. When Matilda died in 1931 of pneumonia, at the age of seventy-five, the young man was no longer there, having gone to his own distant, and unknown, grave fourteen years before; this time it fell to another son, William, to do the needful.

Robert was baptised in Tavistock Parish Church six weeks after his birth. He was slightly unusual among his contemporaries both in being given only one christian name, and in not being required, as far as is known, to perpetuate the name of a recent relative. He was a pupil at the Dolvin Road School. Developing an ambition to become a policeman, he at some point joined the Metropolitan Force. This explains the fact that he was living in London at the time of his enlistment in 1916.

The whereabouts of the remains of Lance Corporal Robert Brooks, No. 86526, 122nd Company, Machine Gun Corps, will never be known. Like so many who died in or around Ypres during the war and have no known resting-place, he is commemorated on the Menin Gate Memorial.

FRANCIS HARRY
Died Sunday 5 August 1917. Aged 32.

Grave in Hospital Farm Cemetery, Belgium

There is something peculiarly beautiful in this spot. It is so sequestered that it seems shut out from all the world. All is tranquil and in harmony.

The century and a half that have passed since Tavistock antiquarian Mrs Bray wrote this description of Crowndale have done nothing to diminish the charm or appeal of the place. The 'crumpled valley' remains a place of peace and seclusion. Here is Crowndale Farm, the site of Drake's birthplace. Close by, between the road and the river, are four cottages. At No. 3, on Friday 14 November 1884, Francis Harry was born.

Francis was the fourth child in the family, following Emily, William, and Charles. Their father was a farm labourer called William, who had been born at Exbourne in 1854, and who, at the time of his marriage in 1876, was living and working at Wringworthy Farm. His bride, at their Tavistock Register Office nuptuals, was Elizabeth Warren, born the daughter of a farm worker at Hatherleigh in 1857, but at the time living at 21 Kilworthy Cottages. They brought up their family at Crowndale, but later moved across town to Wilminstone Cottage. It was here that William senior spent his last years, working as a gardener at Hazeldon House and dying in 1922 at the age of sixty-seven. Elizabeth lived on until 1934. Their daughter Emily, meanwhile, married Reginald Cox. And two of their sons, William and Francis, joined the army, to be killed within two months of each other. They both fell in the Third Battle of Ypres in 1917, Francis on 5 August and William on 27 September.

During the period of his middle and late teens, the early years of the new century, Francis Harry first got a job as a domestic stable lad living in the household of Thomas Sleeman, a retired builder, at Seaton Villa, on Watts Road. He then became a well-known figure in the town for two reasons. He worked as a driver, and established a number of contacts through plying a trade that was, at that time, in increasing demand. In 1908 he was describing himself as a 'contractor's carter', and in 1915 as a 'domestic chauffeur'. His other high-profile activity was playing the organ at the Congregational Church. The choir and congregation at this impressively spired place of worship in Duke Street had a well-earned reputation for the quality of their music. Under Rev. F.T. Astbury, the minister during the first decade of the century, and his successors, much fine choral music was produced, and the role of organist was a key one.

Francis married Winifred Wilmot West, who had been born in 1887, the daughter of a gamekeeper called William West, who had worked successively on the Earl of Devon's estates at Powderham and Walreddon. The young couple lived first at 38 Bannawell Street, where a daughter was born in December 1908. By the time that a second child, a son, arrived, in 1915, they had moved to 28 West Street. Conservative in their name-choosing, Winifred and Francis called their children Winifred and Francis, or familiarly Winnie and Franky. It was soon after the birth of Franky that the family moved away, when Francis got a fresh job at Crediton, working as the chauffeur for a doctor. It was while they were there that Francis enlisted. In July 1916, at Exeter, he became Private Harry, No M2/191945, in the 18th Corps Heavy Artillery, Royal Army Service Corps.

The attritional warfare in Flanders throughout the First World War gave way, on three occasions, to determined efforts by one side or the other to break the enemy lines. The centrepiece of each of these battles was the town of Ypres. The Third Battle of Ypres, which was fought between July and November 1917, was called, alternatively, the Battle of Passchendaele. Its objective was not confined to the capture of that village. It was, in fact, a sustained British offensive to break through and reach the German submarine bases on the Belgian coast. By November, the limit of the British advance at any one point was five miles, made at a cost of 250,000 casualties. It worked out at twenty-eight casualties for each yard gained. Private Harry died in one of the early skirmishes of the battle. As his Commanding Officer reported rather baldly to his widow 'Pte Harry was killed in action this afternoon whilst on duty at the battery'. He was buried in the Hospital Farm Cemetery, one of about 500 war graveyards that had been established in the Ypres area by the end of the war. This, one of the smaller cemeteries with about 100 graves, lies about four miles west of Ypres town centre.

Winifred, left with responsibility for two young children, returned to Tavistock after Francis's death, and bought a small greengrocery business next to the Tavistock Inn in Brook Street. She ran this on her own for some years. In 1925 she married Maurice Oates, a carman like her first husband. After retiring from the business in 1940 she lived at Little Cot on Kilworthy Hill until her death in 1964 at the age of seventy-six. Her daughter Winnie married Frederick Waldron in 1929, and in 1940 her son Frankie married Florence Tonkin. Francis junior inherited from his father not only a name but a duty as organist of the Congregational Church.

REGINALD KERSWILL
Died Tuesday 7 August 1917. Aged 26.

Attestation return for Reginald S. Kerswell

On 13 August 1917 the 'Winnipeg Evening Tribune', the main evening newspaper for that mid-western Canadian city, carried the following piece:

> Pte R.S. Kerswill was buried with full military honors in St. James's Cemetery Friday. Captain F.W. Goodeve officiated at the service. The body was conveyed from 522 Richmond Street escorted by the 10th Forestry draft. The firing party and buglers were supplied by No 10 Special Service Company. Pte Kerswill is survived by his mother, who lives in England.

The essentials are there: the funeral of a soldier whose next-of-kin is his widowed mother back in the old country. The lack of further detail may simply reflect the fact that in 1917 the death of a Canadian serviceman was not an uncommon occurrence. What made this one different from most was that the death and funeral had taken place thousands of miles away from the scenes of battle in which the young soldier had been involved.

The 'mother who lives in England' was Ellen Kerswill. Ellen had been born in Peter Tavy in 1864, the daughter of a miner called William Palmer and his wife Caroline, and had been brought up in Lamerton. In 1888 she married John Kerswill, who had been born in Tavistock in 1863, and who became a carpenter like his father Samuel. The newly-weds lived in one of the Wharf Cottages in Canal Road, and there Florence was born, followed by Reginald, Olive, and Wilfred. By 1901 the family had moved into a Westbridge Cottage, where Ellen was to continue to live until her death in 1929.

Reginald, who was born on 25 June 1891, and was given the same second name, Sidney, as his father, followed the family tradition and became another Kerswill carpenter. That is what he was later to enter as his trade on his enlistment form. He does appear, however, to have explored other fields. For a time he worked for Frederick Bolt, who ran a grocery business in Brook Street. And he developed an interest in photography; in 1914 a Canadian magazine published some of his pictures showing the uniforms and equipment of the Canadian troops who were about to leave for France. There seems to have been a certain restlessness about him. Few, perhaps, would have been surprised at his decision to join the exodus and catch the boat for Canada.

Reginald arrived in Canada in his early twenties, and settled in Winnipeg, in the province of Manitoba. By that time his father had died, succumbing to liver disease in 1911 at the age of forty-seven. The young emigrant found life in the New World very congenial. Work was easy to find, and he enjoyed the companionship of the local militia. And then came the war, and Canada's instantaneous commitment to it. Reginald enlisted on 6 January 1915. He joined Princess Patricia's Canadian Light Infantry, a recently formed regiment named after the daughter of the Duke of Connaught, who was Governor General of Canada. 65% of its members had, like Private Kerswill, been born in England, and another 15% were Scots. The remaining fifth were equally divided between those born in Ireland and native Canadians. The Patricias, as they were always called, were the first troops from anywhere in the overseas empire to arrive at the war. Reginald sailed in February 1915, and reached France on 16 March. His army papers describe him at the time as being 5′ 9″ tall, with a dark complexion, blue eyes, and black hair.

Immediately on his arrival in France, Private Kerswill found himself involved in the Battle of Neuve Chapelle, part of a major allied offensive in the Artois region. The Patricias, coming to the end of a long stint in the trenches, were responsible for the section of line near St Eloi, and they were involved in some heavy fighting. On 24 March Reginald, having been in the thick of this, began to show the symptoms which a subsequent medical report described as:

Profuse rash, covering the whole body. While on active service in France, eyes have become inflamed and face broke out in painful rash. Condition has been fluctuating from almost complete recovery to a very severe condition since. Appears to be easily aggravated by exposure to sun and winds. The cause is obscure. Had same condition when a boy of fourteen.

The name given to the condition was psoriasis. The patient was admitted first to a casualty clearing station, and then to a succession of hospitals in England. In September a further examination concluded that 'this type of psoriasis is very pernicious, and, after a few days improvement, relapses'. Discharge was advised. In April 1916 he returned to Canada. In August 1917 he died.

There remain two plausible explanations for Reginald's death. One is that his condition was inherited. It is known that psoriasis runs in families, and the first medical report did mention that he had suffered similarly at the age of fourteen. The alternative theory is that the young man was showing the symptoms that one would expect to see in the victim of a gas attack. The Battle of Neuve Chapelle was one of the earliest occasions on which chlorine gas was used by the Germans on the Western Front.

FREDERICK PERKIN
Died Wednesday 15 August 1917. Aged 29.

Saint Jean-les Ypres. 31 July 1917 – 15 days before the death of Frederick Perkin

If the names on the Tavistock War Memorial had been arranged according to the battles in which they fell, it would be seen that Robert Brooks, Francis Harry, Frederick Perkin, Harold Goodman, William Walkem, Edward Skinner, Reginald Northway, William Harry, Harry Bath, and Isaac Watts were all lost in the Third Battle of Ypres. This battle, which stretched from 7 June to 10 November 1917, included a series of engagements, of which one of the last was the struggle to take, from the Germans, the Passchendaele Ridge. Though forming only a part of the battle, the fighting at Passchendaele became so deeply etched in the national memory that the name came to cover the whole six months of this desperate campaign. To this day, Passchendaele evokes images of warfare at its most horrific, in which blood and mud combined to produce a canvas that, to the visiting Prince Of Wales for example, was 'the nearest thing possible to hell'. The British forces suffered 250,000 casualties for insignificant gains. Of these, 70,000 were killed, 42,000 of whom never had their bodies recovered. Some were blown to pieces. Some simply sank into the mud and disappeared. Siegfried Sassoon wrote that 'They died in hell; they called it Passchendaele'. It is said that when General Kiggell, the Chief of Staff of General Sir Douglas Haig, made his first visit to the battlefield, soon after the hostilities had subsided in November 1917, he looked across the stretch of swampland which had claimed so many lives, burst into tears, and cried 'Good God! Did we really send men to fight in this?'

Frederick Perkin, who was one of the 70,000 killed in the battle, was a Lance

Corporal in the 2nd Battalion, the Devonshire Regiment. By the summer of 1917 he was an experienced Tommy, having enlisted back in 1910 at the age of twenty-two. With seven years of soldiering now behind him, including three years of war service mainly in France and Egypt, he was something of a veteran. The 2nd Devons were, in July 1917, the only battalion of the regiment who were in Flanders. They were in the line, and responsible for a section of it, in the notorious Ypres Salient. One of their tasks at this time, a popular one no doubt, was the construction of a new trench in No Man's Land. The offensive that launched the new phase of the Third Battle of Ypres was planned for 31 July, and Perkin's battalion, taking its place in the 23rd Brigade, was assigned two particular objectives, the two ridges at Bellewaerde and Westhoek. At 3.50 on that morning the 2nd Devons went over the top, and, with effective covering fire, had taken Bellewaerde Ridge within the hour. Thereafter heavy German machine gun fire checked the attack, and the Devons sustained considerable losses. For the rest of that day, and for the following day, they were heavily involved in repelling spirited German counter-attacks. They were then relieved, and, on the night of 1 August, trudged back to their camp on the other side of Ypres, in the pouring rain that had been falling incessantly since the start of the attack. Over the two days the battalion had suffered 242 casualties. Of these, 170 were wounded, most as a result of machine-gun or shell fire. Lance Corporal Perkin, No. 9068, was one of them. He died two weeks later, on Wednesday 15 August, and was buried in the Brandhoek New Military Cemetery at Vlamertinghe, some four miles west of Ypres. The 500 graves are all of men who fell in that area in the months of July and August 1917.

When Frederick Perkin was born on 9 July 1888 his family was living in Lakeside, Tavistock. Two years later they moved to Whitchurch. His parents were called James and Emma. James worked for the Great Western Railway as a platelayer. He had been born at Stowford in 1846. In 1867, at Sampford Spiney Church, he had married Emma Damerell, who had been born in that village. Both bride and groom were twenty. They proceeded to raise thirteen children. Frederick was the twelfth, leaving Charles, born in 1890, after the move to Whitchurch, as his only junior. A manuscript source listing Tavistock men who served in the war has Edwin and Charles both enlisting in the Devonshire Regiment, in 1914 and 1910 respectively, and serving abroad in the war. Edwin was wounded in January 1917. A notice in the *Tavistock Gazette* on 9 August 1918 refers to the death, in April of that year, of George, son of James and brother of Frederick, who was 'late Devon Reg'. It would appear, therefore, that four of the brothers served in the same regiment, one being killed, one dying after discharge from causes possibly unconnected with the war, and two surviving. Their father James died in the Tavistock Workhouse Infirmary at the age of seventy on 5 August 1917, ten days before his son Frederick. The family had, by then, been living for some time at No. 1 Vigo Bridge Road. Emma, in widowhood, moved to 34 College Avenue, and died, also in the Workhouse Infirmary, at the age of eighty-three in August 1930.

HAROLD GOODMAN
Died Thursday 16 August 1917. Aged 27.

Harold Henry Goodman

The boys who came out of West Bridge Cottages made a bigger contribution to the military effort than one might have expected in terms both of the numbers in uniform and of the size of the casualty lists. They belonged, as did their counterparts in the terraces at Fitzford and at Parkwood, to the second, or possibly third, generation to be brought up in the Duke of Bedford's Model Cottages, built in the middle of the nineteenth century to provide decent housing for working class families. Harold Goodman lived at West Bridge as a boy, in turn at Nos 26 and 13. But he had been born, across town, at No. 4 Parkwood Cottages.

Harold's father was Albert Venning Goodman, who had been born in Launceston in 1862, the son of a butcher who died when Albert was still a child. In his mid teens, Albert was lodging in Tavistock and working as a grocer's assistant, and in his mid twenties he married Bessie Down. The 1891 census shows his two infant sons, Albert junior, aged two, and Harold, aged one, living at 4 Parkwood Cottages with their mother, Bessie Goodman, aged twenty-five. Bessie's younger brother, Trestrick, a railway porter, also lives there, for this is the Down family home. Its head is Bessie's mother, fifty-five year old Harriet, the widow of railway worker George Down. There is no mention of Bessie's husband. Albert Venning Goodman's absence on the day of the census was not prolonged: a succession of sons, Arthur, Conway, Howard, and Redvers, appeared thereafter at regular intervals. The family, which had also come to include two daughters, Freda and Ivy, had, meanwhile, re-settled at West Bridge.

The youngest of the eight Goodman children, the one who had been given the names of two of the British commanders in the South African War when he was christened Redvers Roberts, died in infancy. The others all attended the Dolvin Road National School. And four of the five surviving sons, Arthur, Conway, Harold, and Howard, went on to the Grammar School. This represented ambitious thinking for a working class family. It must also have imposed a considerable financial burden on the parents. Albert Venning probably did not earn much working as a traveller for Grafton and Scott, the Duke Street grocers. His situation improved to some extent when the local council appointed him caretaker of the newly constructed sewage plant at Crowndale, a job that offered the additional advantage of being relatively close to his home at West Bridge.

Harold entered the Grammar School in May 1907, at the age of seventeen, after a spell as a pupil-teacher at the Council School. He took Oxford Local Examinations, and left in 1909. There followed a period of private tuition, which obviously bore fruit because he was offered a place at Exeter College, Oxford. He matriculated in 1911, but joined up, in 1914, before taking his final examinations. He was twenty-four years old when he became a Royal Fusilier, serving in the ranks in the 20th Battalion, a unit composed of former public school and university men. There followed training spells at Epsom and Leatherhead. In May 1915 he was commissioned in the Devonshire Regiment, joining the 3rd Battalion at Devonport, where it formed the Plymouth Garrison. At some point he became attached to the 2nd Battalion, which served in Flanders for almost the whole duration of the war. He was subsequently promoted to the rank of Acting Captain.

The 2nd Devons had distinguished themselves in the opening engagements of the Third Battle of Ypres, or the Battle of Passchendaele, as it became universally known. The Battalion had been in the thick of the action on 31 July and 1 August, when it had suffered 242 casualties, including Lance Corporal Frederick Perkin from Tavistock. Thirteen officers were either dead or wounded. In the inevitable reorganisation that followed, Captain Goodman was given command of C Company. The British attack, which had been suspended on 1 August, was resumed on 16 August. On that day C Company, having advanced in support of the 2nd Battalion, Middlesex Regiment, found themselves held up by persistent machine gun fire. A withdrawal was ordered, and C Company was given the task of providing covering fire for the retreating troops. The Battalion War Diary recorded that 'The Company assisted the withdrawal by hanging on to the position as long as possible and opening a covering fire with rifles and Lewis guns, killing large numbers of the enemy'. The Regimental History added that Captain Goodman 'who had given a fine example, and handled his men most skilfully, was killed in directing their fire'. Battalion casualties for the day numbered ninety-three.

Harold's name is inscribed on the Tyne Cot Memorial to the Missing. The two brothers who were in uniform at the time of his death, Albert and Howard, survived the war, though the latter was wounded twice. Albert eventually emigrated to America, while Howard joined the teaching staff at Tavistock Grammar School. Their mother, Bessie, died at her West Bridge home in 1929, at the age of sixty-four. Albert Venning later re-married, his second wife being Minnie Bale. He died in 1939 at the age of seventy-six.

WILLIAM WALKEM
Died Friday 24 August 1917. Aged 23.

Grave in Ypres Reservoir Cemetery

William George Charles Walkem was a farmer's son. He was born, on 12 June 1894, at Hartshole, a 350 acre farm some three miles to the south-west of Tavistock on the road to Bere Ferrers. Farming communities were often associated with late marriages, and, at a time when the ages at which the couple married continued to be overwhelmingly the major factor in determining the number of children they had, farmers' families tended, as a general but not invariable rule, to be small. The school friends and contemporaries of William Walkem who lived, say, in Exeter Street or Fitzford Cottages, and whose fathers were miners or labourers, might have ten brothers and sisters, their parents having married in their early twenties. William's father was in his thirties when he wed. He had one son and one daughter. And, a generation earlier, William's grandfather and grandmother married in their early thirties, started their family in their mid thirties, and stopped at three, a family of modest size by the standards of the late nineteenth century.

The grandfather and grandmother in question were Charles and Ann Walkem, whom the 1881 census located at Hartshole, both in their late fifties. Charles was a native of Tavistock. Ann had been born in the Cornish Tamarside hamlet of Boyton, later to be described by John Betjeman as 'a few trees and houses almost islanded in Devon and high up'. In 1881 there were three children, aged between twenty-four and nineteen, still living at home, and the household was completed by two young servants. The youngest of the three children was William, who had been born at Sydenham Damerel. In 1886 Charles died at the age of sixty-six, and William took over the running of the farm. By 1891 his elder brother and sister had both left home, and William was living at the farm with his widowed mother. In the following year he married Ella Elizabeth Masters, twelve years his junior, the daughter of the keeper of a refreshment house in Bristol. Their daughter, Ethel, was born in 1893. Their son, called William after his father, but generally to be known by his second name, George, followed in 1894. On Census Day 1901 the Hartshole household comprised William and his wife, his mother, the two children, and four servants.

The nearest church and school to Hartshole were at Gulworthy, and the Walkem family was associated with both. Young William George attended the school from the age of five. Then, when he was ten, he was admitted to Tavistock Grammar School, where he remained for six years before leaving to work on the farm. Events appeared to be taking a predictable course. The plan was that he would increasingly share the load of work, and the responsibility for running the farm, with his father, and would, in his thirties, take over from the old man, so that the generation-cycle could take another turn. Before that, however, came the Duke of Bedford's sale in 1912. William, now fifty, decided that the purchase of Hocklake Farm, Bere Alston, would provide a more secure inheritance for his son. The move was made. For this family, as for countless others, so many carefully laid plans, and so many fervently held hopes and ambitions, were destroyed by the war.

Young William enlisted as a Gunner in 'C' Battery, 306th Brigade, Royal Field Artillery. He was with his regiment in Flanders in 1917 when the Third Battle of Ypres was fought. In early August he returned to the front after some home leave. He found himself employed mainly in the dangerous job of driving loads of ammunition up to the guns from railheads and storage areas behind the lines. His parents were told, in the letter they received from his Commanding Officer, what happened when he was busying himself with these duties on the afternoon of Friday 24 August:

> Your son was bringing up ammunition to the guns in company with other drivers, when a shell burst in the road right in front of him and the dear fellow was killed. The wind at the time was very strong, and he was unable to hear the shell coming, so there was no possible chance of getting under cover, as we often have to do.

William's grave is among 2500 in the Reservoir Cemetery in Ypres, a burial-ground that occupies a site close to the western gate of the old town. Back home, the notice of his death that appeared in the *Tavistock Gazette* referred to him as 'Only son of Mr and Mrs Walkem, brother of Mrs Wainwright, and dear friend of Arthur Dillon of Moorlands, Princetown'. Sister Ethel had married Joseph Wainwright. She was to survive her brother by only two years, dying in September 1919 at the age of twenty-six. She was buried in the family plot in Gulworthy Churchyard, alongside her grandparents. Her father William was also laid to rest here in 1929. Ella, now having lost her husband and both children, tended the plot, and decided that an omission among the inscriptions should be rectified. She arranged for a final sentence to be added to the stone. It read:

> George, only son of W and E Walkem, killed in action Aug 24 1917 aged 23 and buried at Ypres.

JAMES CRAZE
Died Wednesday 5 September 1917. Aged 32.

Dedication of Tavistock War Memorial 1921

The Mesopotamian Campaign ran, throughout the length of the First World War, as a sideshow to the main events. Whether the thousands of British soldiers who found themselves caught up in it saw themselves as side-stage supporting acts is another matter. They may frequently have been bewildered by uncertainties over the strategic objectives of the campaign. They would certainly have been concerned at the problems arising from erratic supplies and lack of local knowledge. In a number of ways the conflict fore-shadowed the kind of war that the twentieth century was to see repeated in such theatres as Afghanistan and Vietnam. Beginning as a limited show of strength by an imperial power in one of its claimed spheres of influence, it expanded inexorably into a full-scale conflict which imposed an ever-increasing drain on manpower and resources without yielding the kind of victory that would have justified the sacrifice. And at the end of it, the toll was seen to have been heavy. The campaign cost 97,579 Anglo-Indian casualties, including 31,109 deaths.

The 2nd Garrison Battalion of the Northumberland Fusiliers had its home at Newcastle-on-Tyne. Formed in October 1915, it specialised in the protection and guardianship of bases, depots, and prisoner-of-war camps. Its ranks tended to be filled by men who, because of either age or medical condition, had been relieved of the front-line duties that they had carried out with other units. In February 1916 this infant Battalion, 937 strong, sailed from Devonport for service in India. There followed a year based at Sialkot, before the unit was transferred to Ahmednagar in January 1917. At this base the numbers increased to over 5000, as drafts, en route to Mesopotamia, arrived, and were transferred to the Battalion. Ahmednagar continued to be the base for these activities throughout the war.

It is not clear when and how Private James Craze No. 53471 became involved with the 2nd Garrison Battalion of the Northumberlands. He died on 5 September 1917, 'from inflammation', according to the death notice in the local press. Whether his death was related to a wound that he had received six months earlier is not known. Nor is it clear how long he had been in Mesopotamia when his end came. He had certainly arrived there before the end of July, at which time he and a group of fellow Devonians in the unit wrote a letter to the *Tavistock Gazette* in which, among other things, they asked their friends back home to send them 'more comforts'. He had enlisted, at Tavistock, at the beginning of the war, but the details of his career over the next three years remain obscure. It is likely that his transfer to the 2nd Garrison Battalion came as a result of his being wounded in February 1917, in which case his earlier service would probably have been with the Devons. He died in hospital at Basra, the town on the River Shatt-al-Arab, within sixty miles of its mouth on the Persian Gulf. Basra had been, from the beginning of the campaign, the base from which the Anglo-Indian operations to the north had been conducted, and it contained all the essential supplies and medical facilities. It also housed a War Cemetery, which had been opened in December 1914. The Commonwealth War Graves Commission, in describing the Basra War Cemetery, gives the following information: 'The headstones marking the 1914–1918 graves were removed in 1935 after severe problems were encountered with the salts. Instead, the names of the casualties buried in these graves are recorded on a screen wall'. Private Craze lies buried here. He was the fifth of the 'Tavistock names' to die in Mesopotamia. The others, James Harris, the Chenhall brothers, and Max Teglio, lie buried in Baghdad. There was to be a sixth. Arthur Whittome has no known grave.

James's second name, Richards, came from the mother's side of his family. Rebecca Richards had been born in Ford Street, Tavistock in 1843, the daughter of a shoemaker called Henry and his wife Ann. The fourth in a family of seven children, she became a domestic servant, and in 1861 was living and working in a house in West Street. In September 1868, when she was twenty-four, she married John Rowe Craze, who was thirty and lived in Bannawell Street, the second son of another shoemaker called William. The wedding took place at the Tavistock Register Office, and the first married home was 49 West Street. Rebecca and John proceeded to raise a family which eventually consisted of five sons and one daughter. John was an ironmoulder, but either his work or other factors appear to have taken him away from his family for some periods; the 1881 census, for example, found him lodging in Plymouth, while the rest of his family were back home in 38 Bannawell Street. They were, on the other hand, all together on Census Days 1891 and 1901. On the latter occasion all the children were in work. James, who was the baby of the family, was aged fifteen, and, following in his father's footsteps, was working as an iron moulder's apprentice. He had been born, in Bannawell Street, on 21 July 1885. He was to outlive his father by only four years; John senior died of cystitis in 1913.

EDWARD SKINNER
Died Sunday 9 September 1917. Aged 25.

Edward Dudley Skinner

Harold Goodman and Edward Skinner were two men with certain things in common, apart from having local connections. They were both army officers, of roughly the same age, and they fell in the same battle, within a month of each other. Their backgrounds, however, offer a stark contrast. Goodman was the son of a grocer's assistant, brought up in a West Bridge Cottage and educated at an elementary school, who burst through the barriers, and, against all the odds, rocketed through grammar school and on to university. Skinner was reared in the scholarly atmosphere of a country vicarage, went to public school, and joined the colonial aristocracy in Ceylon. The former is an illustration of the fact that, in relation to the army, as to other institutions and public offices, British society has long shown itself to be sufficiently adaptable to offer 'the career open to talent'. The latter represented the more conventional background from which the British Army recruited the bulk of its officer class.

Edward Dudley Skinner took his first name from his father, a clergyman called Ernest Edward Becher Skinner, who had been born in East India in 1862, and his second name from his mother, who had been born in Staffordshire in the following year, and who had been Diana Dudley before her marriage. The Rev. Skinner began his ministry with a curacy in Staffordshire, and followed this with one at Stevenage, where their children Edward and Dorothy were born. Edward, who was born on 9 April 1892, retained happy childhood memories of three years at the end of the century growing up on the North Devon coast, during his father's third curacy at Mortehoe. Then, in 1900, the family moved to Gulworthy Vicarage, when Mr. Skinner was appointed to a living that he was to hold for fifteen years. Edward became a pupil at Kelly College in 1905, and remained there for five years as a Day Boy. The Kelly College Register records him as representing the school at both rugby and senior fives. On leaving school he decided to emigrate, rather than to seek the university path, and in 1912 he took up an appointment with a tea planting concern in Ceylon. He was to spend two years there.

Young Edward appears not to have hesitated too long about what he should do when the news of the outbreak of war reached him. In November 1914 he returned to England with the first group of volunteers from the island colony, who were known as the Millward Contingent. On 13 December he enlisted in London, joining the Rifle Brigade, a natural choice, given the two years experience that he had had as a member of the Ceylon Planters' Rifle Corps. There followed a period of two months at Winchester, during which he applied for a commission. This he received on 28 February 1915, when he became a 2nd Lieutenant in the Manchester Regiment, joining the 15th, and subsequently becoming attached to the 1/8th, Battalion. In January 1916 he began a spell of duty in Egypt, and this was followed by service in France. The summer of 1917 found him near Ypres as the Battle of Paschendaele began.

The Battalion War Diary recorded that on Friday 7 September 1917 2nd Lieut Skinner was one of eighteen officers and 538 men who went into the front line at Square Farm via a train journey to the Asylum Station in Ypres and a march through the Menin Gate. Two days later Square Farm was the scene of an artillery duel. The Diary summarised the day's casualties as six killed, including Lieut Skinner, twenty-two wounded, and thirteen gassed. A fellow officer gave some more detail:

> Lieut Skinner was observing the results of a practice barrage our guns were putting down, as it was one under which he would have to attack a few days later. Both the enemy's guns and ours were shelling heavily. At noon one shell burst on his trench and killed him instantly. The men of his platoon carried him down that night, and he was buried in the British Cemetery established near the prison at Ypres.

The burial site was the Reservoir Cemetery, where William Walkem had been buried two weeks earlier.

Two years before his death, Edward's family had moved from Gulworthy, first to a fresh living near Banbury, and then to a short retirement in Bognor Regis, where the Rev. Skinner died in 1931. Edward's ties with Tavistock remained close in spite of the move, and the inclusion of his name on the Town Memorial is a fitting reminder that he spent many formative years here. Of the tributes to him that came via school or friends, one was from the regimental chaplain, who wrote of 'his quiet presence at Communion and his wish that the men should not lack the opportunity to worship God'. A fellow officer wrote:

> He was so happy and hopeful, and no officer in the battalion was braver than he. Only the night previously he had been in charge of a patrol and had been caught between two lines of fire, but he stayed out until he had obtained the information required, and then brought his men in without loss. Our mess will never be the same without him.

REGINALD NORTHWAY
Died Friday 14 September 1917. Aged 20.

Reginald Claud Northway

The sense of grief and loss, as a generation of young men disappeared within five years, affected practically every community in the land. Within the family context these generalised emotions became more heightened and sharpened, and acquired, according to the relationship involved, a particular focus. Thus members of the same family would all see a bereavement in terms of having been deprived of a loved one, but to one the extra hurt might be the loss of an heir, while to another it might be the death of a favourite son. Others might see in the tragedy the loss of a brother who was a best friend, or an exemplar, or someone with a special talent. To young widows poverty, through the loss of the breadwinner, might compound the heartbreak of separation. The reaction of children to the disappearance of their father obviously depended on age, but to many the memory of fleeting furlough visits, together with the ever-present picture of the uniformed figure looking down from its position of prominence on the parlour wall, must have conjured up some very distinctive images.

Reginald Claude Northway left no wife or children. But when he died, at the age of twenty, on 14 September 1917, there were eight people in the family home to receive the news and to respond to it in their own particular ways. Father and mother, Charlie and Elizabeth Northway, were in their early forties. Reginald had been their eldest child. Their other children, two daughters and four sons, ranged in age from seventeen to three. They lived at that time in Swansea, and there, indeed, Charlie and Elizabeth were to spend the rest of their days.

But the Northway roots were not in South Wales, but in the soil of West Devon.

On 16 March 1867, in Mary Tavy Parish Church, a local girl called Mary Lucas married a farm worker from Lifton called William Northway. William, like so many of his generation, felt that he could better himself by exchanging the low pay and poor prospects associated with an industry then teetering on the edge of depression, in favour of the higher rewards and brighter future that the copper mining industry still appeared to offer. He became a miner, and settled in a cottage at Mill Hill, where he and Mary raised six children. Shortly after the birth of the youngest, in 1887, Mary died in her early forties. The 1891 census found father William and two of his sons working in the mines, while the eldest daughter ran the house and looked after the youngest three. In the middle was Charlie, a miner, aged sixteen.

A few years before William Northway and Mary Lucas had gone to the altar in Mary Tavy, John Bennett, a Tavistock clockmaker, had married Ann Lane from Bradford, in Devon. The couple ran, for some years, a grocery shop in King Street. Living above the shop, they raised six children, of whom the youngest, Elizabeth, was born in 1876. The 1891 census listed her as a milliner's apprentice. Five years later, on 30 July 1896, at Tavistock Parish Church, she married Charlie Northway, the young miner from Mill Hill.

According to the family tradition, Elizabeth Northway was a determined woman, ambitious for her husband and children, of whom she had nine. She may well have pushed Charlie into applying for, and securing, a job in the Customs and Excise Service. As a result, for much of the time up to 1914 Charlie and Elizabeth took their ever-growing family round the country, moving between addresses, among them Sharpness, Plymouth, and Swansea, as the job required. The 1901 census glimpsed them at Hinton in Gloucestershire with their children Reginald, aged four, and Ruby, eleven months. The last of the moves, to Swansea, appears to have taken place in 1914, at about the time that the last child, Marcel, was born. Reginald, the eldest of the seven surviving children (two had died in infancy) was then seventeen years old, having been born at 19 Higher Market Street, Tavistock on New Year's Day 1897.

The circumstances of Reginald's enlistment are not entirely clear, but he had for some time been working as a clerk in the Post Office Savings Bank in London, and had been living in West Kensington. He joined the 12th Battalion, the London Regiment (The Rangers), which was affiliated to the King's Royal Rifle Corps. Certain memories of him as a soldier were to become part of family lore, like the occasion, in January 1916, when he played two violin solos at a concert given by members of his battalion, or the last home leave at the end of the same year, that covered Christmas and his twentieth birthday. In July 1917, back in the trenches, he fell to a German shell, and was invalided to Britain, where, in spite of treatment at the Military Hospital at Pendleton in Lancashire, he died on 14 September. His body was brought home to Tavistock, and was buried in a family plot, having been borne to the grave by eight marines.

It was a short life, tragically unfulfilled. If anything illustrates this point, it is that the eight lives that were nearest to his own, those of his parents, brothers, and sisters, extended beyond his death by a sum total of 444 years.

ALBERT GRAINGER
Died Tuesday 18 September 1917. Aged 30.

Cap badge for RN Petty Officer

The only qualification for inclusion in the list of names on the War Memorial, apart from the obvious one, was the approval of the next-of-kin. Not all the names on the Tavistock monument were of men who had been born in the town, or who had resided there. In each case, however, those closest to them felt that the ties were sufficiently strong to justify a wish for inclusion. There was also the consideration that the appearance of the name, in a visible form and in a public place, might be judged to play a helpful part in the grieving process, and in this sense to play a similar role to that of a headstone in a cemetery. Such conscious thoughts, or subconscious wishes, may well have featured in the desire expressed by John and Mary Grainger of No. 3 Fitzford Cottages to have the name of their son Albert included on the Memorial. Albert had lived the first part of his life in Sussex, and the last part either at sea or in Plymouth. Nevertheless he knew Tavistock, and his parents had made their retirement home there. Moreover, there was no grave, and could be no headstone. Petty Officer Stoker Albert Dunstone Grainger had died at sea. To have his name memorialised both in the local town and on the Plymouth Hoe monument would be of some comfort to those bereaved, the parents in Tavistock and the young widow in Plymouth.

John Gulley Grainger (or Granger, as it was frequently spelt by both official and unofficial sources) and Mary Grace Hurrell had both been born in Plymouth, he in 1852, she in 1849. By 1881, soon after their marriage, they were living in the parish of Eastdean, which included that famous feature of the Sussex coast known

136

as Beachy Head. John worked for Trinity House as a Light Keeper. He lived and worked at the Beachy Head Lighthouse. Here a daughter was born in 1879, followed by three sons. John's job involved at least one move. The 1901 census found him, and his family, at Sunderland. Albert was the youngest of the children, and was born on 10 October 1886. His sister, Mary, was later to marry a Captain W. Zappert. Of his two brothers, one met with a fatal accident while still a young man, while the other enlisted in the war and served in the Royal York Infantry.

The sea had an obvious influence on Albert from the beginning. It can hardly have been otherwise for a child of Plymouth parents, whose father and grandfather had both been mariners, and who was himself born in a lighthouse. In September 1905 he gave up his job as a labourer and, at the age of eighteen, enlisted in the Royal Navy, becoming a Stoker. He did a substantial spell of service in the Persian Gulf, for which he was decorated. When hostilities began he was in that area aboard H.M.S. 'Dartmouth', and the ship was speedily engaged in such duties as taking troops to Egypt and to India. He was present at the bombardment that preceded the Gallipoli landings in 1915, and was on board H.M.S. 'Revenge' when she took part in the Battle of Jutland in 1916. He had, by then, had experience of all the main roles that the Royal Navy had been required to carry out, from escort duties to coastal protection and from troop carrying to combat. He took what was to be his last leave in the Summer of 1917. By then he had been married for seven years.

Albert Grainger probably met Kathleen May in Plymouth during one of the periods when he was ashore between assignments. The marriage took place at the Plymouth Register Office on 6 November 1910. The bride had been born at Fowey, the daughter of Joseph May, a labourer who became a marine. Albert and Kathleen lived for a time at the May family home at 156 King Gardens, Plymouth, where the young sailor had in recent times lodged when on leave. Later they moved to 6 Clarendon Place, near The Hoe. It was here that the couple were living at the time of the last leave in 1917. When he returned to duty at the end of that leave he was transferred to H.M.S. 'Contest'.

The 'Contest' was a torpedo-boat destroyer of 935 tons. One of the Acasta Class of destroyers, she had been built by Hawthorne Leslie and launched in January 1913. She carried three four-inch guns, and had a complement of seventy-three. Her role was as a part of the Fourth Destroyer Flotilla. On Tuesday 18 September 1917 she was torpedoed in the Channel. Among the casualties was No. K/352 Petty Officer Stoker Grainger. His name, along with those of thirty-one of his shipmates, feature on the Plymouth Naval Memorial. Two other members of the crew of the 'Contest' are similarly commemorated, one on the Chatham and one on the Portsmouth Memorial.

When John Gulley Grainger retired from his responsible and rather romantic duties, he and Mary Grace, having to leave their 'tied cottage', decided to return closer to their roots. There was also the question of living closer to Albert and Kathleen. In 1912 they moved to No. 3 Fitzford Cottages, Tavistock. Here they were when they received the news of Albert's death.

WILLIAM HARRY
Died Thursday 27 September 1917. Aged 38.

Tyne Cot Cemetery, Paschendaele

Six miles to the north-east of the town of Ypres, near the village of Zonnebeke, lies the largest British military cemetery in the world. This is Tyne Cot. It holds 11,976 graves. At the rear of the cemetery, and forming its north-eastern boundary, is the Memorial to the Missing, on which are inscribed the names of a further 35,000 who died at Ypres between August 1917 and October 1918. The majority of them fell during the Third Battle of Ypres, otherwise known as Passchendaele. One feature of this battle was that the bodies of a large number of casualties were never recovered because they disappeared into the all-enveloping mud of the battlefield. Hence the 35,000 names at Tyne Cot of men with no known graves. Two panels of the Memorial carry the names of casualties from the Royal Welsh Fusiliers. Among them is that of Private William Harry, No. 60423, of the 10th Battalion.

William was born at No. 3 Crowndale Cottages on Tuesday 22 October 1878. The birthplace was one of a row of four cottages lying between the Tavy and Crowndale Road, about a mile from the centre of Tavistock and close to the site of Drake's birthplace. He was the second in a family of five, coming after Emily and before Charles, Francis, and Elizabeth. In the 1881 census he was recorded as a two year old, who had been named William after his father, a twenty-seven year old farm labourer. William senior had been born at Exbourne in 1854. His wife was listed as Elizabeth, aged twenty-four, who had herself been brought up in a farm worker's home. Born in Hatherleigh in 1857, Elizabeth Warren was, on the eve of her marriage to William in 1876, living at 21 Kilworthy Cottages. When their children had grown up, and moved on, William senior and Elizabeth moved across the town from west to east, and re-settled in an equally secluded area at Wilminstone. Here they were to live out the rest of their lives, William abandoning farm labouring in favour of domestic gardening, and here they were to confront the agonising news of the deaths, within a very short space of each other, of two of their sons.

The pattern of the lives of the two Harry brothers who were to die in uniform had, despite a six year difference in their ages, produced some striking similarities. Both had worked as drivers, and had married and fathered children before enlisting in the same regiment in the same year. It is not fanciful to see in this an attempt by a younger brother to emulate an older one. Paradoxically, when it came to their deaths, in the same theatre of war and within two months of each other, it was the younger man who set the course.

Through the twenty-five years that William Harry spent between leaving school and joining the army he was a driver. This brief job description encompassed, at different times, varying occupations. He appears to have spent the earlier years as a coachman working for a family. The 1901 census, for example, found him living at Parkwood House and working there as a domestic coachman. He later drove a conveyance for one of the town's hotels. By 1912, he was describing himself as a coachman at livery stables, and thereafter he re-appears as either chauffeur or taxi driver. The last part of this career, which straddled the worlds of horse and internal combustion engine, was spent in the employ of John Backwell, undertaker, and coach and car engineer and excursionist.

William met Edith Annie Endacott when she was working as a housemaid for the Tarner family, who lived in Morfe Lodge on Watts Road. She hailed from Ashburton, which was where the wedding took place in 1905. William and Edith had four children. Edith arrived in 1905, when they were living at 27 College Avenue. The other three, Nancy in 1908, William in 1911, and Emily in 1912, were all born at No 7 Parkwood Cottages. William died of bronchitis at the age of five, shortly before his father went to war. The three daughters were all eventually to be married, Edith to Frederick Sussex, Nancy to Harry Lang, and Emily to Francis Reddicliffe.

When he enlisted at Plymouth in October 1916, in the same week as his thirty-eighth birthday, William Harry joined the Royal Army Service Corps. He then transferred to the 10th Battalion, the Royal Welsh Fusiliers, and, with them, saw action on the Somme front. The Battalion Diary gives an account of what happened when, in September 1917, the 10th was relieved on the Somme, and was re-directed to Flanders, where the Third Battle of Ypres was raging. The Battalion arrived at Ypres Asylum Railway Station on the evening of 25 September, their train having been bombed on the way. At 3.40 on the following morning a heavy bombardment and an artillery duel provided the overture to an eight-day contest for Polygon Wood. Advances by the Fusiliers, alongside two other battalions, were met with resistance and counter-attacks, and three days of stiff combat ensued. Over that period, before being relieved by a battalion of Australian infantry, the 10th Battalion lost forty-nine dead. One of them was No. 60423 Pte W Harry.

HARRY BATH
Died Thursday 4 October 1917. Aged 31.

Bannawell Street in 1920, with No. 2 the second on the left

Bannawell Street, following the course of the valley down which the Fishlake tumbles in its hasty rush towards the Tavy, is one of the oldest thoroughfares in the town. It has also been traditionally one of the most populous of the town centre streets. Here, in 1891, were sixty-nine numbered addresses plus four uninhabited dwellings. The sixty-nine occupied residences supported 137 separate households and 534 people. Two of the houses, Nos 67 and 69, housed twenty-six persons each. This street saw the births of six of the men whose names appear on the memorial. Percy Adams first saw the light of day at No. 10, and the Tucker brothers at No. 40, while Frederick Maker and William Hellier were born, twenty-five years apart, at No. 50. Harry Bath was born near the foot of the street, at No. 2. When he was three years old, the railway viaduct, which went virtually over the top of his home, was constructed.

Harry was born on 1 September 1886. His parents, John and Mary, came from local families, and both had been born in Tavistock, John in 1847 and Mary in 1850. John was a second-generation miner who had been brought up at Crowndale in a family of four children. Mary's father, Edward Metherell, was also a miner. John and Mary married at Tavistock Parish Church on 22 December 1867, when he was twenty and she was seventeen. Their first child, William, was born in Tavistock in the following year, but soon after that the young couple decided to seek their fortunes elsewhere, and John took his copper mining skills and experience to the coal mining area of the north-east. Here they spent the 1870s, and here, in Newcastle-on-Tyne, were born George, Bessy, and Ada. In 1879 or 1880 John and Mary, now in their thirties, returned to Tavistock and settled in Taylor Square, and then, a few yards away, in Bannawell Street. They celebrated their return by adding the final four to their family, as Ethel, Harry, Olive, and Winifred appeared between 1884 and 1891. Harry was thus the sixth of eight children, and the youngest of the three sons. The birth certificate confirms the date of his birth as 1 September 1886. His entry in the parish baptism register, written when that rite was conducted in St. Eustachius three years later, gives the birth-date as 3 August 1886. Perhaps just a spot of forgetfulness on the part of harassed parents.

At the time of the 1901 census, Harry was fourteen and was working as a golf caddy. He enlisted at Tavistock on 1 September 1914, his twenty-eighth birthday, joining the 1st Battalion of the Devonshire Regiment. No sooner was he away than he was back in Tavistock for his mother's funeral. She died of cancer of the liver at the age of sixty-three on 3 November 1914. A few months later his father also died. John, like his wife, had been suffering from cancer for some time, and had had to endure a great deal of pain. On 13 August 1915, at home at 2 Bannawell Street, he cut his throat with a razor. He was sixty-seven. Harry, who was unmarried, had lost both his parents. The family home remained in Bannawell Street, but was now the household of William Jones, a Royal Navy Stoker, who had married one of Harry's sisters. It was here that Harry was to return when on leave.

The 1st Battalion of the Devons did long service on the Western Front throughout the war, and by the Spring of 1917 had become a thoroughly battle-hardened unit. It had, however, suffered significant losses, and periods away from the front line were greeted with relief as opportunities for the troops to recuperate and to receive drafts to replace the casualties. The middle of 1917 saw one of those periods, following weeks of heavy engagement in the Arras Campaign. Between May and September the Battalion was either behind the lines or conducting routine defensive duties in a quiet sector. Then, on 20 September, it was forward to Ypres, to lend a hand in what was promised as 'the final push'. The terrain that greeted them was described by C.T. Anderson in his history of the Devonshire Regiment in the Great War:

> The shelling had shattered trees, had blocked ditches and streams with debris, had torn the surface of the ground to an extent which disorganised completely the ordinary drainage, and would anyhow have reduced the ground near the brooks to swamps. But when the disorganised drainage had to cope with the abnormal rainfall of 1917, conditions became infinitely worse, and the attack had almost more to fear from the ground than from the Germans.

A major attack was planned for 4 October, and at 6 a.m. on that day the Battalion, having taken its place among the assaulting troops, went over the top. In spite of the problems, modest gains were made, and held for some days before the Battalion was relieved. The strength of German resistance had, however, taken its toll. The Battalion had lost, in the action, 111 dead or missing and 204 wounded. In the first category was Private Bath. His body was not recovered. He is commemorated on the Tyne Cot Memorial.

ISAAC WATTS
Died Tuesday 9 October 1917. Aged 23.

Commemoration on the Tyne Cot Memorial

The impressive War Memorial in the churchyard at Gulworthy contains a Roll of Honour of fifteen names. All the names except one, that of William Spry, appear also on the Tavistock Parish Memorial. The list includes the three Watts brothers from Morwellham. They were the sons of John and Susan Watts, who had finally settled into one of the cottages, No. 29, in that quiet, sleepy Tamarside village that had once been a bustling, thriving port. They had earlier moved about in the area quite a bit. Their family, when complete, consisted of two daughters called Elizabeth and Emma and three sons, John, James, and Isaac. Emma died at the age of twenty in July 1907. Of the boys, John had been born in 1888 and James in 1891. When it came to the third son, the constraints which appear to have operated in the naming of the first two, who faced the world with conventional christian names and only one each, seem to have been abandoned. In the parish of Tavistock on Thursday 8 February 1894 Isaac Tregillis Watts was born.

John Watts senior, who was born in London, spent the early part of his working career as a labourer and quarryman in the clay and lime industries of West Devon and East Cornwall. The move to Morwellham came when he got a job as a forester. For the middle-aged parents it may have been the ideal solution: a more congenial job in a calm, peaceful area. For the children, it may have been different. Life in a small remote community could be very routine when the only excitement was provided by the occasional flood. It is not surprising that the three brothers all turned away in a search for new challenges and opportunities, particularly in a period when the local economy appeared to be on the edge of total collapse. John junior moved away to Suffolk. James joined the Royal Navy. Isaac migrated to Yorkshire. All three joined the services and became caught up in the war. James died at sea in October 1914. John enlisted in the Middlesex Regiment and was later attached to the Royal Fusiliers. He was killed in the Battle of Arras in May 1917.

Of the three sons of John and Mary Watts, only one survived to the Summer of 1917, and he was the twenty-three year old Isaac.

Isaac Watts's move to the West Riding of Yorkshire took place before the war began. Living in Otley, he may have got a job in the woollen industry. Certainly the girl he met and planned to marry was a woolcomber. She was Florence Foster, who was two years younger than Isaac, and was the daughter of a Leading Stoker in the Royal Navy called James Foster, who had died before the wedding. It is not clear whether Isaac knew Florence at the time of his enlistment, which took place at Keighley. He joined the 1/5th Battalion of the West Yorkshire Regiment, which was very much the local regiment, and which cherished also the alternative title of 'Prince of Wales Own'.

Isaac and Florence decided to get married in Devon rather than in Yorkshire, and the event took place during what may well have been the bridegroom's last leave. The ceremony was held at the Wesleyan Chapel in Tavistock on 15 February 1917. He was twenty-three and she was twenty-one. They both gave, as their address, the home of Isaac's parents, No. 29 Morwellham. Their married home was to be in Franklyn Street, Bradford. Soon after, Private Watts No. 203129 rejoined his battalion in Flanders. The Third Battle of Ypres was about to begin.

The British Commander-in-Chief, Field Marshall Sir Douglas Haig will always be associated with the policy of attrition on the Western Front. He held to the constant belief that the next push would lead to a breakthrough which would in turn bring an early conclusion to the war. In September 1917 'the next push' meant the capture of Passchendaele Ridge, some seven miles to the east of the town of Ypres. The Germans, it was said, were exhausted, and would withdraw in the face of resolute assault. The Passchendaele offensive would be the final act, and the culminating victory, of the Third Battle of Ypres, and would, furthermore, serve to disarm Haig's critics and hasten the conclusion of the war. A series of attacks were made during the rain-drenched months that followed. One of them, on 9 October, is remembered as the Battle of Poelcappe. Huge casualties were suffered as exhausted attackers, floundering in the mud, met resolute defenders, well supplied with arms, ammunition, and mustard gas. The 1/5th Battalion of the West Yorkshires were heavily involved. Private Watts was one of the day's casualties. Further attempts in succeeding weeks to capture the Ridge proved abortive, and the offensive was called off after British and Canadian troops took the village of Passchendaele on 6 November.

The Third Battle of Ypres took ten of the lives that are commemorated on the Tavistock memorial. Five of these casualties have known graves. Of the other five, Harry Bath, Harold Goodman, William Harry, and Isaac Watts are commemorated on the Tyne Cot Memorial to The Missing, while the name of Robert Brooks features on the Menin Gate Memorial.

THOMAS EDWARDS
Died Wednesday 21 November 1917. Aged 19.

Thomas Walter Edwards

Tom Edwards was officially eighteen, but actually sixteen and a half, when he joined up. His family was well known in Tavistock, where he enlisted, and it is likely that someone in the recruiting agency knew the truth, but the pressures were all in one direction, and young Tom became Drummer, No. 240270, in the 5th Battalion of the Devonshire Regiment. The 5th was one of the four so-called Territorial Battalions in the Regiment (the others were the 4th, 6th, and 7th) that were assembled from members of the volunteer Territorial Force, the part-time soldiers of pre-war Britain. It attracted a number of recruits from the Tavistock area. Two of them, the Chenhall brothers, died in Mesopotamia in 1916. Six more were to follow them onto the town's Roll of Honour; four were to fall in Palestine and two in France. Of those who were casualties of the campaign against the Turks in Palestine between November 1917 and April 1918, the first was Tom Edwards. He was nineteen years old when he died.

The Edwards family was a large one, and Tom was the eldest child. He was born on March 20 1898 at North Hill, in Launceston. His parents, Elizabeth and Walter, were both Launceston people, who had grown up as near neighbours, she having been born in the town in 1875 and he two years earlier. The young couple moved into Tavistock within two years of young Tom's birth. The new home was 45 Exeter Street. The two brothers and five sisters who followed were all born there, in the home where their parents, Elizabeth and Walter, were to live out their days. Their days were, in fact, to stretch into the 1950s, at which time six of their children were still living in Tavistock.

Walter was a blacksmith and, when the couple moved to Tavistock, he had a forge in Paddon's Row. His two younger sons, William and George, both joined their father in his business. Tom, the eldest son, preferred to become a telegraph boy after leaving the Dolvin Road School. More ambitious than many, he attended evening classes at the Institute that then offered a range of vocational courses in the Plymouth Road School buildings. The coming of the war faced him with that formidable combination of pressures, prospects, and opportunities that proved irresistible to him, as to so many. He enlisted in the early days of the war, and soon found himself, with his comrades in the 5th, on the boat to India. The family was by that time complete, with the birth of Elizabeth. She was a sickly child, and her father felt it necessary to warn Tom on his departure that, since he might well not have a home leave for some considerable time, he would probably not see his little sister again. The prophecy proved to be true, but not in the way that Walter had intended it. Elizabeth recalled the occasion from a distance of eighty-five years, as she saw out the twentieth century in good health.

The army in India was required to carry out the functions of defence and internal security that it had discharged throughout the period of British rule. It served an additional purpose after 1914 in that it constituted a reservoir of troops who could be deployed in one or other of the armed engagements in the general area. In Britain there was, throughout the war, a fundamental dispute over the conduct of the conflict, between those who felt that there should be concentration on the Western Front as the key to victory and those who felt that the cause would be best served by diversionary operations, particularly those aimed at weakening the position of Turkey in relation to her empire in the Near and Middle East. The members of the latter group, which included Winston Churchill, tended to be labelled 'easterners'. Their influence was responsible for the mounting of four campaigns, those at Gallipoli, Salonika, Mesopotamia, and Palestine, in which Indian-based troops were used against what were considered to be vulnerable points in the Ottoman Empire. The 5th Battalion of the Devons played a significant part in both the Mesopotamian Campaign in 1916 and the Palestine operations in 1917.

It was the beginning of November 1917 when the Battalion became heavily engaged in fighting on the Palestine front. Gaza, in the south, was taken, and a determined advance towards Jerusalem was launched. The weather was cold and wet, and the Turkish counter-attacks were fiercely mounted. Villages within nine miles of Jerusalem were reached on 21 October, a day that saw incessant fighting. The 5th had been in the thick of the fray, but their casualties were lighter than those of other units involved. In three days they had lost only eight killed and twenty-nine wounded. But one of the killed was Tom Edwards. He did not live to take part in the entry into Jerusalem that followed the surrender of the city in December. His own entry was a funereal one. A Military Cemetery was begun in the newly-occupied city. Here, Tom Edwards lies buried. Something over 2500 First World War casualties are commemorated on this site, which lies three miles to the north of the walled city.

CHARLES BICKLE
Died Saturday 24 November 1917. Aged 22.

A group of Devons in Palestine

Charles Bickle and Thomas Edwards may have known each other for most of their lives. Their ages were not far apart (Charles was the elder by about three years). They might well have been friends at school, or teenage companions as young men about town. They could have enlisted on the same day. They certainly joined up in the same battalion of the same regiment, and found themselves fighting the same enemy in the same remote places. They died within three days of each other. They lie in the same Middle Eastern War Cemetery.

Being in the 5th Battalion of the Devonshire Regiment, one of four Territorial Battalions in the Regiment, meant, in 1914, a passage to India, and the prospect of a long period of service overseas uninterrupted by home leave. Many members of the Battalion who survived the war found that their reward for three years in India, during which time they were drafted to one of the areas where campaigns were being waged against the Turks, was a year on the Western Front, and that they did not see their families for four years. The same fate would probably have befallen young Edwards and Bickle, had they survived.

The impact of the Indian experience on a teenage lad whose world, before enlistment, had been confined by severe limits, both social and geographical, can only be guessed at. Any help in the process of adjustment was welcomed. An example was Florence Camozzi. She had been brought up in Tavistock, the daughter of a prosperous tradesman who lived in Glanville Road. She emigrated to India, and for many years taught at Queen Mary College, Lahore. This was the arrival point in India for the 5th Devons. Knowing that the Battalion contained many men from her old home area, she organised a welcome for them, which included teas and tennis parties in the grounds of the college. Many Tavistock men retained happy memories of these first few days on the sub continent, though it can hardly have prepared them for some of the hardships that they were to have to endure.

By the Autumn of 1917 the men of the 5th Devons, who had been together now for three years through training and operations in India, were deployed in the campaign against the Turks in Palestine. Here they found themselves in the kind of fierce combat situations that they had not known before. The major objective of the advance north-eastwards, from bases in Egypt, was the capture of Jerusalem. By the middle of November the goal was in sight, but before the final thrust could be made it was necessary to take El Jib, strategically important and 3000 feet high. The attack on it took place on 23 November. The hill was well defended, and the Battalion suffered fearful casualties as Turkish riflemen and machine-gunners caught them on open land. Twenty-six were killed and 120 wounded. In the latter category was No. 240971 Private Bickle. He died of his wounds on the next day. In the following month, when Jerusalem had fallen, he was among the first to be buried in the War Cemetery in that city. Five years later his parents marked the anniversary of his death by publishing in the local press a couplet that, one guesses, they would have liked to have seen on his tombstone:

Out in the desert he heard the cry,
Wounded and helpless he had to die.

Charles Bickle's short life began on 2 November 1895 at 29 Exeter Street in Tavistock. His father, John, was employed by the Great Western Railway as a packer. John had been born in Lamerton in 1868, the son of a carpenter. He had married Charles's mother, Mary Jane, at Tavistock Register Office in July 1894. She was the daughter of a Thrushelton tailor named George Hearn, and was two years older than her husband. Her marriage to John was her second. Her first husband, whose name was Whistlecraft, had died, leaving her with three children, William, George, and Louie, to be brought up by John and Mary Jane alongside the two that they had together, Charles Edgar and Gwendoline May. At some point the family moved, via King Street, to No. 1 Fortescue Terrace, the first in that row of houses off the Old Launceston Road that were built principally to accommodate employees at the nearby Manor House.

On 26 February 1916 at Tavistock Parish Church, Charles married Louisa White. Four years older than her husband, Louisa was the daughter of William White, originally from Widecombe-in-the-Moor but now living at Hartwell Farm, Lamerton. She was, at the time of her marriage, working as a domestic servant at Tor View, in Courtenay Road, Tavistock. During their very brief married life together Charles and Louisa lived in the Bickle family home in Fortescue Terrace. After Charles's death, the old home broke up. John and Mary Jane moved to 12 College Avenue, John taking on a new job as a delivery driver for a brewery. He died there in 1956, six years after Mary Jane. Meanwhile Louisa, having spent the first years of her widowhood in West Street, re-married in 1921, and in so doing reverted to her original name. Her new husband was a Dartmouth man called Frederick White.

ERNEST HARRIS
Died Thursday 29 November 1917. Aged 35.

Trainer Cottage, Albaston

The Parish of Calstock covers a large area, and includes within its boundaries such settlements as Gunnislake and Albaston. Between these two villages lies the cemetery, at the entrance to which is the Calstock Parish War Memorial. It contains one of the names that also appears on the Tavistock monument, that of Ernest Stanley John Harris. It is appropriate that this should be so. Ernest Harris had connections with Tavistock. But he also had the strongest links, through family, birth, upbringing, and marriage, with East Cornwall. The Calstock Memorial is within a stone's throw of his last home.

The story begins in the Tamarside parish of St Dominick, one of Calstock's sister-parishes in East Cornwall. Here lived the Harris family. John, a farm labourer, had been born at South Petherwin in 1845. His wife, Grace, nee Stephens, who was three years his elder, came from Landrake. She was twenty-eight when they had their first child, Mary, in 1870, and forty when they had their fifth and last, Ernest, in 1882. In between came Albert, Emma, and Sarah. They were all born in St Dominick.

Ernest was born at the family home, Burraton, on 12 July 1882. After attending the local village school, he followed his father onto the land. When he married, at the age of thirty, he was working on a farm at Cotehele. His father had by then died. (His mother was to die at the age of eighty-nine in the Tavistock Workhouse Infirmary.) The wedding took place at the Tavistock Register Office on 15 April 1913, and the bride was Mary Paynter. She was a year older than Ernest, and worked as a domestic servant. Her father Henry had been a farmer, but had died before his daughter's marriage. The couple belonged to the same parish, Mary giving an address at Halton Quay. They began their married life together at Trainer Cottage in the village of Albaston. They had two daughters. The elder one left home at an early stage, possibly emigrating to Canada, and had six children. The younger one stayed in the village, and died childless.

Ernest enlisted at Exeter, joining the Royal Army Medical Corps. His service in the Corps was with the 100th Field Ambulance. He lost his life as a result of wounds received in November 1917. The British launched, on the 20th, an assault on the Artois section of the Hindenburg Line, the name given to the defensive arrangements that the Germans had been developing since September 1916 as a system of linked fortified areas, running behind the front lines from Verdun to the sea. The Battle of Cambrai was one of a series of abortive attempts to break this line. It did, however, see one novelty. It was the scene of the first effective movement of tanks en masse. The possible role of the tank, as a device to break the stalemate of trench warfare, had been discussed since the early days of the war. Its performance on the Somme in 1916 and at Ypres in 1917 had, however, been disappointing, in spite of the shock that its early appearances was supposed to have registered among the German troops. The machines were heavy, and tended to get bogged down in the kind of conditions in which they were required to operate. They also tended to be used in small numbers. The champions of the tank argued that a mass attack on firm terrain would be the only fair test of the new vehicle's military viability. The first day of the Battle of Cambrai appeared to prove them right. The day began with a surprise attack, unannounced by a preliminary bombardment, in which the movement of some 400 tanks, combined with infantry, and artillery, contrived to punch a hole, deep and wide, in the German lines. It was the clearest evidence of what was possible, and as such it had an influence over operations for the rest of the war. In the short term, however, the absence of adequate reserves, the failure to deploy the cavalry, and the inability to exploit the situation that had been created, led to the gains of the first day being nullified. The following day the battle degenerated into another attritional confrontation, with some particularly bloody fighting at Bourlon Wood. It was here that Ernest Harris received his fatal wounds. He was one of some 40,000 British casualties suffered in two weeks of combat which ended with both sides occupying positions very close to those that had obtained when the first shot was fired.

Private Harris, No. 74444, was buried in the British Cemetery in the village of Grevillers, a few miles from the scene of his last battle, and just outside the town of Bapaume. Some forty-two years later, in January 1960, his widow, Mary, who had continued to live in Albaston, was laid to rest in the local cemetery, a few yards from where the War Memorial recorded her husband's sacrifice. She had continued to live in Trainer Cottage for some years, before moving to a bungalow near Gunnislake Station. She was cared for, towards the end, by her younger daughter Verona, who married a signwriter from Callington called Melville Thomas. Verona and Melville died within nine days of each other, in November 1984.

GEORGE CLOAK
Died Monday 10 December 1917. Aged 37.

George Henry Cloak

West Bridge Cottages in 1891 accommodated about 5% of the population of Tavistock. There was, however, none of the multi-occupancy that characterised older working-class streets in the town centre. The 1891 census revealed that the sixty-four separate dwellings housed sixty-three households. The total population was 287. Here, at No. 35, George Henry Cloak was born. He was the seventh child in the family. When he was born, on 28 April 1880, he had five sisters, Bessie who was fourteen, Elizabeth thirteen, Mary nine, Edith seven, and Clara five, and one brother, William, who was two. His father, John, was thirty-nine years old, and his mother, Elizabeth, was thirty-eight. John was a copper miner, who had in 1863 married Elizabeth Woodley, the daughter of a labourer called Robert Woodley from Sampford Courtenay. Elizabeth had been working for some time as a domestic servant at the Duke of York Inn in Ford Street. Between 1863 and 1880 she and John gradually filled 35 West Bridge Cottages as their family increased. And then, ten weeks after the birth of William, the baby of the family, tragedy struck. John and two of his fellow-miners were drowned when water from the flooded Tavy swept into the East Crebor Mine on the afternoon of 13 July 1880. The accident produced such a wave of public sympathy that £400 was raised, and a trust fund for the three widows, and the thirteen children who were left fatherless, was established. Elizabeth Cloak was to receive twelve shillings a week. A stone in the Dolvin Road Cemetery marks the three graves, and is inscribed:

We left our homes in perfect health and little thought of death,
One moment busy at our work, the next we lost our breath.

In the aftermath of the tragedy, Elizabeth moved her family to live with her father, who was a widower, on Plymouth Road. There they stayed for some time, while the five daughters, successively, grew up, got jobs, and fled the nest. By the end of the 1880s only the two sons, William and George, remained. Their mother had, by this time, re-married. Samuel Standlake was a labourer who, like Elizabeth, had been born in Sampford Courtenay. He was ten years her junior. Both the 1891 and 1901 censuses found them living at 24 West Bridge Cottages. It was the second of three West Bridge addresses that were to be home to George Cloak.

George earned a living as a general labourer after leaving school. In 1901 the census listed him as a railway labourer. In June of the same year, at Devonport, he married Maud Knott. He was twenty-one. His bride, who was nineteen, came from a mining family. The daughter of James and Sophia Knott, she had been born at 11 Ford Street, and brought up at 47 West Street. Her father had died when she was young, and her mother, Sophia, had maintained the family by running a small dressmaking business, to which, from a young age, Maud had made a contribution. She and George now began their married life at No. 9 West Bridge. Daughter Clara arrived in December 1901, to be followed by Charles in 1908 and Violet in 1912. Violet was to die, at the age of five, a victim of the influenza epidemic that swept Britain, and many other countries, at the end of the decade, and which was responsible for more deaths than the war itself. She died ten months after her father.

George had been working for some time at a local coal store, and had become a foreman there, when he enlisted at Plymouth on 31 August 1916. It was at this time that married men became eligible for conscription on the same basis as had applied to their single counterparts since March. All men could now be called up, provided they were not in reserved occupations. Local committees were established to adjudicate in cases where exemptions were being sought.

Private Cloak, No. 28293, joined the 2nd Battalion, Grenadier Guards. He spent most of 1917 in France. The last battle of that year saw a determined attempt by the British to break the Hindenburg Line by the use of tanks en masse along with infantry and artillery. The spectacular gains made on the first day of the Battle of Cambrai were nullified over the next two weeks by the failure to exploit these early successes, and when the fighting died down on 6 December it was seen that scarcely any gains had been made to compensate for the 40,000 casualties that the British Army had suffered. George Cloak was wounded in the later stages of this campaign. He was taken to Le Treport, an important hospital centre on the coast some fifteen miles north-east of Dieppe. There he died on 10 December. He lies buried in the Mont Huon Military Cemetery in Le Treport, a burial-ground that holds the graves of some 2000 World War One casualties.

Maud Cloak, George's widow, died at 30 Crelake Park in 1962. Of her two surviving children, Clara Simonds provided a home for her mother in old age, while Charles Cloak's widow, Nellie, was still living at No. 4 The Nook as the twentieth century came to an end.

WILLIAM GOULD
Died Thursday 13 December 1917. Aged 24.

Royal Navy War Memorial, Portsmouth

The opening, in 1890, of the London and South Western Railway line through Tavistock brought a number of new jobs to the town, some of which were filled by people moving into the area. Some were direct employees of the company: signalmen, engineers, clerks, porters etc. Others were engaged in ancillary occupations such as caterers and cabmen. In the second category was Charles Gould who had worked, for some time, as a clerk to a wine dealer. Now, in his mid twenties, he moved from Torquay, where he had been born, to work at the W.H.Smith newsagency stall on the new LSWR station at Tavistock. He was joined by a young man from Surrey called Henry Legg, who was taking up a similar job. The two men found lodging at a boarding house at 67 West Street, the proprietor of which was a widow called Jane Pearce. Mrs Pearce's husband William had, until his recent death, run a gas-fitting business from these premises. Within a short space of time Charles had married an Ada Jane Pearce, who was probably related to his elderly landlady. The couple set up home at No. 1 Broadpark Terrace, Whitchurch. There, on 4 November 1893, William Henry Felix was born. The choice of the relatively unusual name of Felix is a further indication of the likelihood of a family relationship with the long-time business people of 67 West Street. William and Jane Pearce had had a son who had died at the age of twenty-three; his second name was Felix.

Young William was sent first to William Winney's Spring Hill House School, nestling below the hospital, and then, at the age of eight, to Tavistock Grammar

School. Here he remained for seven years, leaving in 1909 to join the Merchant Navy. A four-year apprenticeship followed, in which he managed to travel all over the world in the employ of Messrs Milne and Company, who operated, from Aberdeen, the Inver line of sailing ships. At the age of twenty he passed the Second Mates' Examination. When war broke out he was serving on a steamer trading in the Black Sea. This was one of the last British ships to pass through the Straits before hostilities began.

Charles Gould's business career seems to have been a successful one. As far as the station bookstall business was concerned, he was able to take advantage of a number of converging trends which were likely to benefit his trade, among them the growth of mass literacy, the dramatic expansion in the scale of the popular press, and the rapid increase in the popularity of rail travel. By 1914 he had been able to move into one of the most select parts of the town, the stately villas on Plymouth Road. The family occupied in turn houses in Woburn Terrace and Endsleigh Terrace. Named, with due respect, after two of the Duke of Bedford's dwellings, these adjacent terraces, built on the north side of the road, added to the dignity of the impressive boulevard that had been created to provide easier access to West Bridge from the town centre.

Charles and Ada had a daughter called Caroline. They also had another son, who was called after his father. Charles junior went through the same educational experience as his brother, and then joined the army, serving in France throughout almost the whole of the war. A 2nd Lieutenant in the Somerset Light Infantry, he was awarded the MC in 1914, and was wounded at the Somme on 1 July 1916, when he was mentioned in despatches. He survived the war.

William Gould was an experienced, and well qualified, seaman when the war came. In 1914 he was aboard S.S. 'Euston', and in the following year he was engaged in admiralty work on S.S. 'Hermione'. Towards the end of 1916, having passed further qualifying examinations, and obtaining distinctions in signals, he was given a commission in the Royal Naval Reserve. On 1 March 1917 he was appointed to H.M.S. 'Stephen Furness'. This was a merchant vessel that had been commissioned for wartime duties, having retained a name that commemorated a member of the Furness family, the owners of a large-scale shipowning and merchant business. An ex squadron supply ship, 'Stephen Furness' was used as an armed boarding steamer. The last that William's family heard from him was a letter written on 8 December in which he wrote that he would be leaving 'his northern base' in two days time, and heading for Liverpool. He would be home at No 2 Woburn Terrace for Christmas. On 13 December, three days out on its final voyage, the 'Stephen Furness' was intercepted in the Irish Sea by a German submarine, and was torpedoed.

The name of Sub Lieutenant William Gould appears on the Naval Monument at Portsmouth. At home it was to feature on both the Town Memorial and the tablet that was erected in his old school. J.J. Alexander, his old headmaster paid a tribute to his former pupil, who was sitting in the audience, at one of his wartime speech days. William's work as an officer in the transport service was commended as 'being as important and dangerous as if he were actually in the firing line'. And so, indeed, it proved.

GEORGE ADAMS
Died Saturday 22 December 1917. Aged 31.

Part of New Buildings, Broadclyst, 2000

Haslar Naval Cemetery in Hampshire holds the grave of one of the men whose names appear on the Tavistock War Memorial. George Adams died three days before Christmas 1917 and four months after his thirty-first birthday. His younger brother Percy, who, like him, had joined the Royal Navy, had died at the Battle of Coronel in the first year of the war. George's death was to leave one remaining brother in the forces. He was John, the baby of the family, and he was to survive.

George's parents, William and Elizabeth, had been married in 1875 at Broadclyst, where Elizabeth, previously Miss Clark, had been born twenty years earlier. William, who had been born in Tavistock, was two years older than his bride. He was a Permanent Way Inspector employed by the London and South Western Railway Company, and his transfer to Tavistock in 1890 was the result of the Company's achievement in constructing, in that year, its line through the town, thus completing the direct link between Plymouth and its London terminus at Waterloo. The move enabled William to pursue his career in the town of his birth. He brought with him his wife and the seven children who had since 1876 appeared biennially with the precision of LSWR trains. They were William, Thomas, Mary, Edwin, Lucy, George, and Selina. Having settled, handily for the railway station, in the new family home at 10 Bannawell Street, the schedule was re-applied, and the size of the family was increased from seven to ten, with the addition of Bertram, Percy, and John. At about the same time the older children were preparing to enter the world of work, with William and Thomas already contemplating following their father into the railway industry.

George was the sixth child and the fourth son of the family. He had been baptised at Broadclyst on 8 August 1886. Like all his brothers and sisters he attended the Tavistock Board School on Plymouth Road, which was about to come under the control of Devon County Council. After four years working as a railway porter he embarked upon a naval career, enlisting at Devonport in November 1903. The normal twelve year period of service brought him to 1915, at which point he joined the Royal Naval Reserve and immediately volunteered again for service. He had by then risen to the rank of Stoker Petty Officer, and had served on sixteen ships or shore establishments. He was described at the time of his re-enlistment as 5' 6" tall with dark brown hair and hazel eyes, and aged twenty-nine. It was therefore as something of a veteran that George Adams, No. 305399, found himself, in 1917, aboard His Majesty's Torpedo Boat Number 14.

The prosaically named TB No. 14 was a Torpedo Boat that had been built by J.S. White and launched in September 1907. It was one of thirty-six coastal destroyers built around that time. During the war it served with flotillas in the North Sea and on coastal defence duties. In December 1917 it was in Portsmouth Harbour, with Petty Officer Adams aboard. What happened to him on 22 December remains a mystery. It was almost three months later that his family received news of his death from the naval authorities. On 22 March the following 'In Memoriam' appeared in the *Tavistock Gazette*:

In loving memory of G Adams S.P.O. H.M.T.B.14, son of E.S. Adams, 10 Bannawell Street, Tavistock. Sadly missed by Mother, Brothers, and Sisters.

The same issue carried a report that George's body had been 'recently recovered from the water at Portsmouth'. The report went on:

He has been missing since December 22nd 1917. H. Lucy, warrant officer, identified the remains by the tattoo marks on the arm, a ring, and a belt. He also saw the deceased on December 22nd. On the following morning he was reported missing, and a thorough search was organised, but without success. Able Seaman A.Lipscombe said that he saw the body floating in the water and helped to recover it. A verdict of 'Found Drowned' was returned. The deceased was much liked in his boat, and all his officers and shipmates spoke highly of him and greatly regretted his death. Great sympathy is felt for Mrs Adams, who lost another son, Percy, on the 'Monmouth'.

George's remains were buried at Gosport, close to where his body had been found. His grave is one of 766 World War One burials in the Haslar Royal Naval Cemetery. Close by is the Haslar Naval Hospital occupying a tongue of land near Spithead. At home in Tavistock the bare details were inscribed on the stone marking the family plot in the Plymouth Road Cemetery. His name follows those of his father, mother, and brother Percy. His father had died in Plymouth some years before these sad events. The stone records that 'William, for 20 years Inspector L and SWR, died April 12th 1904, aged 52'. George's mother, Elizabeth Sophia, died at 10 Pinhoe Road in Exeter in 1919, at the age of sixty-four, having only recently given up the old family home in Bannawell Street. William and Elizabeth share the plot with one of their daughters, Selina, who died in 1974 at the age of eighty-five. And T.B.14? When the war ended the navy no longer needed her. She was sold.

CHRISTOPHER HOSKYNS-ABRAHALL Jnr
Died Saturday 22 December 1917. Aged 18.

Christopher Hoskyns-Abrahall Jnr

The Royal Air Force did not come into being until the last year of the war. It did, however, have a precursor. The Royal Flying Corps came into existence in 1912. It was considered at that time to be no more than an auxiliary branch of the army, and the 150 machines that it had on the outbreak of war were seen as having limited functions, generally in the area of reconnaisance. Few people were able to glimpse the immense potential of air power in those early months of the war. The Corps did, however, right from the start, offer to a certain kind of recruit the tempting prospect of a life of adventure, of risk-taking, of glamour, and of popular acclaim. Many young men found the allure and the challenge irresistible. Some were restrained by the kind of fears that close relatives naturally expressed. Not so Christopher Hoskyns-Abrahall. He had no ties or obligations, domestic or emotional. He was eighteen years old and unmarried, and both his parents were dead. A 2nd Lieutenant in the Royal Field Artillery, he had already had practical experience of service life, and had been given opportunities to show his sense of initiative. This, together with a background of having been brought up in an army family and sent to public school, made him the kind of recruit that the Flying Corps was looking for in 1917 as it developed its programme of expansion to enable it to widen its roles, particularly in combat situations and bombing exercises. The young subaltern successfully applied for attachment to the Corps. He was sent for training to Yatesbury Camp, near Calne in Wiltshire, where No. 17 Training Squadron had its headquarters. And here, three days before Christmas

1917, he was flying, single-handed, a D.H.C.1953, 90IIP plane, WD/1909, when, close to the ground, the engine stalled and the machine turned upside down and crashed. Death was instantaneous. A Court of Enquiry subsequently decided that:

> The accident was due to no defect in the machine or engine, but by the machine getting on its back (there is no evidence to show how he got into that position). Endeavouring to right the machine at a dangerously low altitude caused a nosedive to earth.

Members of the Court inspected the wreckage, but concluded that no further evidence could be obtained. The Commanding Officer wrote of Christopher:

> His instructors spoke most highly of him; he was getting on extremely well. He is a great loss. His brother officers of the squadron spoke most warmly of his character and said how much he was beloved and respected by them all and how very much they miss him.

Borne to his Tavistock grave by fellow-officers on the afternoon of December 27th, he was given full military honours, including a firing party provided by the Royal Marines.

Christopher Henry Hoskyns-Abrahall had been born on 19 January 1899, at Woolwich. His father, from whom he took all his names, was then in the middle of a career as a Regular Officer in the Royal Marines. He was to die in the Gallipoli Campaign in 1915. By that time young Christopher had also lost his mother, who died at the age of twenty-three, when he was five. He was a pupil at Kelly College from 1911 to 1915, joining, unsurprisingly, the College's Officer Training Corps. During this period his father retired from the army, emigrated to Australia to join his eldest son James, and returned as a reservist to play his part in the war. It was in his last term at Kelly that Christopher junior received news of his father's death. There followed a short period with a private tutor, before he moved on, at the age of sixteen, to the Royal Military Academy at Woolwich. After completing his training at the Academy, he took, at the age of seventeen, the next logical step. In May 1916 he received his commission as a 2nd Lieutenant in the Royal Field Artillery. At some point thereafter he decided that he wanted to fly. He took the fateful, if characteristic, step that led to Yatesbury and to the evergreen-lined grave in Plymouth Road.

Christopher's application papers for entry to the Academy at Woolwich were signed by his guardian, his father's elder brother John, a retired army officer. Uncle John had installed himself at Malvern Villa on Watts Road, and this became Christopher's permanent residence for the last years of his life. When he was on leave the young man also regularly visited his widowed grandmother, who lived on Spring Hill, and who predeceased her grandson by just ten days. In reaching old age, she was an exception in the Hoskyns-Abrahall family during that period. Young Christopher's father died at forty-three, his mother at twenty-three, and his sister at twenty-four. Of the immediate family only his brother James survived. He was awarded the Military Medal, and, although wounded, made it back home to Australia.

Later generations have been able to see Christopher and his kind as the natural forerunners of the young flyers who were to win the Battle of Britain twenty years on. And so, in many ways, they were.

WILLIAM HOLMAN
Died Sunday 23 December 1917. Aged 30.

Tavistock War Memorial scene, Remembrance Day 1921

The function of the destroyer in the British fleet during the First World War was essentially a defensive one, in spite of the attacking role for which this type of ship was originally intended. One of its chief duties was to act in a protective capacity in relation to any other friendly vessels, naval or merchant. Ships of whatever size and in whatever numbers during the war would seek, before going to sea, the chaperon services of a destroyer. H.M.S. 'Tornado' was an R Class Destroyer. Built by A. Stephen, she was launched in 1917, and was put into service in the North Sea on escort missions. On 23 December of that year she was one of four destroyers on duty off the Dutch coast and assigned to provide escort for a Dutch convoy. The practice in such situations was that the warships did not enter Dutch waters, but rendezvoused with the convoy off the Maas Light Buoy. The area was mined. On the night in question, the eve of Christmas Eve, two of the small protective cluster of destroyers were mined. The 'Tornado' tried to get clear by going astern, but in the process she struck two further mines and sank quickly. The last of the four ships involved escaped unscathed. Total casualties from the other three numbered 252. Of those who were aboard the 'Tornado', two are commemorated on the monument at Chatham and four on the one at Portsmouth, while sixty-two have their names on the memorial at Plymouth. Among those in the latter category are Able Seaman No. 223270 William Charles Victor Holman, and Engineer Lieutenant Commander George Joseph Mathews. They both also have their places on the Tavistock Memorial.

William Holman was thirty years old and unmarried when he went down with the 'Tornado'. He held the rank of Able Seaman, which carried with it a wage of 1s 10d (9p) a day. He had been born on 31 May 1887 at No. 2, St Levan Road East, Morice Town, in the Plymouth parish of Stoke Damerel. His father was a sailor called John Henry Holman, who had been born in 1860, and who served for some years as a Stoker in the Royal Navy. John Henry's father was a labourer called William, whose home was in Exeter Street in Charles Parish. On one of his furloughs ashore John Henry, then based at the family home in Exeter Street, married, at the age of twenty-one. His bride, at Charles Church on 2 April 1882, was eighteen year old Elizabeth Ann. She had been born at Rix Hill, in Whitchurch Parish, in 1863. Her father was John Hill, described at different times as farm worker and miner. She was the second of six children, two girls and four boys, born between 1861 and 1874. Coming after William, she preceded John, George, Eliza, and Charles. After leaving school she went into service at Anderton Farm, very close to her Rix Hill home, where she was working on the eve of her wedding, and where her father was also employed at the time as a farm labourer.

The 1901 census picked up William Holman, aged thirteen, living in Devonport, with a mother who is by now widowed, and who is working as a 'general sweet dealer'.

William enlisted at Devonport on 31 May 1905, joining a service in which his father had spent many years, and which, in essentials, had changed little over that period of years. He entered the navy straight from school, on his eighteenth birthday, having previously attended the Greenwich Hospital School. This institution, founded in 1712, had established its reputation when its first master, Thomas Watson, obtained a Royal Warrant to teach Navigation. William's enlistment papers described him as 5' 2" high, with dark brown hair, hazel eyes, and a fresh complexion. The next fourteen years were to see him pursuing a career which, typically, included service aboard eleven different ships, interspersed with five periods in shore-based establishments. He became an Able Seaman in 1907. His association with 'Tornado' began soon after she entered service in 1917.

Twelve days after William Holman lost his life on the 'Tornado', the *Tavistock Gazette* printed a short obituary. They referred to him as 'the only grandson of Mrs Hill and the late John Hill, of Rix Hill', and as 'the beloved nephew of F and E Bale, of Tor Grove Cottage'. Frederick and Eliza Bale continued to live at Tor Grove, Rix Hill, for some years after the war. It is known that William's father had died, and it seems likely from the content of the obituary that his mother also had predeceased him. In these circumstances his Tavistock family, seeing themselves with 'next of kin' responsibilities, felt that it was their duty to do whatever was necessary to honour the young man and his memory. It was, obviously, the grandmother, uncle, and aunt who arranged for William's name to be included in the list which finally appeared on the Tavistock Memorial. The wish to have something close at hand, in the absence of a grave, which could act as a focus for grief and remembrance, was, from their point of view, a perfectly understandable one. Moreover, since the family link with Plymouth was now broken, where better than Tavistock to have his memory preserved.

GEORGE MATHEWS
Died Sunday 23 December 1917. Aged 35.

Tavistock Grammar School

Two Tavistock men were lost when their ship, H.M.S. 'Tornado', was mined off the Dutch coast, two days before Christmas 1917. Whether William Holman and George Mathews knew each other in civilian life, or whether their naval careers had touched at any points before they found themselves aboard the same destroyer on patrol duties in the North Sea, is not clear. What is certain is that they shared the fate of the seventy members of the crew of the 'Tornado', who died when their ship was mined as she waited for the convoy that she had been detailed to escort. The two names are recorded on both the Plymouth Naval Memorial and the Tavistock Parish Monument.

The death at sea of Lieutenant Commander George Joseph Mathews brought to an end a period of some seventy years in which the Mathews family established itself as one of Tavistock's best-known dynasties. The period, which embraced three generations, acquired a certain identity. George Joseph was an engineer. So was his father, George Young. And so was his grandfather, Joseph. The youngest of the trio was given, appropriately, one name from each of his predecessors. And there was a centre of gravity. From the middle of the century until well after its close the dynasty was associated with houses in Watts Road and Glanville Road, those boulevards that reflected so clearly the success enjoyed by those who promoted the economic boom in early Victorian Tavistock.

Joseph Mathews was born in 1821, at Camborne, the son of a civil engineer. He came to Tavistock in 1846 as a partner in the firm that operated the Bedford Iron

Foundry in Lakeside, a business that later moved to Parkwood. His other two principal interests were the local detachment of Volunteers, of which he became commander with the rank of major, and the Masonic Lodge. In January 1901 he laid the foundation-stone of the new Freemasons' Hall in Pym Street. He died in May 1908 at the age of eighty-seven, and was buried in the Dolvin Road cemetery. He and his wife Mary Ann had had six children. The second one, born in 1851, was christened George Young. He qualified as a mechanical engineer, and appears to have travelled abroad in his profession as a young man, both before and after his marriage to Sarah, the sixth of the eight children of Daniel Westaway, who farmed 240 acres at Burnford, near Grendon. George and Sarah were married in Tavistock Parish Church on 15 June 1881. Their eldest child, George Joseph, was born on 19 April 1882, when his father was thirty-one and his mother twenty-eight. The couple were, at that time, living in Norway, where, presumably, George Young was involved in some engineering projects. George Joseph was born in the city which was then known as Christiania, but which the twentieth century was to know as Oslo.

George Joseph's background was one in which both his parents came from families of some substance. The domestic setting was a comfortable one. His earliest home, after the family's return from Norway, was Trebarwith, in Glanville Road, quite close to his grandfather's house in Watts Road. It would have been an obvious step for him to have enrolled at the Grammar School, but when he reached the appropriate age there was no such institution, as the town was enduring an enforced interval following the closure of the old school in 1888. The new Grammar School, on Plymouth Road, opened its doors in the Spring of 1895, and on 19 June, at the age of thirteen, George Joseph became one of the pioneers of its first year. He stayed for two years. During this period his growing desire to pursue a naval career was supported by professional advice from within the family. The result was a decision to attend the Naval Engineering College at Devonport. He passed out of the College in 1903, and two years later was appointed an Engineer Lieutenant. At about the same time George Young and his family bought Hillside, on Watts Road. Here the family was to remain, Sarah dying there at the age of eighty-three in 1937, and George Young living a further six years, into his ninety-third year, so perpetuating the family reputation for longevity, to which his elder son was such a sad exception.

When the war came George Joseph was a thirty-two year old Engineer Lieutenant Commander, serving in the Mediterranean aboard the Flagship H.M.S.'Inflexible'. Within a month of the declaration of war he was a patient in the Royal Naval Hospital at Plymouth. This was not the result of action, but of what the press discreetly described as 'mishaps on board during the patrolling of the North Sea'. George Joseph was one of 120 who suffered significant injuries as a result of the 'mishaps'. He survived, as did the ship, which proceeded to inflict some damage on the German fleet in the South Atlantic by the end of the year. By 1916 Lieut. Commander Mathews was serving with a destroyer flotilla in the Grand Fleet, and he was present at the Battle of Jutland. In 1917 he was serving aboard a new R Class Destroyer, the 'Tornado', when the ship, and its seventy-man crew, met their fate.

WILLIAM HELLIER
Died Monday 24 December 1917. Aged 20.

Henry and Lucy Hellier

The death of William John Hellier was a further loss to the 5th Battalion, the Devonshire Regiment. William was the fifth Tavistock-based member of the Battalion to lose his life in Middle East campaigns within eighteen months. The local community, understandably, saw the event from a different perspective. As the year 1917 came to an end, and news of the death of William reached the town, it was natural to wonder, and to fear, how many more families in Exeter Street would suffer this ordeal before it was all over. The Helliers lived at No 48. Here Henry and Lucy had brought up three sons and two daughters, though it appears that the middle son, Herbert, died at a young age. They had now lost their youngest son, William, Billy to all his friends and relations. Their eldest son, young Henry, was in khaki somewhere in France. Their dominant emotions, grief for the loss of one and apprehension for the fate of the other, were easily understood.

Henry James Hellier, William's father, was born at Colaton Raleigh, near Sidmouth, in 1855. As a young man he served for twelve years in the Royal Artillery, and, following his discharge in 1886, he maintained his strong interest in military affairs by enlisting in the county militia. At about this time he moved to Tavistock, and he was living in Ford Street and working as a labourer when, in 1890, in Tavistock Parish Church, he married Lucy Moyle. She was thirty-three years old, two years younger than her husband, and was the daughter of a miner called John Moyle. Though she had lived in Tavistock for some time, she had been born in the village of Breage, near Helston, in Cornwall. Henry and Lucy lived for a short time in Ford Street, and then at No. 6 Madge Lane, but by the time William was born, in 1896, they were at 50 Bannawell Street. There followed an interlude when the family moved to Bridewell Road in Devonport, where Henry senior was working as a labourer on extension works. The 1901 census captured them here, with William, aged four, already going to school. Soon after that they returned to Tavistock, making their final move, to 48 Exeter Street. Here the children grew up, and here Henry James was to die in 1926 and Lucy in 1932, both in their seventies.

Henry, the elder son, who was given his father's name, also inherited his father's military interests. He enlisted in the 3rd Battalion, Devonshire Regiment when only sixteen, and served for eleven years, surviving the war in spite of being severely wounded in France in 1918. The pressures on William were, no doubt, considerable, and the evidence is that he responded willingly. Born on Boxing Day 1896, he was still only fifteen when he enlisted in the local Territorial Force in September 1912. When war came he joined the 5th, one of the Devonshire Regiment's Territorial Battalions, and was soon sailing for India. After a long spell of duty there he was, with many of his comrades, posted to Egypt, the base from which operations against the Turks were mounted. By the Autumn of 1917 they were in Palestine. In November the 5th Devons became heavily engaged in a crucial phase of this campaign, the assault on Turkish positions guarding the approach to the city of Jerusalem. Lance Corporal Hellier No. 240234 found himself at the centre of some fierce combat, with the Turks showing a stubborn will to resist and using their machine guns to good effect. The last few days in which he saw action must have been among the most difficult he had encountered in his service career, with the cold, wet weather, and shortages of rations and other supplies, adding to the difficulties of unknown terrain and the dangers of enemy action. On 23 November the Battalion assaulted the Turkish stronghold of El Jib, seen as the gateway to Jerusalem, and suffered heavy losses, and it was another three weeks before the city was taken. Thereafter, the 5th was in action for some time in the area between Jerusalem and the sea, taking over, on 15 December, a section of the front line near Beit Nabala. With the Devons in their trenches battered by the incessant rain, finding it impossible to lie down, and living mainly on soaked bread, Turkish snipers and machine gunners took their toll. Lance Corporal Hellier was one of the casualties, suffering a gunshot wound in the chest. He was moved to a base hospital at Cairo, and his family was informed that he was dangerously ill. He died on Christmas Eve, within two days of his twenty-first birthday. His grave is in the Cairo War Memorial Cemetery, some three miles to the south-east of the centre of the city. Cairo was the headquarters of the British garrison in Egypt and a major transit centre. A great many British troops passed through it. Of those who died there, like Lance Corporal Hellier, more than 2000 were buried in what had been originally the New British Protestant Cemetery, before its name was changed to the War Memorial Cemetery.

William's death notice appeared in the *Tavistock Gazette* on 4 January. He was described as 'the loving brother of Harry, Cissie, and Louie and a loving and bright son.'

HARRY GREENING
Died Sunday 30 December 1917. Aged 50.

Grave in Tavistock Plymouth Road Cemetery

Many of the casualties of the First World War were young men, some of them still boys, in their teens and twenties. This was not the case with Harry Greening. The Commonwealth War Graves Commission archive, and the standard Commission headstone that marks his grave, both give his age at death as forty-nine. In fact he was fifty. Born on 16 April 1867, he died on 30 December 1917. There were, of course, special reasons why a man of that age should find himself still on active service. He had, after a long period in the Royal Navy, retired from that service before the war, and had settled into civilian life with a job and a growing family. Then, in 1916, came a call. Some of the skills that he had developed in his naval career and retained thereafter would be of considerable use in some of the specialist projects being undertaken by the Royal Engineers. In the summer of that year he enlisted at Plymouth, and became Sapper Greening No. 294182.

The particular work to which the former Petty Officer was assigned was concerned with the development and exploitation of inland water transport in France and Belgium. When he joined the army in 1916 an agency existed that was responsible for the carriage inland from the channel ports, via the canal network, of less urgent war materials, such as hay, oats, timber, and, occasionally, ammunition. This was known as the Inland Water Transport organisation, or the I.W.T. The trade for which it was responsible grew in volume, as did cross-channel traffic, with increasing amounts of ammunition being carried. In addition, canals were used more and more to carry troops to the Front by barge and to bring the wounded back. The work of the agency was to develop these functions and thus to supplement, and in some cases to substitute for, the railway transport system. Recruits to the I.W.T. at all levels were enlisted as Royal Engineers. Hence Harry's return to a uniform. He worked for the agency, on both sides of the channel, for eighteen months. Then, in December 1917, he fell ill, and became a patient in the Mile End Military Hospital in London. There he died of pneumonia on Sunday 30 December. His widow had his body returned to Tavistock, where it was buried, with full military honours, in the Plymouth Road cemetery. Joining their mother on that winter afternoon were four of her and Harry's daughters, one of whom was in the uniform of the Women's Army Auxiliary Corps.

A particularly distressing feature of so many of the war deaths was the struggle of parents to come to terms with a reversal of the natural order in which generations succeed each other. This aspect, at least, was missing in the mourning that followed Harry's passing. Both his parents pre-deceased him. His father William, a farm labourer, had been born in Lifton in 1842. At the age of twenty he had married Rebecca Masters from Milton Abbot, who was also the child of a farm worker. Thomas and Ann Masters had had four children, of whom Rebecca was the eldest. The marriage between William and Rebecca took place at the Tavistock Register Office in February 1863. Two sons followed: William in 1864 and Harry in 1867.

Harry Greening was born in the parish of Milton Abbot on Tuesday 16 April 1867. He had left home by the time he was fourteen, the 1881 census finding him living, and working as a general servant, at Great Haye Farm in Lamerton, not far away from the parental home, which was Boldhay Cottage in the same village. In 1886 he joined the Royal Navy, so launching a career as a stoker that was to last for twenty-one years. At an early stage in this career, while he was aboard H.M.S. 'Malabar', he married Jessie Thorn. The ceremony took place in Tavistock Parish Church in May 1889, when Harry was twenty-two. Jessie, who was twenty, was the eldest child of a railway plate layer called William Thorn of 40 West Bridge Cottages, Tavistock. William was a native of Bradford, near Holsworthy, and his wife Ann, Jessie's mother, hailed from Tavistock. Jessie herself had been born in Whitchurch. She was, at the time of her marriage, still quite young, and it is not surprising, given the long absences away at sea by her young husband, that she continued for some time to live at her parents' home at West Bridge. Children did not start appearing until 1894, when William was born. Thereafter they arrived at fairly regular intervals, Sydney in 1897, Winifred in 1899, Hilda in 1902, Gladys in 1904, Jessie in 1906, and Clara in 1910. By the time Clara was born, Harry had retired from the navy, and was back home, still working as a stoker, but now with a gas company.

Home, for Harry and Jessie and their young family, was first 12 Ford Street, and then 31 West Bridge Cottages. At the latter address Harry's mother, Rebecca, died in 1916. And here his widow, Jessie, was to die in 1939. For Harry the house offered the prospect of a retirement home, but in this it failed to deliver. The Great War saw to that.

WILLIAM HAYMAN
Died Thursday 31 January 1918. Aged 34.

Submarine 'K5'

Some elements of the fighting services in the First World War acquired a particular reputation for audacity and daring. Aircraft pilots, members of tank crews, and submariners fall into this category. A common thread usually to be found between such groups is that of a readiness to face the risks inherent in applying new, relatively untried, technology to the art of war, whether in the air, on the land, or at sea. According to the popular image, the men who took up this challenge tended to be young, short of experience, but full of reckless courage and derring-do. The reality did not always fit the image. William Hayman, when he died, was a middle-aged career sailor with fifteen years of service behind him and a wife and child at home. He was also one of the pioneer generation of submariners.

William Henry Hayman was born on 2 May 1883 at Bedminster, near Bristol. His father, after whom he was named, was a wheelwright. His mother, before her marriage, had been Emma Gibbings. Both had been born at Woodbury in Devon, he in 1852, she in 1853. The family appears to have moved to Teignmouth at some point. Young William must have experienced the call of the sea at an early age, for, when he enlisted in the Royal Navy, at Devonport in November 1903, he entered his pre-service occupation as 'seaman'. This could explain his absence from the family home at the time of the 1901 census. He was described at the time of his enlistment as twenty years old, 5' 2" high, with brown hair, grey eyes and a fresh complexion. He was destined to spend the rest of his life in the senior service.

On 3 December 1911, in Tavistock Parish Church, William married Mary Gilbert. Mary was, at twenty-seven, a year older than her husband. She was a native of Lifton, and was the fourth in a family of five children born to John Gilbert, a farm worker, and his wife Mary, nee Cowling. When she was very young

Mary's family moved into one of the cottages at the tiny settlement of Mana Butts, some two miles north of Tavistock, and there Mary continued to live with her mother, widowed in 1900, until her marriage, mother working as a charwoman and daughter as a domestic servant. After the wedding the newly-weds set up home at No. 3 Vigo Bridge Road, where a son was born in 1912. Following father and grandfather, the infant became William Henry Hayman the Third.

By the time the war came, Acting Leading Stoker William Hayman, No. 305390, had banked a good deal of naval experience. The switch to submarines came in 1916, following the construction, in that year, of a new type, the K class, of steam-driven submarine vessels. Hayman was to serve, and to die, on one of these, the prosaically named 'K4'.

'K4' had been built by Vickers and launched in July 1916. It had a complement of fifty-nine. On the night in question, 31 January 1918, it was involved in an exercise in which elements of the Grand Fleet put out to sea from the Firth of Forth. Included in the force were 'K4' and eight other K submarines, each known by a number, in two flotillas. The night was pitch black, and, in order to simulate a real operation, there were no lights and no wireless communication. What ensued was given the tragically ironic label of the Battle of May Island. There was no battle. What occurred, as this impressive naval procession left the shelter of the Firth for the open sea, was a series of collisions. May Island lies some five miles off the Fife coast. On that black January night the seas round it became the scene of mayhem. As fate would have it, at the centre of the confusion was the cruiser 'Fearless', on which Stoker Hayman had recently served. Astern of the 'Fearless', 'K4' swung out of line to port to avoid the melee, and stopped. Aboard 'K6' they tried to do the same, but only succeeded in ploughing into 'K4', cutting her in half. As 'K4' settled in the water, she was run down by another of the pack, 'K7', which bumped over her sinking hull. 'K4' and another submarine, and their entire crews, were lost.

Experts were divided about how to apportion blame for the tragedy. Lord Geddes, the First Lord of the Admiralty, was disposed to blame the officers. Others criticised the performance of the K submarines, which, according to one observer, combined 'the speed of a destroyer, the turning circle of a battleship, and the bridge control facilities of a picket boat'. The sense of sadness at the loss of 103 brave submariners was intensified by the feeling that the sacrifice was needless and avoidable.

The majority of the names of the casualties of May Island are commemorated on the Naval Monuments at Portsmouth and Chatham. Twenty of them, however, appear on the Plymouth Memorial, and among the latter is the name of William Henry Hayman. There is a sad postscript. William left a five year old son, who bore his name. When the boy was nine, he died of acute kidney disease in Tavistock Hospital. The bereaved mother was, meanwhile, adjusting to a period of widowhood that was to last until 1963, and her eightieth year.

HARRY WAYE
Died Wednesday 20 February 1918. Aged 19.

Grave in British Naval Cemetery, Bermuda

As a final resting-place for a casualty of the Great War, the British Naval Cemetery on Bermuda must be among the most unlikely of settings, distant as it is from any of the theatres of war. There can, however, be few locations that offer such a sense of restfulness and serenity. It lies near the westernmost part of Bermuda, close to where, for more than a century, the British maintained a naval dockyard as the Royal Navy's Western Atlantic base. The cemetery dates from 1800, and holds more than 1600 graves, though only thirty-four are war graves. Plot No 332 has an inscribed headstone. The cemetery record adds a little by recording this as the grave of 'Henry Waye. Private RMLI. H.M.S. "Carnarvon". Died 20th February 1918 aged 18.'

H.M.S. 'Carnarvon' was a cruiser of 10,850 tons, which had been launched in 1903 and re-commissioned at Devonport in 1912. One of the Devonshire Class of large cruisers, she saw service, successively, in the Mediterranean, the Atlantic, and in home waters. When war came she was sent to the South Atlantic, where she led the cruisers in the Battle of the Falklands. Thereafter, for the rest of the war, she served in North American and Caribbean stations. It was during this long stint in the North Atlantic that she called in at Bermuda in February 1918. It may have been a scheduled visit or, more likely, an emergency stop. There had been an accident of some kind on board, and a young Royal Marine, Private Harry Waye, needed medical attention. He was taken ashore to the Bermuda Hospital. He died there on 20 February.

The cemetery record contain two errors which can be corrected by reference to Private Waye's birth record. He was born on 21 November 1898, so that his age at the time of his death was nineteen and not eighteen. And his name was Harry. It would have been perfectly natural for his superiors on board the 'Carnarvon', and for the hospital and burial authorities in Bermuda, to assume that every Harry was really a Henry. But this time they were wrong.

Harry Waye was the youngest in a family of nine children. His father, William, was a miner, who, according to the 1901 census, had been born at Milton in 1856. The same source has his mother, Mary Ann, being born at Lewdown in 1854. By 1901 their family was probably complete. William and John had been born at Milton, Thomas and James at Plymouth, and Elizabeth, Charles, Francis, Alfred, and Harry, in the parish of Calstock. The ages ranged from eighteen to two, and only the two oldest were earning a living. In 1901 the family was living at Higherland in Stoke Climsland. Harry was the baby of the family. When he was born his mother was forty-five and his father forty-three. At some point thereafter the Wayes made another of their many moves, this time to Orestocks, in the Gulworthy area, and, since that was the family home at the time of Harry's death, it is not surprising to find his name on the Memorial in St. Paul's churchyard as well as on the main Tavistock Parish Monument.

Harry Waye enlisted on 16 October 1915, following an interview on that day at the Royal Marines Recruiting Office at Plymouth. Like so many young, enthusiastic volunteers, he was impatient to be given an opportunity to display his manhood in conflict, and found it necessary to give the Recruiting Officer a false birth-date. The Marines were ready to accept suitable volunteers at seventeen, but on the day of the interview Harry was five weeks short of his seventeenth birthday. He therefore claimed that he was already seventeen, and entered his date-of-birth on the Attestation Form as 1 October 1898, instead of the true date, which was 21 November. One can only speculate as to the part that the interviewing officer played in this; both parties duly signed the form which carried threats of heavy punishment for those guilty of providing false information. Young Waye gave his trade as that of a 'horse driver', and was described on enlistment as 5' 4" in height with a dark complexion, dark brown hair, and hazel eyes. He signed on for the statutory minimum period of service in the Marines, which was twelve years. He was said to be 'Very Good' at both Reading and Writing. He did, however, in the first few weeks experience some problems. For six days he went absent without leave, a period which ended with an arrest at Tavistock and a punishment of being confined to barracks for ten days. The period of his absence, significantly, included the date of his real, as distinct from his official, birthday. Twelve months later, when he joined his ship, such youthful indiscretions had been long forgotten, and his character was said to be 'Very Good'.

Harry's father, William Waye, died at Tuckermarsh Cottages, Bere Alston, in July 1927 at the age of seventy-one. He and Mary had moved there a year before, from Gulworthy, to live with one of their sons. The press account of his funeral reported that 'he was taken to Gulworthy to be buried there among his people'. Mary followed him two years later. She died, aged seventy-five, in the Tavistock Workhouse Infirmary.

ERNEST ACKFORD
Died Thursday 7 March 1918. Aged 38.

Tavistock Parish Church War Memorial

Each year, on 7 March, fresh flowers appeared on the War Memorial in Tavistock Parish Church. The custom began at the end of the Great War and continued for more than half a century. The donor was a lady called Edith Ackford. Mrs Ackford's origins were in the area, but in middle age she had moved away to live with her niece Beatrice in London. The annual observance of the anniversary was strictly maintained throughout her long life. The widow from Wimbledon was honouring her soldier-husband by marking, each year, the date of his death.

Edith Mary Kellaway, as she then was, had married Ernest Alfred Ackford at Lewtrenchard Parish Church on 2 February 1910. The daughter of a labourer called James Kellaway and his wife Joanna, she was twenty-nine years old at the time of her marriage. Ernest, who was thirty, hailed from Sourton. Born on 3 June 1879, he was also the child of a labourer, his father, Thomas, working in a lime quarry. Thomas, whose life began in Bridestowe and ended down the road in Sourton, was, for many years in between, in the Royal Navy. After completing his service he re-settled in his native district, and, in his forties, he married Mary Friend, who was thirteen years his junior. She had been born in the East Cornish parish of St Stephen's. Thomas and Mary are known to have had three children, William, Ernest, and Cordelia. Thomas died in 1887 when he was fifty-seven and the children were still very young. Ernest, the middle child, was then eight years old. The influence on him of his mother, Mary, was considerable over the next few years. She was to die in 1919, within days of the first anniversary of her son's death.

At some point after Thomas Ackford's death, his family moved into Tavistock and occupied a Parkwood Cottage. Ernest moved to Devonport, where, for a time, he worked as a platelayer. He subsequently got a job as a mail cart driver in Tavistock. This was his occupation at the time of his marriage in 1910. Soon after that he began a five year spell as an employee of John Backwell, the coach and carriage operator. His particular job was to drive the bus that conveyed passengers between the Bedford Hotel and the two railway stations in the town. During this period he and Edith lived at No. 3 Vigo Bridge Road. They had two children. Alfred died of 'congenital debility' at the age of three weeks. Mary lived for ten months before succumbing to bronchopneumonia. The family, during this period of distress, were co-tenants at 3 Vigo Bridge Road with the Haymans, who were themselves to suffer domestic tragedy. The two husbands, William Hayman and Ernest Ackford, were to die within five weeks of each other.

Ernest enlisted at Tavistock on 1 November 1915, when he was thirty-six years old. He joined the 20th Siege Battery, the Royal Garrison Artillery. While he went off to fight at Arras and Ypres, and to earn both respect and rapid promotion, Edith left the Vigo Bridge home, which held painful memories, and moved to No 5 Parkwood Cottages, where she helped to look after her ageing mother-in-law. There were also long stays at the London home of her niece.

Ernest's last leave was in September 1917. He then returned to France, to be promoted sergeant. On Monday 11 March Ethel received the last letter that he wrote, in which he told her that he was well. On the following morning a letter arrived dated Friday 8th and signed by the regimental chaplain. It read:

Just a few lines to express my very sincere sympathy with you in the terrible loss you have sustained in the death of your husband, which, as you will no doubt have already heard, took place yesterday. A shell hit the billet, and he was killed and one of his comrades wounded. I know that words are of little help at a time like this, but, please God, I can say a little that may be some comfort to you. Death was almost instantaneous, and he was spared that pain and suffering which so many have to face. He was buried today in one of those military cemeteries which will be kept up after the war is over, so that his grave will never be lost sight of. I have been out here for nearly three years, but have never attended or taken a service which showed more plainly the respect and love that his comrades had for the man who was being laid to rest. The service was a voluntary one, but every officer and man who could be spared from the guns was present. May God grant to your husband life eternal, and to you comfort in your sorrow.

The cemetery to be 'kept up after the war is over' was the Gorre British and Indian Cemetery, which already held the grave of George Hill, who had been killed in January 1917.

Edith Ackford also received a letter from her husband's Commanding Officer. In it, he described Ernest as a 'brave and fearless man', and as 'one of the mainstays of the whole battery'. He concluded: 'His steadiness and reliability under the heaviest strain were well known, and his place will never be filled'.

CHARLES SPOONER
Died Wednesday 10 April 1918. Aged 39.

Tavistock Football Club, season 1901–2. Spooner middle of back row

In Tavistock in 1914 one of the few businesses in the town that employed a significantly large number of people was the Tavistock District Laundry in Parkwood Road. In the same period, visitors to Plymouth could hardly fail to notice the large, imposing store that faced St Andrew's Cross. The first of these enterprises had late Victorian roots, whereas the second originated in the early Victorian period, but they had one notable feature in common. Both were expressions of the initiative and enterprise of a particular family. They were the creations of the Spooners.

Spooner's drapery business in Plymouth had been a family concern since its foundation in 1837. In the 1880s it was being managed by Edwin Charles Spooner. Described in the 1881 census as 'master draper', he was at that time thirty-one years old, and was living at 7 Portland Place, Plymouth, with Alice, his South Molton born wife, and their three young children. The chief changes by 1891 had been a move to 9 Queen's Gate, and the completion of a complement of four children. The eldest of the four was named Charles Norman. He was born in Plymouth in 1879.

In 1898 Edwin Spooner decided on major changes to his life, which meant, for him, a career move, and for his family, a new home. He had a brother called John, who, for some years, lived at Brooklands House, off Parkwood Road, in Tavistock. John and Edwin decided that Tavistock needed a laundry, and that Parkwood Road would be a good site for it. In 1899 the building was completed, the business was launched, and Edwin took over as proprietor. The family moved first to Lydford, and then to Tavistock, where they bought Heatherleigh, one of the few houses that then occupied Whitchurch Road. Charles, the oldest of the children, quickly made an impact on the Tavistock scene as a footballer. He played left-back for the town club, and was described in the local press as a robust player and a good and fearless tackler. In 1901 he was a member of the side that almost pulled off a double by winning the County League and being defeated in the final of the Devon Cup before a crowd of 5000. Ten years later his old club was to honour him by making him their president.

Edwin Spooner continued to run the Tavistock District Laundry, which was very successful and employed some eighty people, until 1909. Then, at the age of fifty-nine, he decided that he wanted to retire, and to hand on the management of the business, in time-honoured fashion, to his eldest son. Charles, who had prepared himself for this eventuality by undertaking, for a spell, the duties of managing the steam laundry at Okehampton, felt that this would only be possible if he gave up the time-consuming activities in which he had been involved as an officer in the Devonshire Regiment, with responsibilites for units of, successively, Volunteers and Territorials. He resigned the commission that he had held since 1900. At the age of thirty he became a full-time businessman. The experiment did not last very long. His father, Edwin, after one year of retirement, in which he had become an Urban District Councillor, died. Charles, who was unmarried, and still living at Heatherleigh, must have missed his father both personally and professionally. He began to hanker again for the uniform. In 1913 he re-enlisted in the Devons, joining the 5th Battalion in the rank of Captain.

The outbreak of war found the Tavistock Company of the Territorials, under the command of Captain Spooner, at its annual camp on Woodbury Common. Two months later Spooner was one of the twenty-eight officers and 800 men of the 5th Battalion who sailed for India. There followed two years in the sub-continent, before he embarked, in March 1917, for Egypt, in preparation for involvement in the Palestine Campaign. At Port Said he spent a spell in hospital with malaria, but recovered to take temporary second-in-command of the Battalion and to assume the rank of Acting Major. From August 1917 he was heavily engaged in the campaign. The Regimental Diary describes the events surrounding his death:

> April 9 1918: At 1.30 p.m. an attack was begun against Turkish positions in the village of Berukin, Palestine. Three companies advanced up the slopes outside the village. At 4 p.m. orders were given for the final assault. The three companies, led by Captain Spooner, charged across about 100 yards of flat ground into the village, apparently taking the garrison, who fled, entirely by surprise. Immediately on the village being taken, the battalion came under heavy artillery and machine gun fire from three sides.
>
> April 10 1918: Heavy bombardment was resumed, followed by an attack by Turkish forces, which led to heavy fighting at close quarters. The attack was repulsed, with heavy losses. Among the casualties was Captain Spooner.

The engagement at Berukin was one of the last in which the 5th Battalion was involved before it was ordered to France.

Preparations were quickly put in hand at home for a Memorial Service in St Eustachius, which was held on 22 April. Meanwhile, the body of Captain Charles Norman Spooner was buried in Ramleh War Cemetery, some eight miles south-east of Jaffa, in what is now the state of Israel.

BERTRAM WILKINSON
Died Thursday 18 April 1918. Aged 32.

Former Devon and Cornwall Bank building, West Street, Tavistock

The world of work in 1900 presented a different picture from that which prevailed a century later in a number of significant respects. For example, a young person setting out on a career at the beginning of the twentieth century would probably expect to do the same kind of job throughout his working life. Or again, people tended to be stereotyped according to the occupations they were in. Take, for example, working in a bank. When Bertram Mudge Wilkinson joined the Devon and Cornwall Bank the prospects were that, given a dedicated approach and a willingness to move around a bit, he could expect a series of promotions that would provide him with some security and the prospect of a reasonably comfortable retirement. Such achievement depended on his maintaining, over a long period, acceptable levels of integrity, appearance, and proficiency. His obituary in the *Tavistock Gazette* suggested that the Wilkinson career had, at least, got off on the right foot. It spoke of him joining the Tavistock branch of the bank:

> After Mr Leslie Gould (who is now wounded in Norwich Hospital) joined the army, his place as second cashier in the bank was taken by Mr Wilkinson, a young man of gentlemanly appearance and pleasant manners and exceedingly smart in his work. By his colleagues, and by the bank's customers, he was held in the highest respect and esteem. Indeed, one of the former said on Wednesday "A nicer fellow than Mr Wilkinson never lived".

The young man who made such a good impression in Tavistock was not a local lad. He had been born in Bridgwater in Somerset on 11 June 1885, the elder son of Thomas and Alberta Wilkinson. His father, a native of Shap in Westmorland, was the senior partner in a firm of marble manufacturers. His mother, born Alberta Mudge, came from Albaston, where her father was the landlord of the Queen's Head Inn. Bertram attended the National Elementary School in his native town. His family must have spent some time in the Tavistock area in the mid nineties, because Bertram was, at the age of ten, enrolled at Gulworthy School. The move appears to have been a temporary one, since he resumed his education in Bridgwater, at Dr. Morgan's School, and went on to the Blue Coats School, Christ's Hospital, London. He then joined the Devon and Cornwall Bank at the age of sixteen, and worked successively in branches at Plymouth, Bridport, Axminster, and Tavistock. The latter branch was a well-established institution, having been in West Street since 1836, and in its impressive new premises at Number 8 since 1870. By the time that Bertram arrived the Devon and Cornwall had been taken over by Lloyd's, and one of the changes of the new regime was a move which, in 1915, brought the bank to the northern side of Bedford Square, and began the process that led eventually to the concentration of banking activity in that area.

One of the steps on which Bertram had stood as he climbed the career-ladder was Bridport, and while he had been there he met Henrietta Martha Parsons Cousins of Eype Manor. Henrietta's father, William, was a yeoman farmer, and his family, which included a wife born in Australia and four children raised locally, was well known in that area of coastal Dorset. Bertram and Henrietta were married at Symondsbury in June 1912. In October 1913, at Henrietta's family home at the Manor, Bertram Desmond Cousins Wilkinson was born. The young family's home was Highlands, in Bere Alston.

On 10 December 1915, before a Launceston magistrate, Bertram took the oath, and enlisted 'for the duration'. The form of attestation described him as a 30 year old bank cashier, 5′ 9″ tall, and married with a two year old son. There followed eighteen months in the reserves, before he was mobilised at The Guards Depot at Caterham in June 1917. Appointed to the 3rd Battalion of the Coldstream Guards, Private Wilkinson No 22315 now faced some months at a home depot before being posted to a battle zone. It was 31 March 1918 when he arrived in France. The great German offensive, in which one million troops had been hurled against a 50 mile stretch of the British front line, had been launched in the previous week. It brought significant advance, and the real possibility, in some areas, of decisive breakthrough. As the situation appeared to deteriorate, Haig issued his 'Special Order of the Day', addressed to 'All ranks of the British Army in France and Flanders'. He admitting that 'many amongst us are now tired', but ordered that 'every position must be held to the last man'. And the order ended : 'With our backs to the wall, and believing in the justice of our cause, each one of us must fight on to the end'. One of those who obeyed both the spirit and the letter of the instruction was a private who had been at the Front for just two weeks. On 15 April Pte Wilkinson was involved in an engagement in which he took a gunshot wound to the head as he tried to save a Lewis gun after all the rest of the team had been killed. Three days later he died in hospital at Wimereux, near Boulogne. He lies buried at the Communal Cemetery nearby.

FRANCIS JAGO
Died Wednesday 24 April 1918. Aged 30.

Villers-Bretonneux 1918

Francis George Jago, No. 69049, was a Lance Corporal in the 2nd Battalion, Devonshire Regiment. The Great War brought many battle honours to the 2nd Devons. None were more richly earned in terms of the fortitude shown, or more dearly bought in terms of human cost, than those that were won in the Spring of 1918. For a month the Germans sustained an offensive which at times threatened to overwhelm allied defences. The outcome of the war itself seemed to be on the point of being settled. The British military authorities were far from optimistic about the outcome, and the admission of General Haig, in his April 11th 'Special Order of the Day' that 'many amongst us now are tired' seemed to presage the possible onset of a more resigned outlook. But, of course, the Special Order went on, famously, to insist that 'with our backs to the wall, and believing in the justice of our cause, each one of us must fight on to the end'. The end did, in fact, come during those days for thousands of British troops, among them L Cpl Jago, but the level of the resistance that was shown, the effectiveness of the counter-attacks that were mounted, and the extent to which the Germans were ultimately weakened by the huge commitment of men and resources that they were required to make, all contributed to denying to the German Army the victory that had, in early April, appeared to be within its grasp.

The 'Kaiser's Offensive' was launched on 21 March. The 2nd Devons, forming part of the Eighth Division, were immediately ordered into the front line at Villers-Carbonnel, on the Somme.

They faced a determined, relentless, onslaught, which brought bitter fighting and heavy casualties. German troops crossed the river at a number of points, and continued their advance along a line running east-west towards the city of Amiens. By 1 April, when they were relieved, the Devons had conducted a series of tactical retreats, but could claim some credit for limiting the enemy advance to some twenty miles. The battalion, at that point, withdrew to Ailly-sur-Somme for a break, during which it received a draft of 230 reinforcements to bring it up to strength. On 20 April they returned to the line. The situation had by now deteriorated to the extent that the Germans were close to Villers-Bretonneux, situated on a plateau which held the key to the defence of Amiens. Since the loss of that city would have been catastrophic, in both psychological and strategic terms, the need to halt the German advance at that point was overwhelming. The Eighth Division, including the 2nd Devons, were directed to Villers-Bretonneux. On 24 April they faced a determined attempt to capture the town and the plateau, and so to throw open the door to Amiens.

At 4 o'clock on the morning of 24 April a thunderous bombardment of gas shell, shrapnel, and high explosives marked the beginning of the attack. Then, through the fog, smoke, and dust, there emerged, for the first time, German tanks. Taken by surprise, the troops defending the town fell back, and by 9 a.m. Villers-Bretonneux was in German hands. The arrival, later in the morning, of British tanks, superior in both quality and quantity, redressed the balance. A dramatic day ended with the town having been regained, the advance having been stopped, and Amiens having been saved. For the Devons the cost was a casualty list that deprived the battalion of one third of its strength: 146 were dead or missing, and 198 were wounded. Francis Jago was among the dead. His name is inscribed on the Pozieres Memorial, near the town of Albert, as one of some 14,000 casualties of that phase of the war who have no known graves.

Francis George Jago was born in Plymouth, and enlisted there. His address at the time of his death was Number 4 King Street. His ties with the city are clear and evident. He was born on 18 September 1887. His father, Samuel Ebenezer Jago, was an engine fitter, and his mother's maiden name was Emma Mary Tozer. The family address given at that time was 10 Hood Street, Morice Town. In 1901 the census found the family living in two rooms in Cornwall Street, Devonport. Francis was the second of three sons, and there was also a young widowed daughter with two infant sons. The connection with Tavistock is not so obvious. It is given, in family terms, in the *Tavistock Gazette*'s Death Notice, which described him as the 'dearly loved nephew of Mr and Mrs Gerry and affectionate cousin of Charles, Harry, and Flo, 15 Market Street, Tavistock'. Francis was obviously very close to his uncle and aunt, George and Emma Gerry, and to his cousins, who lived successively in West Street, Taylor Square, and Market Street. They obviously felt that the ties were sufficiently close and strong to justify his name appearing on the Tavistock Memorial. Francis appears to have been unmarried, and the absence of reference, in the Death Notice, to near relatives may suggest that at the time of his death the Gerrys were the closest to him, in terms of either blood or affection, and that he had come to see Tavistock as his second home.

WILLIAM FRIEND
Died Monday 29 April 1918. Aged 43.

William and Louisa Friend with son Frederick Alfred

One of the original residents of the Duke of Bedford's new Model Cottages at Westbridge was James Friend. A farm labourer, James became the first tenant of No. 50, and was housed there with his wife Elizabeth and their six children. The 1851 census, taken soon afterwards, listed John as the eldest child in the family; at the age of fourteen he was, like his father, working on the land. Ten years on, and John had fled the nest, had married Jane Martin from Milton Abbot, and was living in Bannawell Street. He was now working as a road labourer. He and Jane had recently brought Bessie into the world. She was to be the eldest of nine children, six girls and three boys, to appear between 1860 and 1880. It cannot have been easy to feed the ever-growing number of mouths from the meagre wages that John brought home from his labours as a roadman or a farm labourer, and the frequent changes of jobs, and homes, reflect his attempts to improve his lot. The family moved from Tavistock to Whitchurch, to Stowford, to Lifton, and then to Wilminstone, where they settled, more permanently, at 2 Two Bridges Cottages. The situation had eased by 1891, when only the youngest two children remained at home, though John and Jane, now in their mid fifties, could no doubt have done without the added responsibility of a seven month old grandson called Bert.

William Henry was the seventh child of the Friend family, and the third, and youngest, of the sons. He was born in Lifton on 3 October 1874, and was educated at the recently-opened National School in the village. He then worked for a time as a farm servant for George Abel, a middle-aged widower who farmed at

Wilminstone, near to where his parents were then living. By 1901 he was being employed as an ironmonger's waggoner. Meanwhile, growing up at the same time in Barry Cottages, between Whitchurch and Horrabridge, was Louisa Cornish. Born in 1878, the year following her parents' marriage, Louisa was the daughter of an agricultural worker called Joseph Cornish, who was a Whitchurch boy, and his wife Mary, who belonged to Horrabridge. Mary died of cardiac dropsy at the age of thirty, and Joseph subsequently married Emma Luscombe and, following her death, Alice Francis. Louisa had two half-sisters, the daughters of Joseph and Emma.

William Friend, working on a local farm, and Louisa Cornish, who became a domestic servant, formed a relationship, which appears to have met a crisis in 1912, by which time they had both reached their mid thirties. In the Summer of that year William left for Canada, apparently on impulse. His return appeared equally hurried. On 8 September 1912 the couple were married at Tavistock Register Office. William entered his address as Devon Great Consols, and Louisa as 15 Parkwood Cottages. They were to live at the Old Counting House, a surviving feature the great mine that had closed just a few years before. Here their son, Frederick Alfred, was born on 18 November 1912. A second son, George Henry, was to be born in May 1914 and to die four months later, following a bout of convulsions. Both children were baptised in nearby Gulworthy Church.

William probably enlisted in 1916. He was, by then, into his forties, and was close to the upper age limit for recruits. The conscription regulations, first introduced in January 1916, had imposed a ceiling of forty-one. He first joined the Devons, and sailed for France on Christmas Eve 1916. Shortly afterwards he transferred to the Somerset Light Infantry, joining the 1st Battalion as a Private, No. 32067. The Battalion was then operating in the area of the Somme. It remains to be established where and when Pte Friend was captured. He died in a Prisoner of War Camp in Germany on 29 April 1918. The Regimental History describes engagements in the area between Bethune and Lille on 22 and 23 April 1918, in which the Battalion suffered more than thirty casualties, and he may well have been one of these. On the other hand his captivity could have been of longer duration. Regimental sources suggest that he died of wounds. The camp was at Niederzwehren, some eight miles south of the city of Kassell. On a nearby hill a cemetery was laid out in 1915 to hold the graves of Allied Prisoners of War who died in the local camp. Its 3000 graves were augmented after the war when it was chosen as one of four permanent burial grounds into which were concentrated the graves of British servicemen who had died in Germany.

William's parents both pre-deceased him. His father, John, died in December 1914 at the age of seventy-seven, outliving his mother, who died in July 1903 at sixty-seven. They are both buried in Tavistock's Plymouth Road cemetery. William's widow, Louisa, was living at Devon Great Consols when she received news of her husband's death. She was told in August that he had died on 29 April. Soon after that she moved into Bannawell Street, and it was there, at No. 25, that she died at the age of fifty-eight in 1935, pre-deceasing her father. Her son Frederick was seventy-five when he died in Tavistock Hospital in 1987.

SYLVESTER PETHICK
Died Thursday 9 May 1918. Aged 25.

Gulworthy School

Bombardier Sylvester James Pethick, No. 116673, 'B' Battery, 236th Brigade, Royal Field Artillery, spent his twenty-fifth birthday with his comrades-in-arms in the region of the Somme. The landscape was scarred by the effects of some of the bitterest and most intensive fighting of the war, and yet, in territorial terms, neither side had won or lost much, in their stern contest for these blood-soaked acres. It was March 1918. The whole area was blasted, cratered, mined, pockmarked, and littered with the debris of discarded metal and the remnants of men and horses. Everywhere there were rats, and everywhere there was mud. But at least, as Bombardier Pethick celebrated that birthday on 6 March, and dreamed of home, he could comfort himself with the thought that his section of the Front was fairly quiet. It was not to last.

The Spring assault, the so-called Kaiser's Offensive, was launched on 21 March. A heavy and debilitating bombardment was followed by a mighty thrust that sent the British Fifth Army reeling. Within three days the allies lost so much ground that German long-range guns were shelling Paris. Thereafter, the advance was to slow down and the situation to be restored, but the shock and near-panic of those days, with allied armies in full retreat, remained a painful memory. It was during that period that Bombardier Pethick, one of the many thousands thrown into the desperate effort to hold back the tide of German advance, was wounded. The date was 24 March. From the nearby field hospital he was sent home. Admitted to the 3rd General Hospital, in Glasgow, he died there on 9 May. His family decided that his body should be brought home to the parish where he was born. He was buried in the churchyard at Gulworthy. His tombstone reads: 'In loving memory of Sylvester J Pethick, the beloved son of J and L Pethick, who died at the Third General Hospital, Glasgow, May 9th 1918. Age 25 years'.

Sir John Betjeman described Lezant as 'a pastoral, gently undulating parish, with elms and limes and oaks, streams, and the remains of former grandeur'. Here, in this small settlement nestling near the Cornish bank of the Tamar, the Pethick family had its roots. In 1880 two brothers, the sons of a woodman called William Brock Pethick, made the short, but decisive, journey to Tavistock to look for work. They re-settled at the appropriately named Copper Stocks, on the Devon Great Consols Mine site, and worked there as labourers. William brought with him a wife called Ann and a one year old son. The younger brother was James: he was twenty-three and single. James lodged with William and Ann for some years, during which time both brothers, following in their father's footsteps, became foresters.

By 1889 James Pethick, now thirty-three, was living at The Rock and plying his trade as a woodman. In that year he married Mary Laura Lendon. Mary was eleven years younger than her husband. She had been born in Cullompton, the daughter of a Thomas Lendon, a farm labourer, and had, from an early age, earned her living as a domestic servant. When she was thirteen, for example, she was working for the Fuge family in Walkhampton. Later, she got a job at Morwell, close by The Rock, and there she met James. They were married on 9 October 1889 at Tavistock Register Office, and lived for a time in Morwellham. Sylvester James was their eldest son. He was born at the Bedford United Cottage on the Devon Great Consols site on 6 March 1893. He is recorded in the 1901 census as living there with his parents, and he is known to have attended Gulworthy School. Thereafter his whereabouts are far from clear. He enlisted at Rhayader, in the Welsh county of Radnor. At the time of his death he was engaged to be married to Laura Phipps, who lived in Gloucestershire. As for his family, he had a sister, Winifred, born in 1900, and two brothers, Norman and Eric, who appeared, respectively, in 1903 and 1907. The parents of this well-spaced quartet continued to live in the Devon Great Consols area after mining activity there had closed in 1902. His father, James, died at their home there, Russell House, in 1926, of carcinoma of the stomach, at the age of seventy-one. His mother then moved away, to Lewdown, where she died at the age of sixty-seven in 1934, of myocardialitis.

Sylvester's remains lie within a short distance of the places where he was born, baptised, and educated. His grave is in the churchyard of St Paul's at Gulworthy, near the north-east corner of the Church. A family plot is shared with both his parents. A few yards away, in front of the west wall, stands the War Memorial, where his name is recorded, along with those of other sons of Gulworthy who fell in the two World Wars. There is interesting testimony to the tight-knit nature of this small community in the fact that, fifteen months before Sylvester's funeral, the body of another war casualty, John Symons, had been buried here at St Paul's churchyard. Sylvester's uncle, William, had a daughter called Lilian. Lilian Pethick became the wife of John Symons.

SAMUEL BRENTON
Died Tuesday 28 May 1918. Aged 31.

61–64 West Bridge Cottages, Tavistock

William Brenton was one of the best-known characters in Edwardian Tavistock. Employed for over thirty years by the local council, he spent most of his time as a road-sweeper. Although not a native of the town (he had been born in St. Dennis in Cornwall) he was seen as very much a local figure, and he was already living in Tavistock when, in 1880, he married Mary Knight, a dressmaker, who lived in a West Bridge Cottage. Mary had been brought up in Exeter Street, the daughter of a labourer, Samuel Knight, and his wife Mary, whose maiden name was Buckley. Four years older than William, Mary, at the time of the marriage, had a five year old son called James. Two years later Ethel came along, followed fairly quickly by William, Samuel, and Thomas. The family home was 61 West Bridge Cottages, a house that father William, as the sitting tenant, was to buy for £100 in the Duke of Bedford's sale in 1912. He and Mary were both to live out the rest of their lives in this house, and to die here, within a year of each other, in their seventies.

The children, as would have been expected of a Wesleyan family, attended the Council School on Plymouth Road, the elementary school generally favoured by nonconformists. The three boys, with parental encouragement, had ambitions for careers in a uniformed service. And so it was that, when war broke out, William was in the Metropolitan Police, based at Brixton, Samuel was a warder at Parkhurst Prison on the Isle of Wight, and Thomas was a Coldstream Guardsman waiting to be sent to the front. Thomas was an early casualty of the war, dying in a Versailles hospital in October 1914 of wounds received at the First Battle of The Aisne.

Samuel Brenton was the third child of William and Mary. He had been born in Tavistock on 28 June 1886, and was twenty-eight years old when the war began and claimed his kid brother as one of its first victims. He had by then, after a spell working as an errand boy for a confectioner, embarked on a career as a prison officer. He joined the infant Royal Flying Corps, the precursor of the R.A.F., but his activities, and the length of his service, remain unrecorded. At some point he decided on a change. He walked into a Hammersmith recruiting office as Airman No. 19837 and emerged as Private No. 57187, 11th Battalion, Lancashire Fusiliers.

It was as a corporal in 11th Battalion, Lancashire Fusiliers, that Samuel found himself, in May 1918, operating at the Front near the River Aisne. The 11th Battalion had been withdrawn to a quiet and restful sector in exchange for French divisions. They were being given a break on what was considered a somnolent stretch of the Front north of the river. On 26 May two German prisoners revealed, under interrogation, that an attack was imminent. The British, overcoming French scepticism, made certain preparations. The attack was launched, and was sustained through two days of fierce fighting. The allies decided that at that point the German attack had spent itself. This assessment was now shown to have been too sanguine. On the morning of the 28th the Germans broke through on the right. The Regimental War Diaries record what ensued:

> The last report of the 11th Battalion was that they were almost surrounded and heavily engaged. There is little doubt that the CO carried out his orders in maintaining his position to the last. Nothing further has been heard of the battalion. It is presumed they have been taken prisoner or killed.

Missing were the CO, thirteen other officers, and 319 other ranks. A battalion that had lost 1332 men in two months had now ceased to exist. In August it was formally disbanded.

News that their son was missing reached the Brentons in mid August 1918. For some time they clung to the hope that he could have become a prisoner-of-war, but as the armistice came, and time passed, this hope diminished. It was finally extinguished with the official announcement in October 1919, seventeen months after the annihilation of the 11th Battalion, that those hitherto reported as missing must now be presumed dead.

With no known grave, Samuel Brenton's memorial was an inscription on the Soissons Monument, which also bears the names of Bertie Doidge and Alfred Pendry, who were among the other casualties of that summer's campaigns in that sector. The monument stands close to the spot, Huit Voisins Romain, where Samuel died. Not far away lies the body of his brother Thomas, killed in the First Battle of The Aisne. Thomas was killed in the first year of the war and Samuel in the last. Nearly four years, but only a few miles, finally separated the two brothers.

Of those who were closest to Samuel and Thomas, their surviving brother, William, developed a career in the Metropolitan Police Force as a motor patrol officer. Ethel, their sister, remained unmarried, and lived in the family home at West Bridge. Father William died in 1930 at the age of seventy-four, after failing to recover from a road accident. His widow Mary died just a year later.

BERTIE DOIDGE
Died Wednesday 29 May 1918. Aged 30.

Dedicating the battlefield monument to the 2nd Devons at Bois Des Buttes

Some of the most ferocious fighting in the Great War took place in its final months. One reflection of this can be found in the casualty figures. In the case of Tavistock, for example, one-third of the total number of deaths occurred within the twelve months leading to the Armistice on 11 November 1918. The Spring and Summer of 1918 saw a crucial struggle on the Western Front, in which the centre-pieces were the Battles of the Aisne and the Marne. The German plan was to break through and establish a position of ascendency before the full weight of the recent American intervention could be felt on the battlefield. British troops, often in small numbers, were required to conduct a 'backs to the wall' operation in the face of this determined attack, and they played, in the words of the Commonwealth War Graves Commission, 'a conspicuous part in defeat and in victory'. Distinguishing itself over this period was the 2nd Battalion of the Devons. In the last days of May this unit carried out a remarkable defensive action against heavy odds, with its centrepiece at a place called Bois Des Buttes. Among the ranks of its casualties during those days was a thirty year old corporal from Tavistock called Bertie Doidge.

The 1851 census for Broadwoodwidger recorded a family called Doidge living in a house called Raxton, in that scattered Tamarside parish. Richard, a road labourer, lived with his wife, Sophia, whose maiden name was Rixon, and their three children. The eldest child was Thomas. He had been born in the village in 1841. Thomas became a farm labourer, and, in his early thirties, he married

Harriet Kerslake, who also lived in Broadwoodwidger and was a dressmaker. Harriet had been born at Broadwood Town in 1847, the youngest of six children of George and Jane Kerslake. Thomas and Harriet moved to Tavistock. In 1881 they were living at Crease Farm, and Thomas was working as a farm labourer. In 1887 their address was given as Crays, while the 1891 census had them at a house in Pixon Lane. Bertie was the fourth of their five children, following Emily, Harriet, and Frank, and preceding Gertrude. When he was born, on 12 June 1887, his father was forty-six and his mother forty.

Young Bertie ('Bertie' was not a diminutive, but his given name) lived for a time, after leaving school, with his uncle and aunt, John and Harriet Doidge, and their eight children. They farmed at West Rowden, in Stowford. Later, he was employed by Thomas Tozer, who ran a grocery business in King Street. It was during this period that the family moved into a West Bridge Cottage. Here, at No. 25, Harriet, Bertie's mother, died in 1912 at the age of sixty-five, followed four years later by Thomas, at the age of seventy-five. Bertie formally registered the deaths of both parents, who were both buried in the Plymouth Road cemetery. Three months after his father's death, he joined the army. Enlisting at Tavistock in April 1916, at the age of twenty-eight, he became No. 21657, 2nd Battalion, Devonshire Regiment.

The Bois Des Buttes is an undistinguished feature of the Aisne Valley, to the north of Rheims and about seventy miles west of Paris. The 'buttes' are two pimples surmounting a small hill. In May 1918 this was a well fortified stronghold on the British line, which the defenders, by an elaborate system of tunnels, had developed into a reasonably comfortable, as well as a relatively safe, bastion. The frontage in this sector, some six miles long, was the responsibility of the Eighth Division. Of the three brigades that made up this division, one, the 23rd Brigade, which included the 2nd Battalion of the Devons, took the stretch to the left. This included the well-appointed Bois Des Buttes. At one o'clock on the morning of Monday 27 May the Germans launched a gas and artillery attack on the hill, followed by an infantry charge. The Devons, their number already reduced to below 800, found themselves, in the words of one eye witness, 'merely an island in the midst of an innumerable and determined foe'. Casualties were very heavy. Over a period of five days the Germans were able to press their attack from the Aisne to the Marne, but, starting at Bois Des Buttes, a series of stubborn and prolonged defensive actions slowed down this advance, and, in the words of the French General Maistre 'allowed of the formation of a dyke against which the hostile flood was in the end to break itself and to be held'. The 2nd Battalion of the Devons, whose crucial contribution towards the construction of this 'dyke' had been the stand at Bois Des Buttes, became the first British unit to receive the Croix de Guerre. The Battalion that limped back to its headquarters on 12 June, bloody but unbowed, numbered two junior officers and ninety men. One of the many they left behind was Corporal Bertie Doidge. He is commemorated on the Memorial in the main square of the town of Soissons on the left bank of the River Aisne. The figures of three soldiers guard a cenotaph, behind which a three-sided wall bears the names of nearly 4000 British soldiers who died in this theatre and have no known graves.

ERNEST COLLINS
Died Sunday 2 June 1918. Aged 18.

A battlefield burial party

Daniel Patrick Collins was born in 1860. His name reveals his roots; he was brought up among the Irish community in Liverpool. It appears that the family did, however, move, when he was quite young, to Salwayash, close to the border between Devon and Dorset. As a young man Daniel went to sea, and the 1881 census found him, an Ordinary Seaman, aboard H.M.S. 'Seagull'. It is not clear what brought him to Tavistock, but by 1888 he was living at 20 Barleymarket Street, and working as a labourer. Barleymarket Street, before it was bisected in 1890 by the construction of Drake Road, stretched from the foot of Exeter Street to Bank Square, and housed a large population in conditions of multi-occupancy. One of the families who shared No. 20 were the Kingdons. Daniel Kingdon was a shoemaker who had been born at Lewdown. His wife, who had been born Fanny Rich, in Tavistock, was a charwoman. They had four children, the third of whom, Mary, was born on 30 May 1869. When she was nineteen, Mary married Daniel Collins. The wedding took place at Tavistock Parish Church on 4 June 1888.

At the time of her marriage, Mary Jane Andrews Kingdon was still living with her parents at 20 Barleymarket Street. Daniel was given the same address. He was eight years older than his bride. Mary and Daniel eventually settled at 22 West Bridge Cottages, though the fact that they do not appear locally in the 1891 census may suggest that they spent some time away before that. They had seven children. Catherine was born in 1889. There followed, during the 1890s, Frances, Albert, Lottie, and Ernest, in that order. The turn of the century brought two more arrivals. A son, with initials G.E., was to register their father's death, and another son, Richard, eventually married Nelly Tucker, and moved away to live and work in Bedford.

Ernest Frederick Collins was born in Tavistock on 28 August 1899, a fifth child and a second son. One can now only imagine the privations suffered a century ago by the likes of Mary Collins, struggling, on a labourer's wage and without state support, to bring up a family, all of whom, at one point, were of school age or below. Reared at West Bridge, Ernest attended the Plymouth Road School. In September 1917, at the age of eighteen, he enlisted, initially in the Hampshire Regiment. At an early stage in his military career he transferred to the London Regiment, joining the 1/19th Battalion as a Private, No. G/44651. It was with this unit that he saw action in France in 1918.

A great many of the casualties of the war, on both sides, occurred in combat situations in the great set-piece engagements, the names of which resound in both military history and in folklore. It is also true, however, that significant losses were incurred throughout the war, on a continuing basis, through a natural, inevitable, process of haemorrhage. Given the conditions that existed on the Western Front, it would be unusual, in some sectors, for a day to go by without some deaths, whether from mishap, accident, bad luck, a stray shell, an unanticipated mine, a change of wind direction, a hundred-to-one hit from a sniper's bullet, or from any other of scores of incidents that were bound to arise in the situations that prevailed. Young Private Collins, for example, appears to stand in that endless line of victims who was killed in action, not in the heat of some pitched battle but in the routine circumstances of constant danger that surrounded all the players in this great drama. It was June 1918. A fierce contest was going on some way to the south as efforts were made to check the German advance from the Aisne. Collins was with his unit on the Somme. The blood-soaked killing fields of 1916 had seen some heavy fighting a month or so earlier, but attention had now been diverted elsewhere. On 14 June the *Tavistock Gazette* carried the one-sentence report that: 'News has been received by Mrs Collins, 22 West Bridge Cottages, that her son, Pte E Collins, of the London Regiment, was killed in action in France on the 3rd (sic) inst.' One week later, with the date corrected, there appeared a notice: 'In ever loving memory of our dear son and brother, Pte Ernest Collins of the 1/19th London Regiment, who was killed by shell in France'. It was signed by parents, sisters, and brothers.

Ernest's final resting place is the Communal Cemetery in the village of Montigny, some twelve miles east of Amiens, and on the road from that city to Contay. Village and cemetery lie near the heart of the old Somme battlefields. Here the London Regiment buried some of its dead in the summer months of 1918. The site holds some fifty graves of British soldiers.

Daniel Collins died in March 1927 at the age of sixty-five, having worked mainly, in his last years, as a night watchman. Mary lived until she was eighty-five, and died in November 1955. Both she and Daniel lived out their years at 22 West Bridge. Both lie buried in Plymouth Road cemetery.

REGINALD SPURWAY
Died Wednesday 5 June 1918. Aged 20.

Dolvin Road School, Tavistock

The Germans, in their Spring Offensive, were most successful, in territorial terms, in the sector between the Rivers Aisne and Marne, where their gains came close to threatening Paris. Many towns in this area underwent the experience of being captured in the late Spring and retaken, within three months, in the high Summer. One such town was Fismes, which lies to the north-west of Rheims, about halfway between that city and Soissons. Having, in May, occupied the region, the German authorities established, at Fismes, a field hospital to treat some of the wounded from the area, in which the combat had been fierce. On 28 May the hospital admitted a young British private who had received a severe neck wound earlier in the day, and had been taken prisoner. He died eight days later, and was buried in the military cemetery that the German authorities had laid out in the grounds of the hospital. And there he remained until the authorities embarked on the post-war programme of consolidating graves into larger, more accessible, sites that could more effectively be cared for. They discovered, at Fismes, a solitary British grave, and transferred it to the Marfaux British Cemetery midway between Rheims and Epernay. And there, one of over 1000 casualties of the Battles of the Aisne and the Marne, lies the young British private. He was No. 42992, and belonged to the 10th Battalion of the Worcestershire Regiment. His name was Reginald Gordon Spurway, and his home was in Exeter Street, Tavistock.

The inhabitants of Exeter Street must have felt, by the Summer of 1918, that the grim reaper had exacted his full toll from them. No street in the town had paid a higher price, in terms of the loss of their young men. And then, in mid-June,

John Spurway, who lived at No. 24, received a letter from the Red Cross telling him that his son Reginald had been seriously wounded and was a prisoner of war. There followed a long and agonising period of uncertainty before, in early October, a week before the date of Reginald's twenty-first birthday, a further letter arrived at No. 24 from the organisation normally referred to at that time as the Geneva Cross. This time the Spurways heard what they had been dreading but expecting. Reginald, it was confirmed, had died four months earlier, on 5 June.

Reginald's father John was a well-known Tavistock personality. Born in Honiton in 1864, he had had a military career, in the middle of which he had married Annie Heller from Newlyn. Between 1888 and 1895 they had had five children: James had been born at Exeter, William at Aldershot, Beatrice in Egypt, and Lilian and Harold in India. Reginald and Cyril, born in Tavistock, were to complete the family after John had, in 1897, moved into civilian life and into 24 Exeter Street. He then became the drill sergeant and instructor of the local Volunteers, the fore-runners of the Territorials. He was also for a time the secretary of the Unionist Club in Drake Road, and after the war, he served for nine years as secretary of the Tavistock Library in Court Gate, holding with the job, as was customary, the tenancy of the cottage next door, on the corner of Guildhall Square. For her part, Annie, in the early years of the century, took advantage of the last of her children emerging from infancy to open a little shop in the front of their Exeter Street home.

Reginald was the sixth child. He was born in Exeter Street on 18 October 1897. He attended the Dolvin Road School, where the Log Book recorded his performance in the annual R.I. examination in 1908 as meriting special mention. In joining the army, he was not only, presumably, responding to the hopes of his father, but was following the path of his younger brother. Cyril Spurway had joined the Devons, earned two stripes, served in France, and been awarded the DCM. He was to survive the war. Reginald did not follow him into the local regiment. On 1 December 1916, at the age of nineteen, he enlisted in the Worcestershire Regiment, joining the 10th Battalion.

The 10th was a battle-hardened unit, having been in France since July 1915. The most heroic chapter in its history was written in the last days of May 1918, when its contribution to the Battle of the Aisne was made at such a high cost that it was considered impossible to bring it back up to strength. On the 30th the Left Flank Company of the Battalion lost all its officers and two-thirds of its total strength. The inevitable outcome of this, and of further losses over the next few days, was the absorption of the remains of the 10th into another battalion. Private Spurway was one of the last of the 800 to lose their lives in the ranks of the 10th during a history that was short but full of stern challenges.

John and Ann Spurway continued to live in the town for some years after the war. Thereafter, however, they moved to Scotland, to live with their daughter Lilian, who had married George Mitchell and settled in Arbroath. From that distant town there came, for many years, regular reminders, through wreaths and newspaper notices, of young Reginald.

CHARLES HORNE
Died Thursday 13 June 1918. Aged 41.

Grave in Lambeth Cemetery, London

When, towards the end of June 1918, the news reached Tavistock of the death of Charles Horne, the story appeared bizarre. The latest in the line of Tavistock-born war casualties had died while on active service, not on some foreign field, but, of all places, at Stonehenge. A story in the *Tavistock Gazette* served to increase curiosity and to add a layer of mystery. 'The work on which he had been engaged had just been completed', reported the paper, conscious of its duty not to say anything that might be construed as being of some use to an enemy, 'but the information that has reached his distressed relatives is that he died from a fractured skull'. The inscription that was to appear on his tombstone did nothing to make the situation clearer. It records that Charles 'was killed by an accident while on military service at Stonehenge aerodrome'. If it had been widely known at the time that he was a member of one of the so-called Special Companies within his regiment, the Royal Engineers, who were involved in research on Gas Warfare, then public interest might have been even higher.

The news of Charles Horne's death reached Tavistock in a letter to his parents. They lived in one of Browne's Memorial Cottages, a group of eight semi-detached cottages on the Launceston Road. These constituted, at that time, a comparatively new feature of the Tavistock landscape, having been built in 1914 in accordance with the will of Joseph Browne, whose gift was targeted at providing accommodation for 'poor and deserving persons of the age of sixty and above'. John and Elizabeth Horne were among the first to benefit from this bequest. John had worked as a carpenter all his life. The son of a mine labourer called William, he had been born at Ottery in December 1847. Elizabeth was a native of Bridestowe, the daughter of a miner named Richard Pine and his wife Ann. After their marriage John and Elizabeth lived for a time at Mill Hill, and then at 30 Fitzford Cottages. There appeared, at regular intervals during the 1870s, Elizabeth, William, Charles, and Edith. Charles Thomas, the third of the four children, was born on 24 June 1876. The 1891 census found the family intact, with its members all still living at Fitzford. The two elder boys were working, one as a plumber and one in a jeweller's shop. Charles and Edith, respectively fourteen and twelve, were both still at school.

Charles Horne followed in his father's footsteps and became a joiner. He had left the family home by 1901, at which date the census found him in London, lodging in Lambeth with the family of a fellow-joiner called Robert Addicott. Robert and his wife Emma both hailed from Devon, he from Witheridge and she from Crediton. In 1906, at Stockwell, Charles married their daughter, Alice, a schoolteacher. The newly-weds acquired what one obituarist described as 'a nice residence off Brixton Hill'. Charles enlisted at Camberwell, joining the Royal West Surrey Regiment, but he later transferred to the Royal Engineers. Here he became involved with 'J' Company. 'J' was one of twenty-one Special Companies established within the Royal Engineers to be involved with work in the field of Gas Warfare. They were spread over five battalions; 'J' was one of four operating within the 3rd Battalion. This was the work with which Sapper Horne, No. 368999, had been concerned for some time before he met his fatal accident. On the day in question, 13 June 1918, he was working at the aerodrome near Stonehenge. Salisbury Plain was an obvious site for an air base, both because of the proximity of the Channel and because of the flatness of the terrain. A certain amount of construction and repair work was being carried out to buildings at the base. Two Royal Engineers who were stationed at the camp were detailed to work on one particular building. One of them, Sapper E. Phillips, told an inquest jury on the following day what had happened to the other, Sapper C.T. Horne. According to the report in the *Salisbury Times* he explained that:

> Horne was holding the roofing sheets which he was nailing down, and was partly behind him (Phillips). Hearing a noise, he looked round and saw Horne fall head downwards on to the floor below. Descending to the floor he found Horne lying in a pool of blood, and apparently very seriously hurt. He did not consider that there was any special danger in the job.

A sergeant in the Medical Corps then gave his opinion that death had been practically instantaneous. The jury returned a verdict of accidental death.

The funeral took place six days after the accident. Charles was buried in Lambeth Cemetery. He was to be joined there thirty-six years later by his widow Alice, who died in November 1956 at the age of eighty. Back in Tavistock, John Horne survived his son by six months, dying on New Year's Eve 1918 at the age of seventy-one. His tombstone in the Plymouth Road cemetery also commemorates his wife, Charles's mother. She is, however, not buried there. Elizabeth continued to live at Browne's Cottages for a short time after becoming widowed, but then emigrated to South Africa to live with relatives. She died in 1926, at the age of seventy-seven, in Cape Town.

LEONARD HARRIS
Died Sunday 7 July 1918. Aged 19.

Ypres – Rue au Beurre in 1918

Leonard Cotton Harris was one of those young men who appear, at an early age, to have the main outline of their lives, or at least their careers, clearly defined. When the war broke out he was fifteen, and in his last year at Tavistock Grammar School. He would stay on until December, and would then, with the kind of educational grounding behind him to prepare him for the commercial world, he would do what everyone had for some time assumed that he would do. He would become a draper. It was something that he knew a good deal about, because his father had run a drapery business for some years. There had been a time, many years before, when his father had thought that his elder son Thomas, Leonard's elder brother, might follow him into the trade, but Thomas had shown that his interests lay elsewhere. He had become a clergyman and had gone to minister to a flock in America. Leonard was more conventional, more likely to stay at home and follow the predictable path. There was no reason to think, in August 1914, that the war would make any particular alterations to the plans of lads of his generation. In all probability it would all be over by Christmas. No reason, then, to think that a bright, soundly-educated boy need be deflected from doing what countless of his counterparts had done in the past. The prospect beckoned of fifty rewarding years making a decent living by providing the community with household needs, while at the same time enjoying a happy and respectable family life and carrying out other public functions and good works. It was an honourable enough ambition. Leonard's generation was to experience the pain of having such plans and hopes, and the confidence that underpinned them, shattered by events.

Leonard's father William, and his mother Lydia, both came from Harrowbarrow, where they had both been born in 1856. William was the son of a miner, whose name he inherited. Lydia was the daughter of William Trefry, a house mason. They were married on 30 October 1879 at Tavistock's Bible Christian Chapel in Bannawell Street. William's occupation then was given as a draper's assistant. In 1881 the census found the young couple living in Redruth, with William working in a bookshop. Later in that year a son, Thomas, was born. Two years later, when a second son, John, appeared, the family was living in Liskeard, with William still in the book trade. It is not clear whether there were any more children in the sixteen years that followed before the birth of Leonard, who arrived on 8 April 1899. By that time the family was back in Harrowbarrow, and William had resumed his former career. In 1901 the family moved into Tavistock, and for the next twenty-six years William ran a drapery business in West Street.

Leonard's first school was the Elementary School on Plymouth Road, responsibility for which had recently been transferred from a locally elected School Board to the County Council. He was then, at the age of twelve, admitted to the Grammar School. His father had by this time established a business as a travelling draper, supplying the needs of individuals and families in the surrounding area. His centre of operations was the family home at 27 West Street, a house along the stretch of road between the feet of Rocky Hill and Spring Hill, sometimes referred to as The Reeve. This was to remain the business centre until after the war, when William moved into new premises further down West Street, and on the opposite side of the road, at No. 69. Here the family lived until William retired in the mid 1920s, when they moved to 6 Chapel Street.

In 1917, at the age of eighteen, Leonard interrupted the career in his father's business, into which he had gone after leaving school. He enlisted at Plymouth, joining the 15th Battalion of the Hampshire Regiment. The Battalion did a long stint in 1918 in the seemingly never-ending duty of defending Ypres. Its particular responsibility was the sector south of Potijze, a part of the line described by one diarist as 'all water and no dug-outs'. The beginning of July found the Hampshires doing a shift in the front line. On the 5th they withdrew to a support position, before returning to the front on the 15th. Private Harris, No. 45630, was reported as having been killed in action on 7 July, a date on which the regimental records suggest that he and his colleagues were taking a break. It is possible that his fatal injuries were sustained a few days earlier, during the period between the 1st and the 5th, when the Hampshires were at the front. This interpretation would fit with the fact that he was buried at the Lijssenthoek Military Cemetery at Poperinge, a burial ground close by one of the biggest centres of British field hospitals and field ambulance centres.

Some five months after the death of Leonard in Belgium, his brother Thomas died in the United States at the age of thirty-seven. Their father and mother, outliving both their children, died, respectively, in 1937 and 1938, and lie together in the Plymouth Road cemetery.

ALFRED PENDRY
Died Saturday 20 July 1918. Aged 27.

The football team formed by men from the 5th Devons stationed at Barrackpore in India

In the Summer of 1918 a number of letters appeared in the national and regional press on the subject of the plight of the 5th Battalion of the Devonshire Regiment. They were written by relatives and friends of serving members of the Battalion. On their behalf, also, questions were asked in parliament by members representing constituencies in the county. The theme of the complaints was that many members of the unit had never had home leave throughout the whole duration of the war. The Battalion had mustered in August 1914 and had sailed for India in October. Over the next three and a half years members of the 5th had seen service in India, and had also been drafted into combat operations against Turkish forces in Mesopotamia and in Palestine. Already the unit had suffered heavy casualties, including the loss of six Tavistock men. Now, apparently, its reward for all this was to be an indefinite spell on the Western Front, where reinforcements were urgently needed following the shock of the Kaiser's Offensive. In May 1918 it was announced that the Battalion was on its way to France. There, the war was to continue to exact its toll of the 5th. Two more names were to be added to the six that had already taken their places on the Tavistock Roll of Honour. Alfred Pendry and Robert Roberts were to die at the same place on the same day.

Alfred Pendry, his birth certificate tells us, was born at Gunnislake on 19 April 1891. The surname is given with a second 'e' before the 'y', in a spelling which was to be used frequently throughout his life. His father, Frederick, decided that his son should share his second name, William. Frederick, who recorded the birth on

30 May, was described as a brick maker. He was not a local boy. He had been born in 1858 in the village of Colnbrook in Berkshire. His home patch was, in later years, to be changed out of all recognition through the combined effects of the construction of the M4, the growth of Slough, and the birth and expansion of Heathrow Airport. His father, Isaac, was a labourer. It is not clear what caused Frederick to buck the trend and migrate to the south-west, but by 1880 he was living and working in Gunnislake. In that year, at Tavistock Register Office, he married Mary Ann Jackson Williams, who was working as a domestic servant. Mary, unlike her new husband, had roots in the local area. She had been brought up in the parish of Calstock, the daughter of a farm labourer from Bridestowe called John Williams. At the time of the marriage Mary was twenty and Frederick was twenty-one. The young couple lived for a time with Mary's parents at 5 Under Road, Calstock, and there their first child, Minnie, was born. Two others, Lillie and Alfred, were to follow, but by then the family had moved to 7 Lees Cottages, Gunnislake. The 1891 census listed them at that address, with Frederick and Mary in their early thirties, their two children (Alfred was about to make his entrance), and Mary's father, John Williams, who had gone to live with his daughter when his wife Elizabeth died.

The evidence suggests that Frederick Pendry was a versatile man. He moved between a number of labouring jobs, at local quarries, brickworks, and other industrial sites, and was also, for a time, a rag-and-bone man. Then, in middle age, he became an insurance agent. By 1914 he had moved into Tavistock, and was living at 17 Bannawell Street, from where he operated the insurance business with which he was to continue to be involved into old age. For a time, during the war, he moved to 10 Fitzford Cottages, before taking his wife and his business back across the Tamar to Gunnislake. In the 1920s his address was Turner's Row, and in the 1930s Fore Street. Mary died in 1935 at the age of seventy-six, but Frederick lived on until 1951, dying at ninety-three in the Tavistock Workhouse, which had by then been re-designated 'Gwynntor'. They are buried together in the cemetery at Albaston.

Alfred Pendry enlisted in the first month of the war. He was twenty-three years old, and was at the time living with his parents at their home in Fitzford Cottages. Along with his comrades in the 5th, Territorial, Battalion of the Devons, he sailed for India. He survived the rigours and hazards of service on the sub continent, and later the combination of hostile conditions and enemy action in Palestine, though in the latter campaign he was wounded a month before the Battalion was due to be redeployed to the Western Front. He had been in France for a little over a month when he was killed in action on 20 July. It had been forty-five months since he had left England.

Alfred has no known grave. His battlefield commemoration is an inscription on the Soissons Memorial, in the town of that name on the left bank of the River Aisne. It bears also the name of Bertie Doidge, along with some 4000 others, most of whom fell in the desperate fighting in that area in the last months of the war.

ROBERT ROBERTS
Died Saturday 20 July 1918. Aged 22.

Robert Roberts (left) with brothers Bert (seated) and Harry (right)

The odyssey of the 5th Battalion of the Devonshire Regiment during the First World War deserves a fuller telling than it has yet received. It had all begun on the day that war was declared when the unit, one of the four Territorial Battalions in the Regiment, was diverted from its annual training camp at Exmouth to its Drill Hall in Plymouth. Then, after two months on Salisbury Plain, it was Southampton and embarkation for India. Some 828 officers and men, the complement of the Battalion, left the shores of England in October 1918. Over the next four years many of them, and many of those who joined to fill the gaps that opened in the ranks, went to their graves in places that, before the war, they had not even seen on maps. They, and their comrades who survived, were predominantly local lads. Few, if any, would have been outside the country before their service. Many would not have travelled beyond Devon and Cornwall. Those who made it, and came through, must, one thinks, have emerged as very different men as a result of those years.

   The experience of war is debased by seeing it in terms of theatre. And yet, if it is a dramatic device to leave the biggest bang until the end, then the 5th's story has a finale that is both noisy and chilling. The Battalion, restored to its 1914 strength, sailed from Alexandria on 26 May 1918, and arrived at Marseilles on 1 June. There followed a month's training to introduce 'western front conditions' to men who hitherto had done all their fighting in the Middle East. And then it was the fields of the Aisne and the Marne. On 19 July the Devons moved into position to take part in an attack on German positions planned for the following day. The immediate objectives were the villages of Morfaux and Cuitron in the valley of the River Ardre. The attack was launched at 5.30 on the morning of the 20th. It ran into fierce resistance, and the advance had to be halted after a gain of some 1000 yards. The day's casualties, thirty-six dead and 192 wounded, amounted to about one quarter of the Battalion's strength. Among the dead were Lance Corporal Alfred Pendry and Corporal Robert Roberts. The latter, numbered 240666, was buried at the Marfaux British Cemetery, very close to where he fell. The 5th had experienced its French blooding. Succeeding days were to bring similar ordeals, and similar costs.

The two young men from Tavistock who died at Marfaux on 20 July must, one assumes, have known each other in their home-town days, if only through their membership of the Territorial Force. And this common interest brought them on 4 August 1914, into a war, and thereafter to almost four years of shared experiences.

Robert Roberts's grandfather on his father's side lived in South Tawton. His name was Robert, and he married a Jane Caunter. One of their children, William, was born in May 1860, and became a copper miner, though the registrar, at the time of his death described him as a 'gold miner', adding, in parenthesis, by way of explanation, 'below ground'. The 1881 census recorded him, at the age of twenty, lodging at 37 Fitzford Cottages with a family called Handy. Living in the same house was a nineteen year old servant called Mary Simmons, the daughter of a mine labourer. Before the year was out William and Mary were married, and had set up home together at 16 Ford Street. They were the parents of Robert Roberts.

William Roberts died of tuberculosis, at the age of fifty-four, on 23 May 1914. He left a widow, Mary, and six children, James, Alice, Bertram, Harriet, Robert, and Harry, whose ages ranged from thirty-two to sixteen. Two others, William and George, had died in infancy. Robert had been the seventh child; he had been born on 26 September 1895. When their father died, James had already embarked on a naval career. The other three boys all enlisted on the outbreak of war three months later, in the 5th Battalion of the Devons, graduating smoothly from their days as young Territorials. The thoughts of Mary, so recently widowed, can only be imagined at that time as she feared for Jim, in peril on the seas, and for Bert, Bob, and Harry, preparing to sail to the other side of the world to meet heaven knows what. In the event, three of the four brothers were to survive the war and return, though Bertram was wounded in Palestine in 1917 and had to be invalided home.

Soon after William's death Mary moved to 2 College Avenue, where she was to die in 1942 at the age of eighty. Her relief at the safe return of three of her sons partly offset her grief at the loss of young Bob. Yet again, it was a question of unrealised hopes and ambitions. Many in the town remembered Bob as a footballer who was, it was said, about to be offered professional terms by Leyton Orient. A mother's hopes and regrets tend to be more private and intimate, and she is likely to want to take them with her to the grave.

JESSE MITCHELL
Died Thursday 15 August 1918. Aged 37.

Headstone at Noordwijk Cemetery, Holland

Jesse Mitchell's roots were in East, rather than West, Devon. His father, Richard, was born in the village of Newton Poppleford, close to Sidmouth, in 1852. Richard was a domestic gardener. He married a girl called Emma Pitcher from nearby Honiton when they were both twenty. They appear to have lived in Newton Poppleford until 1878, and to have then moved to Sidmouth. The 1881 census recorded them at the latter address, with their four sons, William eight, George four, Alfred two, and Jessie (sic) five months. Jesse had been born, in Temple Street, Sidmouth, on 14 October 1880, and had been baptised in the Parish Church on 1 December.

One can only speculate on the factors that persuaded young Jesse Mitchell that his was to be a sailor's life. The great national event that took place at about the same time that he enlisted was Queen Victoria's Diamond Jubilee, in 1897. The great outpouring of patriotic feeling that accompanied this occasion was particularly focused on celebrating the success of a number of British institutions. These included the Royal Navy, which was portrayed as the ultimate protector and guarantor of the nation's independence and freedom. The navy might still recruit heavily from some of the rougher parts of British society, but as an institution it seemed impossible to disagree with the claim, made two centuries earlier by Charles II, that 'It is upon the navy that the safety, honour, and welfare of this realm do chiefly attend'. The wish to be among the recipients of the country's gratitude, together with the desire to escape from the severe limitations imposed by rural working-class life, may have been considerations that weighed with Jesse. But also, he was brought up by the sea, while, in the schoolroom, he would have heard the stories of the exploits of Devon seamen, and of none more than Walter Raleigh, born just down the road.

Jesse's impatience to join the service is reflected in the fact that he lied about his age when he enlisted at Devonport on 24 February 1898, declaring himself to be eighteen. The recruiting officer, possibly with a wink, entered the information that the day was the lad's eighteenth birthday. He noted, at the same time, that Jesse was 5′ 5″ tall, and had brown hair, grey eyes, and a fair complexion.

Twenty years after accepting the naval shilling, Jesse was still in the Royal Navy, although now a middle-aged Able Seaman. The coming of the war had, of course, made his life aboard much more dangerous, his long tours of duty exposing him constantly to the attentions of German submarines. It was at this stage in his life that he married. The occasion took place at Tavistock Parish Church on 10 October 1916, and the bride was Edith Acton. She was aged thirty-four, lived at 2 Parkwood Road, and worked in the nearby laundry. Her father, Abraham, was a bootmaker, and her mother was originally Mary Joll. Edith came in the middle of a family of five girls and one boy, who were brought up, successively, at 11 Barleymarket Street and 38 Bannawell Street. Such little time as Jesse and Edith had together in their short married life was spent at 2 Parkwood Road, and here Edith was to spend some years of her widowhood. Her last years were spent at 8 Yelverton Terrace, where she died in 1961 at the age of seventy-nine.

Jesse's last leave, for two days, brought him home in early August 1918. He then returned to his ship, H.M.S. 'Scott'. She was a destroyer of the Scott Class, and had been built by Cammell Laird as one of ten in that class of flotilla leaders. Launched in October 1917, she had a complement of 164. Her last months were spent on duty in the North Sea.

In the war at sea the Battle of Jutland was the turning-point. Until June 1916 it was possible for both sides to conceive of a major struggle in which the two fleets locked horns in a series of pitched-battle confrontations, which would settle the question of maritime superiority, and thereby decide the outcome of the war. After Jutland, this was not going to happen. The German authorities switched the emphasis on to attempting to wear down the enemy by an attritional campaign of unrestricted submarine warfare. German U-boats had considerable success in the last two years of the war in hunting down, and destroying, both naval and merchant shipping. Material losses were heavy. In terms of lives, over the whole period of the war, the Royal Navy lost 23,000, or 4% of those serving. The corresponding figures for the Merchant Navy were 15,000 and 5.5%.

The 'Scott' was, presumably, on escort or patrol duties in the North Sea in August 1918. On the 15th it was just off the Dutch coast when it suffered a torpedo attack and was sunk. It is not clear how many bodies were recovered, but Able Seaman Mitchell, No. 193172, was buried in one of the cemeteries on the North Dutch coast. This may have been one of eighteen burial places from which graves were later transferred to the Noordwijk General Cemetery, or it may have been Noordwijk itself. In any event, it is there that Jesse Mitchell now rests, one of eighty British war casualties, some of them unidentified.

CLAUDE BLYTHE
Died Monday 2 September 1918. Aged 22.

THE ROYAL NORTHUMBERLAND
FUSILIERS

A grenade; on the ball a circle inscribed "Quo Fata Vocant" (Whither the Fates Call), within the circle St. George killing the dragon. For officers the grenade is in gilt or gilding metal, with the exception of the detail on the ball, which is in silver plate. For other ranks the badge is in gilding metal and white metal.

The front lines of the two contending forces on the Western Front stretched through the Somme Department from north to south. Four years of war had made these acres among the most fiercely contested in history, and had made mockery of the fact that the name 'Somme' had derived from the Celtic word for 'tranquillity'. The maps, over those four years, recorded small alterations as an advance was secured here and a tactical withdrawal effected there. It remained the case that on 1 September 1918 the lines were more or less where they had been on 1 September 1914.

For the men and boys of the 14th Northumberland Fusiliers the first day of a new month, September 1918, the fiftieth month of the war, offered nothing that they were not used to. Theirs was a Pioneers Battalion. Much of their work was done between engagements, repairing the ravages of the previous one and preparing for the next. The schedule for the first part of September seemed familiar. Some roads in the area which had been badly damaged were in need of repair so that communication, of both men and material, could be speeded up. There was also the question of maintaining the wiring, and other fortifications, that guarded the front line trenches. These tasks were the bread-and-butter duties that fell to the Pioneers. They were less glamorous than the exploits of some of their colleagues. But they were often no less dangerous. The Battalion War Diary expresses this truth, in a style of controlled terseness:

September 1st – 'A' Coy repaired the Pys-Lesars road. 'C' Coy improved the Miraumont-Courcelette road. 'D' Coy worked on the Eaucourt-Guidecourt road and the Le Barque-Beaulencourt road. September 2nd – 'A' and 'D' Coys wired 680 yards of our line in front of Beaulencourt. Casualties : 2nd Lieut C Constable and 20 ORs. 'C' Coy continued road making. 2nd Lieut G Foster reported for duty.

The twenty-one losses among the wiring party were the victims of one of a number of hazards that might occur during such an operation. The officer-diarist simply records the facts and offers a shrug of resignation.

One of the casualties of 2 September was a young sergeant called Claude Blythe. He was taken, wounded, to a casualty clearing station at the nearby village of Varennes, and there he died. Close by the clearing station was a military cemetery, first used by the British at the height of the Battle of the Somme in August 1916. Here Sgt Blythe, No. 45366, was buried. He was among the last of the thousand or so casualties of the Great War to be commemorated on this site.

Claude Parsons Blythe was a Cornishman. The rural landscape of East Cornwall, that distinctive area to the south of Launceston and between Bodmin Moor and the Tamar, was his home territory. He was born on 8 January 1896 at Down End in the parish of Lewannick. The event was registered a month later by his mother Ann. She was a native of South Petherwin, having been born there in 1864, the eldest child of a couple called John and Elizabeth Veale. John was a dairyman, who had himself been born in Launceston, as had Elizabeth. In 1881 the census found the family living at Hendra, in Launceston, the parents in their mid forties with their two daughters, Ann and Kate. Ann, the elder child, was at that time working as a dressmaker. Later she married Edwin Blythe. His Cornish roots were just as impeccable as hers. Born in Launceston in 1866, he surfaced in 1881 as a farm servant working for a local farmer called Henry Essery. He later worked as a wheelwright. Edwin and Ann were living in Lewannick, in the area where both of them had been reared, when their first son, Stanley, was born in 1894. Claude followed two years later. Ann and Edwin were, it appears, ready to diverge from the practice, faithfully followed by the great majority of other parents of their generation, of choosing names for their offspring from a narrow range of names that were readily associated with their family. When the two boys were still quite young the family moved to Plymouth, where they were living when the 1901 census was undertaken. Their home at that time was 44 Park Street, in Charles Parish. Edwin was still operating as a wheelwright, and the two sons were aged seven and five. At some point the family moved to 42 Gibbon Street, off Plymouth's North Hill, which was the family address at the time of Claude's death.

Claude remains a shadowy figure, and it has proved difficult to establish the links with Tavistock that one might expect to find, except that he enlisted in the town. He originally joined the Devonshire Regiment as No. 1747 in the 7th Cycle Company of the Regiment, but at some stage he transferred to the Northumberland Fusiliers, though he appeared to have no family, or other, connection with that regiment, or that county. He presumably was an effective soldier, effective enough to win three stripes and thereby to qualify, in Kipling's famous description of Sergeant Whatsisname, as 'a man in khaki kit, who could handle men a bit'.

JOHN SARGENT
Died Monday 2 September 1918. Aged 40.

Canadian Memorial, St Julien

The letter from Lieut. N. Anderson to Mrs J.H. Sargent of 9 Exeter Street, Tavistock, was dated 23 September 1918. It read :

> Please accept my sympathy in your bereavement, and I assure you it is very sincere as I knew your husband very well, and he was a true man and an excellent soldier. It appears your husband was with Lieut. Edwards in rather an advanced position on the 2nd inst. Lt Edwards had occasion to leave him for a short time, and during his absence it was necessary for the platoon to retire slightly. Your husband failed to show up, so a corporal went to look for him, and has been reported as 'missing', but another party went out and found that your husband had been killed, apparently instantly, by machine gun fire, so had not any knowledge of being hit. I am always very sorry for all the near and dear ones of the boys who have fallen, as it seems to be that the strain and uncertainty must be very hard to bear, and the losing of one's very dear ones must be terrible, but he has fallen in the greatest cause, that of Justice and Right, that anyone could possibly fight for.
> P.S. In case I can ever be of further use to you, I am at your service.

It was a letter, typical of so many, written by platoon and company commanders to grieving relatives. Families needed to be told that their sons and husbands had been popular and brave comrades, and that their deaths had been instantaneous. Mrs Sargent, we may assume, was comforted by the letter and grateful to the young officer who had written it.

The Sargents had been married for less than two years when John was killed in France. The wedding had taken place at the Tavistock Wesleyan Church on 5 December 1916. The bride, thirty-nine year old dressmaker Helena Gregory, had been born in Gunnislake in February 1877, the daughter of a miner called Thomas Gregory and his wife Fanny, whose maiden name was Oxenham. The family had subsequently moved into Tavistock to live at 15 Madge Lane and later at 9 Exeter Street. As for the groom, he was enjoying the first leave of his army career. Private John Herbert Sargent, No. 252869, 10th Battalion Canadian Infantry (Alberta Regiment) had arrived in England, with his unit, in mid November. But this was far from being his first sight of England, or of Tavistock, or, perhaps, of Miss Gregory.

John's father, William Sargent, was born in the parish of Clawton, just south of Holsworthy, in 1854. He was working as a farm labourer when he married Anna Maria Collins, four years his senior, who was the daughter of a Peter Tavy miner called John, and his wife, the former Ann Palmer. William and Anna Maria were living in Milton Abbot when their eldest son, John, was born, on 14 July 1878. Soon after that they moved over the Tamar to Lawhitton, and thence to Ottery, where William died in 1901 at the age of forty-seven. At that time young John was working as a farm labourer at Antony, in Cornwall. Anna Maria finally settled at Mill Hill, with her two younger sons (there were four in all), and there she died in September 1916, aged seventy-six. By then John had emigrated to Canada, and had begun a new life as a farmer in the town of Echo, Saskatchewan, close to the border with the United States.

When he enlisted in the Canadian forces on 26 April 1916, John declared himself to be thirty-four. He was, in fact, thirty-seven. His religion was recorded as Methodist, his height as 5' 8", and his appearance as featuring a dark complexion, black hair, and blue eyes. His mother was listed as his next-of-kin; she was to die during the short period between her son's attestation and his embarkation for England. John had been sending her 100 dollars a month since he arrived in Canada. He arrived in England on 11 November. On 20 December the military authorities gave him permission to marry, which was just as well because he had already done so, fifteen days earlier. Both he and Helena were in their late thirties. It would be interesting and surprising to learn that two people who were married on 5 December had been unknown to each other on 11 November, but stranger things than that have happened, particularly in wartime.

Private Sargent's short war career was not uneventful. On 30 December he fell a victim to measles and was hospitalised at Folkestone. Then, when he got to the Front, he was wounded, although he remained on duty. A second leg wound that he received in August 1917 was more severe, and necessitated treatment back in England before he was able to resume normal duties towards the end of the year. Much of 1918 was spent, with his comrades in the 10th, in the Somme region, and it was there, near the village of Hendecourt-les-Cagnicourt, ten miles south-east of Arras, that he was killed while about his duties as a runner. His resting-place, in the Upton Wood Cemetery, is within a mile or so of where he fell.

Helena Sargent died on 4 February 1954 at Crelake, Tavistock, at the age of seventy-six.

FREDERICK WOODROW
Died Monday 9 September 1918. Aged 18.

THE DEVONSHIRE REGIMENT

An eight-pointed star, the uppermost point displaced by a crown; on the star a circle inscribed "The Devonshire Regiment". Within the circle the Castle of Exeter above a scroll inscribed with the motto "Semper Fidelis" (Always Faithful). For officers the star, castle and title circle are in silver plate and the remainder in gilt or gilding metal. For other ranks the badge is in gilding metal.

In September 1916 the German military authorities began the construction of a system of fortifications behind the Western Front, which would provide some insurance in the event of their lines being punctured or overrun. This was the Hindenburg Line, named after the army's Chief of Staff. It stretched from the coast south-east to Metz, and was concentrated on five sectors, which were given the Wagnerian names of Wotan, Siegfried, Alberich, Brunhilde, and Kriemhilde. The first real sign that the end of the war might be in sight came when, in September 1918, first Wotan and then Siegfried came under intense pressure from allied forces. Siegfried occupied the forty miles or so from Cambrai to St Quentin. Here British victories at Amiens and Albert opened the way for further advances and for an attack against the Hindenburg Line itself. Some of the sternest fighting took place in and around the town of Epehy, and it was here that Frederick Charles Woodrow, a young Private in the Devons, sustained his fatal injuries.

The 16th Battalion of the Devonshire Regiment, which Private Woodrow joined, was a successor of the Devon Yeomanry, which had formed the cavalry element of the pre-war Territorial Force. Now a dismounted unit, they served a long spell in the Middle East before being transferred to France in May 1918. Some of the features of Western Front warfare, like trenches, bayonets, and machine guns, were familiar to them, while others, such as aeroplanes, tanks, and gas, were novelties. Some re-training was necessary before the Battalion could take its place in the line, and it was July before it was ready for action. Woodrow had by then joined them direct from England. He had enlisted on New Year's Eve

1917, eleven days after his eighteenth birthday. On 16 July he found himself in contact with the enemy for the first time. For the next six weeks the Battalion was responsible for the Amusoires sector of the front, in the area of the River Lys. Then, at the end of August, came the move to the Somme. Woodrow was wounded soon after this, in one of the earliest of the Devons' engagements. He was taken to the No 1 Hospital at Etretat, a town on the coast fifteen miles north of Le Havre and forty miles west of Dieppe. Here he died on 9 September. The regimental chaplain provided some details in his letter to Frederick's mother:

> He had been wounded in the head and I am sorry to say that he never regained consciousness. There is, therefore, no message I can give you. He had the greatest possible attention, but it was impossible to save his life. If you wish for a photograph of his grave you should write to the War Office. He was laid to rest with full military honours in a beautiful cemetery near the sea.

The 'beautiful cemetery' was the Etretat Churchyard Extension, which now holds the graves of 250 World War One casualties.

It was significant that Frederick (as in so many cases, his second name was the preferred one, and to his family he was Charlie) became a Trooper. In all probability, it was a job as groom or coachman that had taken him to live at Tidworth in Hampshire, and thereby to enlist at Andover, just a few miles down the road, on that New Year's Eve. Working with horses was in the Woodrow blood. Both his father, Richard, and his grandfather, William, were coachmen and grooms. Born at Launceston in 1851, Richard was energetic, resourceful, and long-lived. At the age of twenty-one he married eighteen year old Mary Geake, the daughter of a woodranger called William Geake from Milton Abbot. Mary was living at the time at Foghanger. Richard was grooming at Kilworthy House. Between 1875 and 1899 they produced an ample but well-spaced family of three boys and three girls. Frederick was the youngest. He was born on 20 December 1899, when his parents were both in their forties. Richard, in the 1880s, operated a business from stables at The Wharf, where he advertised 'horses broken to saddle and harness horses taken to livery at moderate charges'. He described himself at that time as a 'trainer', an appellation that on later occasions he amended to 'horse breaker', 'colt breaker', or simply 'horse trainer'. It is easy to see how, given this upbringing, a knowledge of, and interest in, the world of horses stayed with Frederick throughout his short life.

Richard Woodrow had a second trade. His widowed mother, Phoebe, ran a greengrocer's shop at 12 Barley Market Street. Richard and Mary worked in the business, lived on the premises, and brought the first five of their children up here. In 1890 family and business moved to 12 Brook Street, where Frederick was born, and from there, in 1905, to 5 Pepper Street. Richard had by now abandoned colt-breaking for greengrocering, and the whole family was engaged in the business. Richard and Mary did not make a fortune from their hard work and long hours. They retired to a Brown's Charity bungalow; they both died in their eighties in the Workhouse Infirmary. Their eldest son, who had emigrated to Australia before the war, died in an accident in 1912.

HENRY MAKER
Died Wednesday 18 September 1918. Aged 36.

St Eustachius, parish church of Tavistock

Of the four Makers whose names appear on the Tavistock Memorial, Henry was the last to die. Francis and Harold, the two London-based brothers who had been born in Tavistock, had both died of wounds at the ages, respectively, of twenty-two and nineteen. The other pair of brothers, Frederick and Henry, also natives of the town but of a different family, were, on the other hand, both middle-aged when they died. Frederick was forty-five when he succumbed, in September 1916, to an ailment that developed while he was on active service in the East. Henry was within three weeks of his thirty-seventh birthday when he was killed in action on The Somme just two years later.

Henry's paternal grandfather, James, was a carpenter. When the 1851 census was taken he was fifty-two years old, and was living at 49 Bannawell Street with his wife Mary and their three children, Jane, John, and Henry. Also living there were Mary's brother, John Gosling, a master mason, and their widowed mother, Grace. John Maker, the middle child, was sixteen, and was an apprentice mason. Ten years on, and James has become a master carpenter employing five men. Two of the children, Jane and Henry, were still at home, she working as a dressmaker and he as a carpenter. John Gosling was still there, now in his sixties, but old Mrs Gosling has passed on. Of the children, one, John, had moved on, albeit not very far. He was living just down the road, and earning enough as a carpenter to keep his new wife, Newlyn-born Thomasine, and their nine month old daughter Mary. Thomasine, whose maiden name was Bilkey, was to create some concern among those who needed to write down her name. She scarcely emerges with the same spelling on more than one document.

John and Thomasine were the parents of Henry Maker. They were also the parents of Mary, Richard, William, Frederick, John, and Florence, who appeared, in that order, and at fairly regular intervals, between 1861 and 1881. Henry was the baby of the family. He was born on 9 October 1881 at Canal Cottage in Canal Road, which had just become the new family home as well as the business premises of John's successful building enterprise. Henry's baptism took place at the Parish Church on 13 January 1882. By 1891 he was, at the age of nine, one of four of the children who were still living with their parents. He and his sister Florence were still at school. Richard and Frederick were still at home, earning livings as, respectively, carpenter and horse trainer.

Henry enlisted in October 1916, one month after the death, in Gloucestershire, of his brother Frederick. He originally entered the Hertfordshire Regiment, but then transferred to the Essex Regiment, where he joined the 9th Battalion. Regimental records indicate that he enlisted at Plymouth and was, at the time, a resident of Yelverton. But the Essex Regiment's Museum has a book of unattributed press cuttings which contains an entry suggesting that he came from Newmarket. This, together with the fact that he chose two Eastern counties regiments, might suggest that there had been a horse theme in his later career, in which case he had followed the example of his older brother Frederick, who was a professional horseman. Whatever the truth of that, Henry was thirty-five years old when he became a soldier. He was still single. His enlistment, and imminent departure for the Front, would no doubt have been very difficult for his parents to accommodate to, coming so soon after the death of Frederick, had they not both already died, after spending their final years in retirement in a house in Ralph's Court. John succumbed to a cerebral haemorrage in February 1912 at the age of seventy-five, while Thomasine died of hemiplegia three years later aged seventy-nine. They were thus to be allowed what few parents of the war dead were granted: they lived long lives but were spared the grief of losing their children.

Wednesday 18 September 1918 was a crucial date in the British Army's advance on the Hindenburg Line, the taking of which was such a symbolic, as well as strategic, final twist in the story of fluctuating fortunes on the Western Front. The fighting on that day round Epehy involved four corps of the British Third and Fourth Armies, supported by a creeping barrage from 1500 guns and the concentrated fire of 300 machine guns. The success of the operation convinced the military authorities of the allies that the level of German resistance might fall away rapidly and reveal a state of exhaustion. It was therefore the prelude to an approach that was both more aggressive and more coherent in terms of allied co-operation. Private Henry Maker, No. 44405, 9th Battalion, Essex Regiment, was one of those who fought, and died, at Epehy. He was buried nearby. As occurred in many areas after the armistice, graves in small scattered burial grounds were concentrated in larger cemeteries, and this was the case in the town of Peronne. Here the Communal Cemetery Extension gathered graves from eleven scattered sites in the immediate vicinity, and became the final resting place for a total of more than 1500 casualties including Henry Maker.

THOMAS TRICK
Died Wednesday 18 September 1918. Aged 20.

Grave in Tavistock Plymouth Road Cemetery

Private Trick was given a low-key farewell. It was a Saturday in late September, and the setting was Tavistock's Plymouth Road Cemetery. The young soldier was laid to rest on an autumnal afternoon in the same plot as his mother, who had died five years before to the day. They joined a schoolmistress called Charlotte Nettle, presumably a relative, who had died in 1894 at the age of eighty. The young soldier was accompanied to his grave by just thirteen mourners. They included a half-brother, the couple who had fostered him, his former employer, and a handful of friends. It was a subdued end to a short life. Thomas Frederick Trick was only twenty when he was fatally wounded in the back in an engagement on the Western Front near Epehy in September 1918. He was with his unit, the 6th Battalion of the Dorsetshire Regiment. They formed a part of the British Fourth Army that launched an attack on forward outposts of the Hindenburg Line. Brought back to England, Private Trick died in King's Cross Hospital, in London, on 18 September. His foster mother, Mrs Jones, who lived at 2 Bannawell Street, which had been Thomas's home for some years, arranged for his body to be brought to Tavistock and to be buried in his home soil. This was done on the weekend following his death.

Thomas Frederick Trick was born at Coombe, in the parish of Lamerton, on 19 February 1898. His father, George, who worked as a labourer in one of the local mines, had been born in Thrushelton, the son of William and Charity, both of whom were natives of Sourton. George was the young, unmarried labourer who was recorded in successive censuses as a lodger in local hostelries, in 1881 with the Richards family at the Ship Inn at Morwellham, and in 1891 with the family of William Williams at the Hare and Hounds Inn at Chipshop. It could be significant that a Mr and Mrs Williams attended Thomas's funeral. For Thomas's mother, Jane, the marriage to George in January 1898 was her second. Originally Jane Cornish, she had married James Hutchings in 1882 but he had died in 1895, leaving her with three young sons, of whom the youngest, William, was to become a Leading Stoker in the Royal Navy. He was the half-brother who attended Thomas's funeral.

The family lived for a time, when Thomas was young, at Wheal Maria, close to his father's work at the mine, and it was while here that Thomas was baptised, in Gulworthy Church, on 2 August 1900. He attended the Dolvin Road School, where the Log Books for 1910 and 1911 record him as having been commended in both years for his performance in the annual R.I. examination. After leaving school in the latter year he got a job working for Henry Penny, who ran a grocery business at 11 and 12 Market Street. His home at that time was 2 Bannawell Street, a tenement dwelling. In October 1913, when he was fifteen, he lost his mother. Jane Trick was fifty-two when she died, in the Workhouse Infirmary, of cerebral haemorrhage, paralysis, and bed sores. Although she was described as the wife of George, a general labourer, he seems by now to have become a rather elusive figure. There is certainly no mention of him in relation to circumstances surrounding his son's career or death. Thomas and his half-brother appear to have been taken in hand when their mother died by Mrs Jones. She was married to a naval petty officer. Her brother, Harry Bath, had died at Ypres in October 1917.

After working in the grocer's shop in Market Street for some five years, Thomas joined the colours on 13 October 1916, at the age of eighteen. He enlisted at Plymouth, joining the Devons, but subsequently transferring to the Dorset Regiment as a Private, No 19772, in the 6th Battalion. He went to France in the early Summer of 1917. His war ended when he was wounded in fighting on the Somme when British forces advanced against the Hindenburg Line.

In the Plymouth Road Cemetery, separate from the burials of Thomas and his mother, there is a family plot containing the remains of five members of a family called Trick. Four of them are named Thomas, Charity, William, and Henry. They are the father, mother, and sons of a family who had been living at Chipshop in 1881, and who all died within three years of each other, between 1899 and 1902. The family had previously lived at Thrushelton. Thrushelton was where George Trick had been born. The fifth occupant of the family plot is called George. He died at the age of sixty-two, and was buried there on 17 June 1919. The *Tavistock Gazette* had reported, a few days before, the discovery, in The Meadows, of the body of a sixty-two year old man who was later identified as George Trick, who had been living at Peter Tavy. This is, presumably, our Thomas's father. If this is so, he shares a final resting place with his parents and two brothers. By living for sixty-two years he had outlived all the close members of his family, including his wife and son.

JOHN PALMER
Died Saturday 21 September 1918. Aged 19.

Tavistock Grammar School War Memorial

The battle-scarred fields round the medieval Flemish town of Ypres claimed their last Tavistock victim on 21 September 1918. He was Private John Percival James Palmer, No. 72222, of the 6th Battalion of the Cheshire Regiment, who was killed in action. He was nineteen years old. His career with the Cheshires had been comparatively short, because he had previously seen service with the Devon Yeomanry. It became, in the last year or so of the war, quite common for members of cavalry and yeomanry units to join infantry battalions as casualty replacements, and this is probably what happened in the case of young Palmer. It is interesting to note that of the two other lives that were lost in the raid in which Palmer died, one was a man called Alfred Buscall, who was also a former member of the Devon Yeomanry. Possibly the two comrades in death had been friends going back to that earlier period of service.

John Palmer (Percy to friends) was born at Tinhay, the site of a medieval farm in the parish of Lifton, on 30 December 1898. The birth was registered on 11 February. It may be assumed that this latter operation was conducted promptly and accurately, because John's father, John senior, was the Registrar of Births and Deaths for the Lifton area. This was one of two duties that John performed as an employee of the Tavistock Union, a grouping of twenty-five parishes charged with Poor Law responsibilities and some other administrative tasks. The other side of his job was his work as one of three Relieving Officers in the Union. They were required to organise the system of Out Relief, under which paupers could receive weekly payments as an alternative to going into the workhouse. Since, in the last years of the century, about 1000 of the 25,000 who lived in the area of the Union were paupers, this was a considerable undertaking. In 1890, when he was thirty-one, John married Rosina Maria Squire. She was twenty-eight and had been born at Stowford, the daughter of a farmer. The marriage took place at Tavistock Congregational Church. They were to have two children, John junior and Annie.

While the family remained at Lifton, young John attended the local school and then the Grammar School at Launceston. In 1913, however, following a move to Tavistock, he was admitted to Tavistock Grammar School, staying there for two years before leaving to work as an ironmonger. The move had been the result of some changes by the Tavistock Union, in which his father's responsibilities were switched from the north to the south of the area, and the town became his new centre of operations. The new home was 'Nuneham', No. 4, Parkwood Place. John senior continued to work from there until his retirement in 1923, and thereafter to live there until his death in 1939. Rosina Maria died there in 1938.

John Palmer lost his life in a raid launched in the first few minutes of 21 September at a point on the Wulverghen Sector of the line. The Regimental Diary recorded:

An operation carried out by the 6th Battalion against dug-outs was entirely successful, the raiding party advancing 400 yards and cutting out a salient. Fourteen prisoners were captured. Our barrage at zero hour was effective. Hostile artillery reaction was very light, and came down at 12.05 am. There was a little shelling and a few trench mortars were used. The enemy infantry put up a little resistance but, on the approach of our party, the majority turned and ran. Our casualties were three killed and three wounded.

The three killed included John Palmer and Alfred Buscall. The Company Captain was awarded the MC. It was probably he who wrote the letter of condolence to the parents. It read:

We had carried out our attack and gained our objective with great success. My section was told to hold a certain part of the new position and up to five minutes of the time for our relief to come up we had not suffered a single casualty. Then the unlucky shell burst in our midst, killing three and severely wounding another. When I realised what had happened I set to work rendering first aid. Your son was nearest to me, but I discovered at once that his wound was mortal, but I did my best to make his last moments easy. He suffered little and almost immediately became unconscious, and died on his way to the dressing station. May I add that there was no braver soldier mounted the parapet on this occasion.

Private Palmer is one of the 150 Great War casualties who lie buried in the British Cemetery in the village of Westoutre, eight miles south-west of Ypres. The area is 1349 square metres in size and is enclosed by a brick wall. At home, some years later, an addition was made to the inscriptions on the tombstone in the Plymouth Road cemetery commemorating his parents. It read, with a pardonable mistake in putting the tragic event on the wrong side of the border: 'John Percival James, dear only son of the above, who fell in action in France, September 21st 1918, aged 19 years'.

WILLIAM RICH
Died Sunday 29 September 1918. Aged 26.

Grave in Salonika Lembet Road Cemetery, Greece

The Greek town of Salonika (now Thessalonika) is one of those places that offers important reminders that the tragic drama of the Great War was not all conducted on the stage of the Western Front. Here, in the military cemetery, are the graves of soldiers and sailors from Britain, France, Serbia, Italy, and Russia. Among the last of the British servicemen to be buried here before the closure of the British section in October 1918, was William Rich. He is one of two Tavistock men to have their final resting place in this remote and, at first appearance, unlikely place. The first was William Davy, who died in October 1916. Neither he nor Private Rich fell in combat. Salonika, sitting at the head of the gulf that shares its name, was, for most of the war, the base for a large British operation in support of friendly states, Greece and Serbia, against Turkey and her allies. This base housed, among other facilities, eighteen hospitals. And they must have been kept busy, for, while the level of battle casualties was comparatively modest, the losses from disease were considerable. Significantly, neither Private Davy nor Private Rich succumbed to wounds, but to illness, pneumonia in the latter case and probably malaria in the former.

 The men who served in the Balkans Campaign inevitably saw themselves as sidelined and forgotten. The strategy of opening up new fronts, of diverting enemy resources away from other theatres, and of nurturing the friendship of any conceivable Balkan ally, all made sense, but these were limited objectives and did not offer the prospect of clearcut military success. Moreover, the cost of the operation was, by any measure, very high. What effect this had on the morale of the troops involved it is difficult to gauge. They would undoubtedly have been heartened by the way in which Bulgaria, Germany's ally, had shown increasing signs of weakness. These signs became very evident in the summer of 1918, and a final British thrust in September brought the Bulgarian Army to its knees. On 29 September armistice talks began. On the same day Private William Rich died in one of Salonika's hospitals.

William Henry Rich was one of the legion of copper miners who gave a son to the war. He had been born in 1860. The 1881 census had him living at 17 Ford Street with his elder brother and their widowed mother. Both sons worked in the mines. In January 1891 William Henry was married at Tavistock Parish Church. The bride was Mary Maude Westlake. She had been born in Hatherleigh in 1864, the daughter of Simon Westlake, a policeman, and his wife Ann, whose former name was Cobbledick. In her teens Mary Maud moved into Tavistock to work as a domestic servant. At the time of her marriage she was living at 54 West Street. William Henry and Mary Maud were married on 17 January 1891. On 25 November their son, William John, was born. On 17 December Mary Maud died of septicaemia. William Henry was a widower for seven years. During that time he shared both the family home, 17 Ford Street, and the task of bringing up an infant, with his widowed mother, who was now in her seventies. Then, on 3 December 1898, he married Mary Ann Lavis. The same age as her husband, and thus thirty-eight at the time of the marriage, Mary Ann had been a neighbour in Ford Street for some years. She was a native of Bere Alston, but had for some years been living in Tavistock and working as a domestic cook. She now took over a middle-aged husband and a seven year old stepson.

The early adoption, by William junior, of the nickname 'Jack' was, presumably, at least partly intended to differentiate father and son. The young man, after leaving school, got a job in the Brook Street brewery of Messrs Hilton and Sons. He enlisted, at Plymouth, on 31 August 1916, at the age of twenty-four, joining the Army Service Corps. He was 5' 5" high and weighed 119 lbs on the day when he became No. T4/220137. Ten months on the Home Front were followed by a voyage from Southampton to Cherbourg on 27 June 1917 and a train journey from there to Taranto in Italy, from where SS 'Saxon' took him on the final, four-day, leg of a trip that delivered him to Salonika on 15 July. The next fourteen months saw him working there as a munitions loader in the 28th Lines of Communication Company. The fighting was reaching a final climax at that time, but disease continued to take its unrelenting toll of the British forces. Private Rich developed broncho-pneumonia. He died in hospital in Salonika on 29 September. A hospital sister wrote to his father and stepmother:

> Your son passed away this morning at 3.30. Yesterday afternoon there was a change for the worse, but he held his own wonderfully well until just before passing away.

In addition to the grave inscription in the Military Cemetery at Salonika, William is commemorated on the Tavistock Monument and in an inscription in the Plymouth Road Cemetery on the tombstone that records the death of his father, in March 1930, at the age of sixty-nine.

JOHN HARVEY
Died Tuesday 1 October 1918. Aged 28.

Fitzford Church, Tavistock

Of all the agonies that families experienced during the Great War, the feeling of uncertainty must have been among the most difficult to endure. At one level, of course, given the nature of the conflict, the fate of every man in uniform was constantly in the balance. But, for those keeping the home fires burning, there were situations which presented a more intense degree of anxiety. This was often the case where a son or husband was reported to have been taken prisoner, or to have simply disappeared. It was of little comfort to be reminded that all belligerent countries were required under international law to treat prisoners with humanity, and that the Red Cross would exercise its right to visit camps and deliver supplies and post. The fears, intensified by long periods of silence, remained. So it must have been during much of 1918 for the wife and parents of Lance Corporal John Roy Crotch Harvey. The first news to reach the parental home arrived in the middle of June, in the form of a letter from the Chaplain of John's regiment, the Royal Army Medical Corps, telling Mr J.C. Harvey 'that his eldest son, Pte Harvey RAMC, was missing with other comrades on 27 May, and it was believed had been taken prisoner by the Germans'. The beginning of August brought confirmation that he was a prisoner of war. It was 20 December, six weeks after the armistice, before the *Tavistock Gazette* was able to bring the news of the death 'On Oct 1 at Gustrow, Germany, where he was a POW, of J Roy C Harvey, eldest son of John and Penelope Harvey, 10 Parkwood Road, and late Windsor Lane, Plymouth, and beloved husband of Betty (nee Peters).'

Lance Corporal Harvey was serving with his unit, the 24th Field Ambulance, Royal Army Medical Corps, at the Front, when, on 27 May, a German attack heralded the beginning of the Battle of the Aisne. As the advance rolled on, 50,000 prisoners were taken in three days. Harvey was among those captured on the first day. He was interned in a camp at Gustrow in the province of Mecklenburg-Schwerin. He died there on 1 October, and was buried in the adjoining cemetery. At the end of the war the fifty-nine graves of British servicemen in that cemetery were removed to Hamburg as part of an operation which resulted in the concentration of graves from 120 burial sites throughout Germany.

Young Harvey had been prominent in the Territorial movement before the war, and his transfer, when war was declared, to the colours was automatic and immediate. He enlisted at Exeter. Since he joined up on the first day of the war, and died within six weeks of the armistice, the length of his wartime service can have been matched by few other non-survivors. He is one of four members of the Medical Corps to have their names recorded on the Tavistock Monument.

John Harvey was born in Plymouth on 12 December 1889. Three of his four names were taken from his father, who was called John Henry Crotch Harvey. By substituting 'Roy' for 'Henry' his parents gave him at least one distinguishing name, and, inevitably, this was the one that everyone used. Both his parents belonged to Plymouth families. John Henry grew up at 5 Athenaeum Street, the second of three sons of a coachman called John and his wife Charity. The 1881 census revealed that the household also contained four lodgers, an elderly widow, a middle-aged lady's maid, and a young artillery officer and his wife, as well as a young servant. John Henry was listed as a sixteen year old apprentice. He was later to go into the baking business. Not far away, at 6 Bedford Place, lived the Peacock family. John Peacock had made a good living as a coal merchant. He and his wife Mary had three teenage children. Penelope, the middle one, was sixteen and was still at school; she and her younger brother had been born since the family's move down from Wolverhampton. The two sixteen year olds, John Henry Harvey and Penelope Peacock, were later to marry. John Roy, their eldest son, was born in Plymouth in 1889. Their family was to include at least one other son and one daughter.

The Harveys moved from Plymouth to Tavistock in about the year 1908, when John Henry bought a bakery business at 10 Parkwood Road. Home and business were to continue, under that roof, until the Second World War, Penelope and John Henry dying there, in 1934 and 1948 respectively. John Roy was in his late teens at the time of the move to Tavistock. He worked in the family business. He also became a very active member of the congregation of the Fitzford Church.

During his last leave, in November 1917, Private J.R.C. Harvey was married in London. His bride was Bessie Peters. She was the daughter of a Plymouth baker, William Peters, who had died by 1901, leaving a widow and five children. Bessie and her mother both continued to work in the bakery trade. The new Mrs Harvey was, at thirty-four, six years older than her husband. Widowed within a year, she thereupon began a long career on the staff of Tavistock Hospital, which ended with her death at Crelake House in February 1939.

WILLIAM TURNER
Died Thursday 24 October 1918. Aged 34.

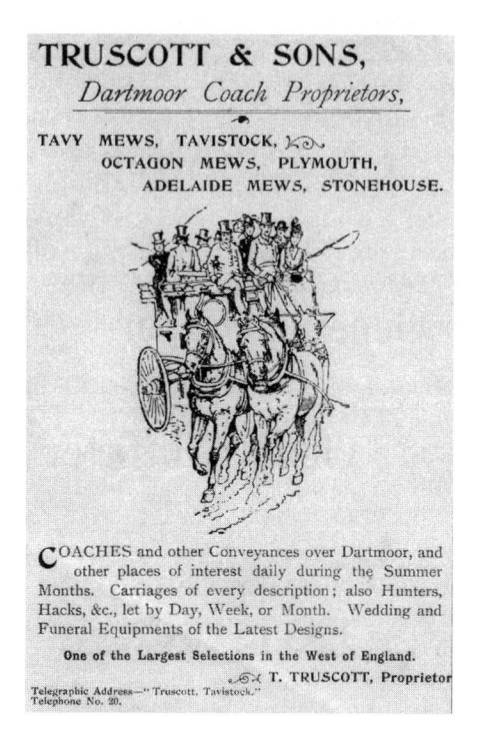

> **TRUSCOTT & SONS,**
> *Dartmoor Coach Proprietors,*
>
> TAVY MEWS, TAVISTOCK,
> OCTAGON MEWS, PLYMOUTH,
> ADELAIDE MEWS, STONEHOUSE.
>
> COACHES and other Conveyances over Dartmoor, and other places of interest daily during the Summer Months. Carriages of every description; also Hunters, Hacks, &c., let by Day, Week, or Month. Wedding and Funeral Equipments of the Latest Designs.
>
> **One of the Largest Selections in the West of England.**
>
> T. TRUSCOTT, Proprietor
> Telegraphic Address—"Truscott, Tavistock."
> Telephone No. 20.

On 16 August 1918 the *Tavistock Gazette* carried the following story:

> Tavistockians will be pleased to hear that Pte W Turner of 7 Exeter Street has been awarded the Military Medal for extreme bravery and smart discipline. He is attached to the Somerset Light Infantry, having transferred from the Devons, and has been twice wounded, but seems to bear a charmed life, having seen most of his old comrades pay the supreme sacrifice. We can only hope he may be spared to return and enjoy a long and useful life in his native town.

Three months later, on 15 November, in the edition that brought news of the armistice, the same paper recorded that 'Pte W Turner of the Somerset L.I., husband of Mrs Turner of 7 Exeter Street, was killed in action in France on October 24th'. William Turner was one of five brothers in the colours. Up to the moment when they received the news of his death, his parents were entitled to think that the whole family bore charmed lives. Now, notwithstanding the fact that the other four sons had survived, the protective spell had been broken.

The parents who received the ominous letter were James Turner and his wife Elizabeth Ann. James, the son of a Thomas Turner, was probably born in 1858, though his chronic uncertainty about his age means that he could have been anything between sixteen and twenty-two when, in December 1880, he married Elizabeth Ann Dawe. She was a domestic servant who had been born at Heathfield, near Tavistock, in October 1857. He was a coachman, who for many years drove four-in-hand coaches for Messrs Truscott of Brook Street. The young couple started their married life in Exeter Street. In 1884 they were living in Paull's Buildings, but the 1891 census found them back in Exeter Street. They had seven sons and three daughters. The third child, and second son, was William John, who was born in Paull's Buildings on 9 August 1884.

William followed in his father's footsteps in becoming a waggoner. He worked for some years for Messrs Hilton and Son, who had a brewery in Brook Street. In February 1909, at Tavistock Parish Church, he married Kate, the daughter of a retired farmer called Isaac Burnard. She had been born in Delabole, and had recently been in service in the employ of Thomas Doidge, the Bedford Square hatter. By 1914 William and Kate had moved to Exeter Street, a road that seemed to continue to arouse the homing instincts of generations of the Turner family. Meanwhile William's parents moved to Plymouth to spend their last years, though they were both to be buried in Tavistock, he in 1931 and she in 1937. James's funeral was distinguished by the carrying out of his request that 'his remains should be borne in the hearse and drawn by the horses which he had been in the habit of using in the course of his employment'.

Five of the seven Turner brothers served in the army during the war. The youngest two became gunners in the Royal Field Artillery, while another became a member of the Service Corps. The oldest, James junior, joined the Worcestershire Regiment, and was taken prisoner-of-war. William opted for his own county regiment, enlisting at Tavistock on 30 November 1915, but he later transferred to the Somerset Light Infantry. He saw plenty of action in France, and was twice wounded. On the second occasion, in August 1917, he was invalided home, and spent some time in hospital at York. His final spell at the Front began in the last week of April 1918, a week that saw the death in a German prisoner-of-war camp of William Friend, a fellow-Tavistockian who had also transferred from the Devons to the Somersets. Private Turner rejoined the 1st Battalion on 1 May, when it was located between Bethune and Lille. His conduct during the combat in which the Battalion was involved throughout that summer earned him the distinction of the Military Medal, awarded 'for bravery in action'. In October, the unit was operating in the area of Haspres and Monchaux, just south of Valenciennes. The Regimental History described William's last day, 24 October, in the following terms:

> At 4 a.m. an attack was launched against the enemy lines, in which the 1st Somersets were involved. They had a very successful day's fighting, and their spirits and morale were excellent. At least 150 prisoners must have been taken, as well as a large number of trench mortars and machine guns. A great many Germans had been killed. But the Battalion had also suffered heavily. Three officers died of their wounds and five more were wounded, while the losses in other ranks were 149 killed, wounded, and missing.

The end of 'a very successful day's fighting' left the bodies of Private Turner MM, No. 27063, and of a number of others, unrecovered.

Near the village of Vis-en-Artois, six miles to the south-east of Arras on the main road to Cambrai, there is a Memorial containing the names of over 9000 men who died in battles in the area during the last two months of the war, and who have no known graves. William Turner, who fell at nearby Valenciennes, is commemorated here.

SIDNEY VINSON
Died Wednesday 6 November 1918. Aged 25.

Sidney Vinson, 2nd from left on the back row, with other members of the Tavistock Battery at Crelake Barracks. n.b. Richard Stranger (see pp 238–9) kneeling on the right of the middle row

Among the first local men to enlist, on the day that war was declared, were the members of the Tavistock Battery. This pre-war artillery unit of part-time volunteers mustered on that day at Crelake, their headquarters off the Whitchurch Road, which was accessed, appropriately, from Battery Lane. Within days they were off to Salisbury, and within weeks to Bombay. Four years on, and the Battery had lost only one of its Tavistock members, Dingle Martin, who had died of malaria in 1915. It was true that seven other members, two from Bere Alston, and one each from Princetown, Dousland, Walkhampton, Exeter, and Topsham, had also succumbed to tropical disease, but none had as yet been killed in conflict. That changed on 6 November 1918 with the death of Gunner Sidney Vinson.

His full name was Sidney Edward Vinson, and he was born on 5 November 1893. His mother, born in Plymouth in 1865, was formerly Adelaide Foster. His father, Charles Harry Vinson, born in Falmouth in 1856, had had a naval career before becoming a painter and decorator. Both parents were to live into old age, Adelaide, who died in 1950, outliving her husband by fifteen years. They had at least six children, four sons and two daughters, all of whom were born in Plymouth. The 1901 census found them all living in Desboro Road in the St. Judes area of the city. Shortly after that they moved to Devon Great Consols. Sidney attended school at Lamerton, and later at Gulworthy. At the age of fourteen he started work as a railway porter. Later, in 1913 and 1914, he was described, successively, as a coachman at livery stables and as a miner. In November 1912 he was married, at Tavistock Register Office, to Annie Creeper, who lived in Market Street and worked as a cook. She was the daughter of a Heathfield farm labourer called Thomas and his wife Hannah, nee Huggins. Hannah, born in the workhouse at Stowford, had been married at seventeen and widowed at nineteen before, at twenty-one, she married Thomas Creeper. She was, however, thirty-nine when her daughter Annie was born.

At the time of their marriage, Annie was thirty-four years old and Sidney was nineteen. When the war came they had a one year old daughter named Dorothy, who had been born at Devon Great Consols, and Annie was eight months pregnant with their second child. Gunner Vinson, No. 865602, was in the middle of the period of training under canvas on Salisbury Plain when Adelaide, known as 'Queenie', was born, on 12 September. He was able to get a little leave before the departure for India, and was therefore able to see his new child. He was not to see wife and children again for almost four years. He celebrated his twenty-first birthday aboard one of a fleet of liners hired for wartime duty as troop carriers by the Royal Navy. The armada of eleven ships and two naval escorts arrived at Bombay on 9 November, and the 12,000 troops were then taken to their bases. On 14 November 1914 the Tavistock Battery arrived at Barrackpore. Gunner Vinson's life, in the period that followed, consisted mainly of spells of training at various locations, movements to mitigate some of the effects of the climate, and border and security operations. Increasingly, troops were redeployed from India to such stations as Greece and Egypt, but there is no evidence that this happened to Sidney. He probably remained in India until June 1918, when he was included in a draft of forty men who left for France. Arriving back in Europe in July, he took some leave before reporting to his unit at the Front in August. His third daughter, Alice, was to be born, in Taylor Square, in the following May.

The last full day of Sidney Vinson's life was his twenty-fifth birthday. On the following day, 6 November 1918, as the allied armies pushed forward against opposition that was close to crumbling, he was killed by shell-fire in an engagement that came five days before the armistice. The setting was the area of the River Sambre, near the town of Le Cateau. A dutiful regimental chaplain found the right words in the letter home:

This morning we reverently laid him to rest, with another comrade who also fell. A large number of his own friends were present. It will always be a proud memory to you to have loved and been loved by such a noble fellow.

The temporary interment in the small burial plot was followed, after the armistice, by removal to a larger, regional, cemetery, where the grave could be properly cared for. This was Cross Roads Cemetery, in the village of Fontaine-au-Bois, six miles from Le Cateau. It holds the graves of 750 casualties.

The widow and her three children drew an allowance of £1.8s (£1.40p) per week, which Annie supplemented by taking a laundry job at the Workhouse. The daughters were eventually to become, respectively, Mrs Horrell, Mrs Cleave, and Mrs Love. Long before that, on the day that the Tavistock War Memorial was unveiled, a large number of wreaths were laid at its foot. One bore the message: 'Dear Daddy, from Dorothy, Queenie, and Alice Maud'.

FREDERICK HICKS
Died Saturday 9 November 1918. Aged 39.

Headstone in Plymouth Road Cemetery, Tavistock

John Hicks was a sawyer. He had been born in the North Cornish parish of Marhamchurch in 1813. His wife, Elizabeth, nee Eddy, was a native of Tavistock, and was two years younger than her husband. That she was not yet twenty, and he only just so, when they married, was not a circumstance that would have occasioned much surprise in working class communities in the nineteenth century. Their first home together was at Walkhampton, where their daughter Kitty was born in 1835. There followed, between 1841 and 1856, John, William, James, Henry, Sarah, Mary, and Elizabeth. During this period, the family lived in Tavistock, successively in Exeter Street and Ford Street. William, the third child, who was born in 1847, became a saddler and harness maker. When he was twenty-two, he married nineteen year old Myra Hodge. Myra's unfamiliar name caused the kind of confusion, on those rare occasions when the name had to be recorded for some official purpose, that led to her becoming Mirah, or Maria, or Mary. Her surname, on the other hand, was well known and quite common. Her father, William Hodge, had been born in the same period as John Hicks. John was a Cornish sawyer who had married a Tavistock girl and settled in the town. William, a mason, was Tavistock-born, as was his wife Ann, whose maiden name was Simmons. And while the Hicks family flowered in Exeter Street and then Ford Street, the Hodges expanded, first in Dolvin Road and then in Back Street. William and Ann had their first child when he was twenty-two and she was twenty. Between 1839 and 1858 they had five children, Mary, William, Myra, Alfred, and

Frederick. Myra, who had been born in 1850, came in the middle of her family, as William Hicks did in his. Here, then, were two working class families in the town, showing similar patterns in the way their lives developed. In January 1869 they became linked through the marriage of William Hicks and Myra Hodge in the Tavistock Register Office.

The 1871 census revealed that William and Ann Hodge had once more been on the move, and were now residing at 48 Exeter Street. Living with her parents were daughter Myra, her husband William Hicks, and their three year old child, Lilian. Ten years on and William Hodge had died. Myra was living with her widowed mother, and was listed as the wife of a harness maker. But there was no sign of her husband. Across town, on that census day 1881, the harness maker was at the house of his father, John Hicks the sawyer, who was now at 20 Fitzford Cottages. Here, William Hicks continued to live. In 1891 he had with him his three children, Lillian, Alfred, and Frederick. There was no sign of Myra, but William remained designated as 'married'.

William and Myra's youngest child was born on 27 October 1879, and was given the Christian names Frederick William Hodge. Like his sister and his brother, he was born in Tavistock. The 1901 census has the three of them, in their twenties, working as coachmen in the case of the men and domestic servant in the case of Lilian, still living at Fitzford with their father William, who is still saddling but is now widowed. William was to die in 1913, at the age of sixty-five, of cirrhosis of the liver. Frederick married Bessie Coombs, and they had one daughter, Ethel Dorothy Hodge Hicks, who was born in September 1907. Frederick and Bessie were at that time living at 18 Chapel Street. They later moved to 14 College Avenue, but their last family home was 46 St Aubyn Street, Devonport, and it was there that Bessie received the news of her husband's death.

Frederick Hicks was thirty-five when he decided to join up. It was March 1915, and the war was in its sixth month. It is not clear why he enlisted in London, and why he joined the Army Service Corps. His civilian experience as a driver would, presumably, have proved valuable to those who were trying to build up the strength of a corps which, although a traditional and specialist branch of the army, had operated on quite a small scale before the war. Transport and supply were the two areas for which the R.A.S.C. was responsible, and in these areas the war machine showed an ever-growing appetite. The Corps expanded tenfold between 1914 and 1916. Men like Lance Corporal Hicks, No. M2/073487, helped to keep moving the 56,000 trucks and 34,000 motor cycles that were, by the end of the war, at the disposal of the British Army on the Western Front.

The circumstances in which Frederick Hicks, in the final stages of the war, received his fatal wounds, are not known. He was invalided home, to the Military Hospital at Compton Chamberlayne, near Salisbury. Here he died on 9 November 1918. Five days later, his body having been brought back to the town of his birth, he was buried in the Plymouth Road cemetery. As is occasionally the case, the headstone provides accurate information on name, date of death, and on regimental affiliation and number, but is less reliable on age. He was thirty-nine, not forty, when he died.

WILFRED CRUZE
Died Thursday 14 November 1918. Aged 22.

Headstone in Plymouth Road Cemetery, Tavistock

The headstones of the Commonwealth War Graves Commission have a distinctive appearance. Seen in large numbers, in the cemeteries of the Western Front for example, they are movingly impressive in both their uniformity and their essential simplicity. Equally affecting can be the sight of a single one, or a scattered handful, in many a British parish graveyard or cemetery, serving as a reminder to the local community of a sacrifice made. There are a number of such headstones in Tavistock's Plymouth Road cemetery, not concentrated in a particular area, but dispersed among the other stones and memorials. They mark the graves of local men who died in this country, but whose deaths were due to the effects of wounds received, or disease contracted, during war service. In some cases the deaths occurred after the date of the formal end of hostilities. The first case in this latter category was that of Wilfred Cruze. The armistice became effective on 11 November 1918. Private Cruze died three days later.

The name 'Cruze' was a fairly common one in Tavistock in the early twentieth century. A local directory for 1916, for example, lists thirteen families of that name as living in the town at the time. One of them was the family of James Edwin Cruze of 6 Parkwood Cottages. James, who was described at various times as a mine labourer and a waggoner, had been born in Lamerton in 1840. He had married a fellow Lamertonian in Elizabeth Jane Botterill, who was eight years younger than her husband. James and Elizabeth moved into 6 Parkwood Cottages, which was to remain their home throughout their married life, and where they were to be joined, for a time, by Elizabeth's widowed mother, Susanna Botterill. They began their family in 1862, but Elizabeth, born in that year, died at the age of one. The next two children, Henry and John, who were born in 1867 and 1872, survived until the ages of thirty-one and twenty-one. John, as his tombstone reveals, was 'drowned whilst bathing in the River Tavy, August 19 1892'. There followed, between 1873 and 1883, five survivors in Mary, Albert, Charles, Jane, and Sidney. And then, on New Year's Day 1886, James and Elizabeth buried the youngest of their nine children, an unnamed infant. The litany of family tragedies was not an exceptional one in Victorian England.

Mary was the fourth child, and the oldest surviving daughter, of James and Elizabeth Cruze. Born in February 1874 at 6 Parkwood Cottages, she was registered, baptised, and schooled in the town, before getting a job as a domestic parlourmaid. By 1891 she was living away from home. She was twenty-two years old when, back at her old home and under her mother's attentive eye, she gave birth to a baby boy. The date was 9 August 1896. Mary registered the child, and called him Wilfred, which might or might not be a clue to the identity of the father whose name was omitted from the birth certificate.

Neither Mary, nor her young son, were present at 6 Parkwood Cottages on census day 1901, yet it is clear that, from an early stage, this was his home. His grandparents assumed parental responsibilities in the fullest sense. Although they were in their fifties during the period of the child's most formative years, yet they felt, presumably with their daughter's willing consent, that this was the solution that offered the fewest problems. Both the solution, and the situation that it was designed to remedy, were more common in that period of English history than has hitherto been recognised. The family appears to have gone as far as it could in formalising the arrangement and giving the required public impression. When news of Wilfred's death was received, the *Tavistock Gazette* published a notice which read: 'On November 14th, Private W Cruze, the beloved son of J and E Cruze, 6 Parkwood Cottages. Sadly missed by sorrowing mother, father, brothers, sisters'. One might guess that, outside Parkwood Road, there were few who knew the truth.

Wilfred attended the Dolvin Road School. What he did immediately thereafter is not recorded, but at the age of twenty, on 16 November 1916, he joined the colours. He was one of those, along with Frank Harry, Frederick Hicks, Charles Philp, and William Rich, who enlisted in the rapidly-expanding Service Corps, largely because of an interest in mechanised transport. Wilfred served as Private No. 43033 in the RASC, and that is how he is remembered on his tombstone. However, according to the Commonwealth War Graves Commission and other sources, he was at some point transferred to the Labour Corps, where he became No 355798 in the 68th Agricultural Company.

Private Cruze died of pneumonia in the No. 1 War Hospital, Exeter, on 14 November 1918 at the age of twenty-two. His body was brought back to Tavistock for burial in the Plymouth Road cemetery. There he shares a family plot with his grandparents, both of whom outlived him. Elizabeth died at 6 Parkwood Cottages in November 1928, at the age of eighty. James, who thereupon moved out of the home he had occupied for more than sixty years, lived for a further eighteen months in Whitchurch, before dying at the age of ninety. Mary, meanwhile, had slipped quietly out of the picture, and had disappeared.

CHARLES HAWKINS
Died Friday 22 November 1918. Aged 27.

Railway Cottages, Trelawny Road, Tavistock

Charles Hawkins was a navy man. He enlisted at Devonport on 8 August 1911 at the age of twenty. Described in his enlistment papers as being 5′ 11″ tall, and having blue eyes and a fresh complexion, he was said to have been employed as a clerk. The place and date of birth were given as Misterton, near Crewkerne in Somerset, and 23 March 1891. The current address was entered as 4 Railway Cottages, Tavistock. Over the next six years he was to serve on a number of ships, as a sick-berth steward. There were spells of duty aboard the 'Doris', and the 'Tamar', followed by a long period in the Royal Naval Hospital at Wei Hai Wei, on the Chinese coast, between March and July 1914, with an undisclosed ailment. Soon after that, war broke out, and he found himself, first aboard the 'Hampshire', the ship that was later to be sunk while taking Lord Kitchener on a mission to Russia, and then with the crew of the 'Romone'. This proved to be his last assignment. In February 1917 he fell ill, perhaps with a recurrence of the problem that had laid him low in the Far East. He was invalided out of the service, and returned home to Tavistock, where he lived for the rest of his life at the family home on Trelawny Road. He died there on 22 November 1918. The cause of death was given as tuberculosis. Though his naval post had been non-pensionable, a gratuity of £15.10s was paid, on death, to his next-of-kin. The death was registered by his younger brother Frederick, who had been present at the end.

Charles Hawkins lived to see the end of the war of which he, and countless number of his contemporaries, were the casualties. The armistice came into effect eleven days before he died. The guns fell silent at the eleventh hour of the eleventh day of the eleventh month. The Great War had delivered the last of its many surprises. In the early weeks of the war all the smart money was going on the idea of a short, sharp, decisive conflict, which would be over by Christmas. Four years on, and in the Summer of 1918 the prospect seemed to be that the war could continue its 'long, long trail of winding' for a long time to come. In both cases the pundits and observers were wrong. The war may, for much of its course, have followed patterns that were hideously predictable, but it retained the capacity to surprise, and never more so than in its last three months. The Kaiser's Spring Offensive was taken at the time as an indication of Germany's impressive reserves of resilience and strength. In fact it represented a final throw, the failure of which left the country exhausted. The end came with dramatic suddenness. In July there was still all to play for. In September the issue had been decided. Armistice Day brought joy, relief, and celebration. It did not, however, draw a line under the suffering, in all its forms, that the war had brought. The fate of Able Seaman Charles Hawkins was an early reminder of that.

Charles was the son of William and Elizabeth Hawkins. In an age when there was a good deal more mobility than has often been recognised, the Hawkins family seemed particularly restless. William's roots were in North Tawton, in mid Devon, where he was born in 1863. He became a railway signalman, employed by the London and South Western Railway Company, and it was while he was at one of his postings that he met, and married, Elizabeth Martha Clarke of West Coker, a village close to Crewkerne. They were both in their early twenties at the time of the marriage, and their first child, Dorothy, arrived in January 1886, when they were living at Misterton. There followed Mary, Elizabeth, Margery, and Charles, also born at Misterton, before another job move, this time to the Exeter area, brought a change of address to Whimple and two more children in Frederick and James. Finally, when William moved to the recently-opened LSWR station at Tavistock, in the late 1890s, the family re-settled, temporarily in 14 Parkwood Cottages, and then more permanently in No. 4 Railway Cottages, one of the company's houses at the end of the long sweep of Trelawny Road, overlooking the station. Here appeared William, Mabel, and Edith. By 1904 the family was complete, with ten children, reduced to nine by the loss in infancy of Elizabeth. Charles, coming in the middle of the family, was born in Misterton, near Crewkerne in Somerset on 23 March 1891. He was young when the family moved to Tavistock, and it was as a Tavistock boy that he went to school, got a job, and decided to go to sea. He was not alone in his family in seeking fresh pastures. Of his eight surviving siblings, four emigrated to Canada, one to Australia, and one to South Africa.

Charles was buried in a family plot in the Plymouth Road cemetery, along with his mother, who died in 1937, and his grandmother. His father William, who died in 1939, was buried in the same cemetery.

PERCY COLES
Died Thursday 27 March 1919. Aged 34.

The Coles family. Front row L to R – Bertram, George, Percy Leopold, Rhoda, Winifred
Back row L to R – Bertha, Florence, Adeline, Alice

In 1844, seven years after the first appearance of 'Oliver Twist', Mary Coles gave birth, in the Okehampton Workhouse, to a male child. She called him George. The child's father was a William Brook. In the Dickens story, of course, the hero manages to break free from the life of deprivation and crime that awaits the workhouse boy. And it has certainly long been claimed that the avenues of English society are sufficiently wide to accommodate refugees from such unpromising starting points as destitution and illegitimacy. Those who seek local examples to support this belief may wish to look at the career of George Coles. He joined the Devon County Constabulary in 1865, when he was twenty-one, and served as a constable at Cheriton Fitzpaine, at Tavistock, and then at Honiton. While at the latter posting he was promoted, and it was with the rank of sergeant that he returned to Tavistock in the mid 1880s. The rest of his life was spent in the town, completing, first, an illustrious and popular career in the police force, followed by a period as Master of the Workhouse. It would be interesting to know whether there are any other examples of a man who had been born in a workhouse becoming the head of such an institution. After retirement he sought voluntary public office, getting himself elected to the Urban District Council.

George Coles had a prominent public career, albeit one conducted within the confines of a small community. He also had a busy family life. During his first assignment, as a young P.C. in Cheriton Fitzpaine, he met, and married, a local girl called Rhoda, the daughter of George Sanders, an agricultural labourer. The third in a family of four children, Rhoda was seventeen at the time of her wedding in 1866. Her husband was twenty-one. During the next four years they had two daughters, Bertha and Florence. A move to Tavistock coincided with the birth of Adeline, and a transfer to Honiton brought further additions to the family in the shapes of Alice, Bertram, and Winifred. A final move, the one that brought him to Tavistock in 1884, occurred at the same time as the last of the births, that of Percy.

The Tavistock Police Station offered residential accommodation for its officers, and here George Coles and his family lived for a time on their return to the town. The appearance, soon after their arrival, of Percy did, however, increase the pressure on space to such an extent that a new home was sought, and found at Mill House, on Parkwood Road. The seventh child proved to be the last. Percy Leopold, born on 29 November 1884, was to be the baby of the family. His mother Rhoda, in spite of her experience in bringing up a family over a period of eighteen years, was still only thirty-six when he was born. Percy was taken, while still a scholar, under the wing of his sister Winifred, who was four years his senior but only one rung up from him on the seniority ladder. She had by then become an assistant school mistress. In 1901 she had set up home at 37 West Street, where her only co-resident was sixteen year old Percy. The young man subsequently chose, we may assume under his sister's guidance, to become a dentist, and to specialise in the manufacture of false teeth. His surgery and business address was across the road from his West Street home.

The recruitment policy of the British Army did not always follow the 'horses for courses' principle, but in the case of Percy Coles it is hardly surprising to find that he joined the Royal Army Medical Corps. He enlisted at Exeter, on 1 October 1915, as a Private, No. 83585, and was described at the time as measuring 5′ 8½″ in height and weighing 132 lbs. Thereafter, following a short period at Aldershot, he served continuously at the Dental School in Dublin, where, as a dental mechanic, he was entitled to an addition to his pay of sixpence a day. He was still there in March 1919 when, on the 19th, he left for home to begin his pre-demobilisation furlough. He died in Tavistock on 27 March, one of the estimated 70 million victims of the influenza pandemic that raged worldwide between the Spring of 1918 and the Summer of 1919. His journey home had required a detour. This is the explanation for a note written a few days after his death by his family doctor, Leslie Watt, in which the doctor informed the military authorities that 'I have no hesitation in saying that the exposure to damp conditions which he had to endure on Salisbury Plain before his return home was the original cause of his illness'.

Percy's elder brother Bertram, who had served throughout in the Duke of Cornwall's Light Infantry, was wounded in the later stages of the war, but survived. Meanwhile his parents had moved in with Winifred in her West Street home. There George had died in June 1908. He was followed into the family plot on Plymouth Road, first by his youngest son, then, in 1926 by his wife Rhoda, and finally, in 1959, by his daughter Winifred.

CHARLES MERRIFIELD
Died Sunday 15 February 1920. Aged 28.

Bodmin War Memorial

The name 'Merrifield' was quite a common one in nineteenth century Tavistock. Within the Tavistock Registration District more than sixty children bearing that name were born between 1837 and the end of the century. The task of disentangling the various branches of the family is made the more difficult by the frequency with which certain 'traditional Merrifield' names, such as William, John, and Charles, were bestowed on new arrivals. It is clear, however, that Charles Willoughby Merrifield, who died in an Exeter hospital in February 1920, was the elder brother of Cecil Edmond York Merrifield, who had been a casualty of the Battle of Jutland in May 1916, and that the family of the two brothers had lived in Tavistock for a long period, certainly since the eighteenth century. Their great-grandfather, John Merrifield, had been born in the town in 1796. For almost all of his eighty-one years he carried on, in Back Street, his trade as a cordwainer, or leather worker specialising in shoemaking. The 1841 census revealed that there were at that time eighty men employed in that particular trade in the town. John had four children, of whom the second, named after his father, graduated from errand-boy to mason, married a local girl called Ann Maker, and moved into one of the newly-built cottages on Trelawny Road, recently named in honour of Sir John Trelawny, Member of Parliament for Tavistock for seventeen years in the middle of the nineteenth century. Here, at No. 23, John junior and Ann brought up eight children. The second child, and the oldest boy, was Charles, who was born in 1864. The 1881 census recorded him as a sixteen year old grocer's apprentice, working for John Carter, the enterprising founder of the Creber grocery dynasty. Charles then embarked on a long, professional career in the military, emerging as a sergeant-major, after which he became the proprietor of the Queen's Head Hotel in Bodmin. An interesting, and varied career ended with a period, in the last part of the war, at Salisbury, where he worked as an inspector of army canteens. It was there that he died in February 1919, one of the countless victims of the influenza epidemic, at the age of fifty-five.

Both of Charles's sons were born during their father's long military career. Cecil, the younger, appeared in India in 1893. Charles Willoughby Merrifield was born in 1891 at Canterbury, while his father was serving in the 8th Hussars. The two boys spent a good deal of their youth, while their father was in uniform, being looked after by their grandparents in their Trelawny Road home. They re-settled in Bodmin when Charles senior returned to civilian life. Charles junior was then fifteen.

Young Charles was called after his father. His second name, however, was a nod in a different direction. For a proud NCO in a prestigious cavalry regiment there could not be a more striking example to offer to the young than Lord Willoughby, a fearless, buccaneering blue-blood who had commanded a regiment of horse during the Civil War. When it came to his own military career, Charles junior was, in spite of his name, not to be found in the cavalry, with its romantic traditions of dashing deeds and carefree, adventurous improvisations but with the more mundane work of supplies, munitions, and administration. He enlisted in the Royal Army Ordnance Corps, the service established to provide the army's needs in terms of material and resources. An idea of the scale and scope of the work of the Corps is given in the official History of the Great War:

> There were issued from Calais alone during the first ten months of 1915: 11,000 prismatic and magnetic compasses, 7000 watches, 40,000 miles of electric cable, 40,000 electric torches, 3,600,000 yards of flannelette, 1,260,000 yards of rot-proof canvas, 25,000 tents, 1,600,000 waterproof sheets, 12,800 bicycles, 20,000 wheels, 6,000,000 anti-gas helmets, 4,000,000 pairs of horse and wheel shoes, 447,000 Lewis-gun magazines, 2,260,000 bars of soap . . .

In this vast exercise, Charles did have a specialist area of interest and responsibility. He is listed in the Burial Register as a former 'sergeant saddler in the army'. It is a description of which, presumably, his father would have approved.

In November 1915 Charles married Ada Eliza Field Weston. The wedding took place at Crediton, where Ada lived. At twenty-six she was two years older than her husband. The daughter of a London-born railway porter, she was the fourth in a family of seven, who, at the turn of the century, had been living in Tavistock, where, presumably, she first met Charles. The couple's new address was Beer Farm, Crediton. They had a daughter called Peggy.

Charles died at the Isolation Hospital at Whipton, near Exeter, on Sunday 15 February 1920, at the age of twenty-eight. Death was said to have resulted from pulmonary tuberculosis and infection of the intestines. The funeral took place six days later, and the sergeant saddler was laid to rest in Tavistock's Plymouth Road cemetery. His widow was to join him thirty-six years later.

The names of the Merrifield brothers feature on the War Memorials of Tavistock and of Bodmin. This is appropriate. Both towns played major formative roles in the lives of those two young men.

REGINALD WHITE
Died Monday 29 March 1920. Aged 39.

Mount Pleasant, Launceston Road, Tavistock, 2002

In nineteenth century Tavistock the commercial heart of the community lay where it had been throughout the history of the town, in Market Street. Or rather in Market Streets, for then there were two linked thoroughfares sharing the name. Lower Market Street was the short stretch from the foot of West Street to Bedford Square. Higher Market Street, from Church Bow northwards towards Taylor Square, was to be allowed, in the twentieth century, to drop the 'Higher'. Here was the nucleus of the medieval town, developing an original identity in the shadow of the great Abbey but staying close to the banks of the Fishlake as it descended the valley to finally empty itself into the Tavy. Market Street, as the name clearly indicates, was the commercial heart of this small community as it grew in prosperity, importance, and self-confidence, and exploited the opportunities opened up by the granting in 1105 of a royal charter that firmly established the market.

In the middle years of the nineteenth century there lived, in Higher Market Street, at No. 5, a brewer called John White. Described also as a maltster and wine and spirit merchant, John, who had been born in Bratton Clovelly in 1801, operated a popular and accessible business. He also headed a substantial household. According to the 1851 census, No. 5 housed also a wife, three children under five, named Mary, John Henry, and Fanny, and three servants, two of whom worked in the home and one in the business. Mary, the wife, who had been born in Tavistock in 1821 and whose maiden name was Skinner, was nineteen years younger than her husband. When John died in middle-age, Mary supervised the running of the business until their son became old enough to take it over. This was John Henry White, who had been born in Higher Market Street in July 1848, and who was to lead White and Company from the 1860s through to the eve of the Great War. Mary, meanwhile, enjoyed a long retirement, outliving her husband by fifty-three years.

Another prosperous business in Higher Market Street in the second half of the nineteenth century was that of Richard Williams, the outfitter, at No. 21. He had been born at St Austell, and had married Elizabeth Kittow, a native of Beal who had moved to live in Tavistock. Their eldest child, Elizabeth, was born in 1848, at Lifton Down. At that time Richard was described as a mason, but shortly afterwards he re-established himself as a tailor with a town-centre business. By 1871 the family had grown, and trade had prospered, to the extent that there had arrived, successively and regularly after Elizabeth, Amelia, Richard, William, Bertha, Emma, Laura, and Rosa. The 1871 census also listed eight employees, six men and two boys. The Williams family had another flourishing business interest in the soft drinks industry; they ran a manufactory producing mineral water, originally in Higher Market Street and later in premises in Brook Street. The fact that Elizabeth was brought up in a strict tradition of fundamentalist anti-drink nonconformism did not prevent her from developing a relationship with the heir to a wine business.

John Henry White and Elizabeth Williams were born within a month of each other. They grew up in the same street and could well have attended the same school. When they were twenty-seven they were married, at Tavistock Wesleyan Church, in October 1875. John Henry was by now in full control of the family business. He and Elizabeth had three sons, John, Richard, and Reginald, born between 1876 and 1880. In November 1883 Elizabeth died, at the age of thirty-five, the cause of death being given as brain congestion and paraplegia. She was buried in the family plot in the Dolvin Road cemetery. The children were at the time each under eight. John relied on his mother a good deal when it came to bringing up his young family, and Grandmother White, in her sixties, shared their Market Street home. Later, a housekeeper was employed. The 1901 census identified her as Rose W Hockaday, who was twenty-five years old and had been born at Bridestowe.

Reginald was the youngest of the family. He had been born, in Market Street, on 4 September 1880. In 1901 he was the only one of the children still living at home, and was described as a dentist's apprentice. He was five years younger than Rose, the housekeeper, whom, it appears, he subsequently married.

The last listing of White and Company appears in the Kelly's 1910 Directory. Shortly after that John Henry retired and left the area. He died at Gravesend in March 1917 at the age of sixty-eight, and was buried in Dolvin Road.

Reginald White died on 29 March 1920. He was described, on the Death Certificate, as 'army pensioner and dentist', and the cause of death was given as tuberculosis. His last home was Mount Pleasant, a country cottage, later to be extended, near the junction of the Launceston Road and the road to Mill Hill. The Death Notice that appeared in the *Tavistock Gazette* referred to him as 'the loving husband of Rose, and youngest son of the late Mr J.H. and Mrs White'. He was buried, on 31 March, in the Plymouth Road Cemetery. He remains a somewhat elusive figure.

ROBERT SMITH
Died Tuesday 27 April 1920. Aged 35.

Headstone in Plymouth Road Cemetery, Tavistock

Private Robert Herbert Smith was given a military funeral. It was Friday 30 April 1920 and the setting was the Plymouth Road cemetery in Tavistock. The body had been brought down from Salisbury, where Robert had died three days earlier. A grave lay open in the plot of the Hawke family. Robert's widow had been a Hawke. He was borne to the graveside by a party from Devonport composed of comrades of his old regiment, the Royal Army Service Corps. A firing party was provided by the Devonshire Regiment. The principal mourners included close relations, mother and sister among them, from Birmingham, a reminder that for Robert Smith the Tavistock connection was one of marriage rather than of birth. He had, in all probability, been born in Birmingham in 1885, the son of a retired prison warder who died when Robert was still young. The family home was in Sarehole Road, Hall Green. Robert left it when he was in his late teens to migrate to Plymouth, where he took a job as a clerk at Brown, Wills, and Nicholson, the firm of provisions merchants in the city. In 1913, at the age of twenty-eight, he married Ida Emily Hawke, and the Tavistock link was forged.

Ida Emily's Tavistock roots extended back at least as far as her grandfather. He was a miner called Francis Hawke, who had married Elizabeth Gundry, and who lived for some years in Exeter Street before moving, in 1850, into No. 12 Westbridge Cottages, thus becoming one of the original tenants on that brand-new estate. His son Richard was one year old when the family moved into its new home. The young man followed his father into the mining industry. He was, however, more ambitious than most, and he was to become a Mine Captain, a post that carried status, authority, and responsibility. In June 1872 at Tavistock Register Office this Richard Hawke, now twenty-three, married Emily Rodda, the nineteen year old daughter of a miner. Between 1876 and 1881 three girls were born, Jessie, Bessie, and Lily, during a period when the family was in America. Back in England in the mid 80s, Richard and Thomas arrived to interrupt the flow of daughters, before normal service was resumed with Ida and Gladys. Jessie died at twenty-six in 1903, Bessie at twenty-seven in 1905, and Lily at twenty-five in 1906. Their father Richard died at the age of sixty-one in 1911. That series of tragic events, four deaths in eight years, was centred on No. 5 Parkwood Place, Tavistock, which was the Hawke family home. As for the rest of the family, only two of them proved to be long-lived. One was the mother, Emily, who was in her eighty-third year when she died in 1934. The other was the fourth daughter, Ida Emily, who died in 1965 at the age of seventy-six. It was Ida who married Robert Herbert Smith.

The marriage between Robert Smith and Ida Hawke, who, at twenty-four was four years younger than her husband, took place at Tavistock Parish Church on 2 June 1913. Robert entered his address as simply 'Plymouth'. The couple were to live at Parkwood Place, and their two children were to be born there, Ida Joan in 1914 and John Hawke in 1920. Between those two dates Robert was away for much of the time, after his clerical job in Plymouth was exchanged for the life of a private in the Service Corps. During the war he served in Egypt as well as at home stations. He was still in uniform when the end came, suddenly and dramatically, in April 1920. On the 30th of that month, the morning of the funeral, the *Tavistock Gazette* broke the news to a local community which, rather like the family, had, one might think, become inured to the effects of bad news. The notice ran:

Deaths: Smith. Suddenly at Salisbury on April 27th. Robert Herbert, husband of Ida E Smith, father of Joan and baby John. Parkwood Place. Aged 35. He was expected to be discharged from the army at the end of this week.

Private Smith had been found dead in a bed in a room of the Chough Hotel, Salisbury. An inquest was held on the following day, Wednesday 28th. Thomas Hawke, the dead man's brother-in-law and a mining engineer, identified the body. A local doctor who had been summoned to the hotel when the body was discovered said that he thought that death was probably caused by gas poisoning, of which the room had smelt strongly. The widow, Mrs Ida Smith, said that she had corresponded four times weekly with her husband. He had told her that he would be demobilised on the Friday (30th) and would return to Tavistock. She could not believe that he had committed suicide. Letters between husband and wife were read, and the jury returned an open verdict, saying that there was insufficient evidence to show how death was brought about.

John, the infant son, later chose to use both parental surnames and was known as John Hawke-Smith. He worked for many years for Creber's, the well-known grocery business, and died in 1998. His elder sister, Joan, became Mrs Golding, and was living on Parkwood Road as the century came to an end.

WILLIAM EXWORTHY
Died Friday 14 May 1920. Aged 29.

William John Thomas Exworthy

The tone of the Death Notice was clear and pointed. It read:

EXWORTHY. On May 14th at 26 Trelawny Road, William J.T. Exworthy, only son of the late W.J. Exworthy and Mrs Exworthy, and brother of Selena and Annie. Aged 29 years. After 4 years and 9 months service in India and Mesopotamia.

The note of exasperation was unmistakeable. The young man had served through the whole of the war. He had survived combat situations and other conditions that had carried off so many of his contemporaries. He had endured it all, to return to the bosom of his family, to the comforts of Trelawny Road, and to the connections and friendships of his native town. And then? And then he died, at home, of pneumonia. It was an illustration of the kind of tragic ironies that wars throw up.

It may be assumed, from the reference to long service in India and Mesopotamia, that William had enlisted in the 5th Battalion of the Devonshire Regiment. He may, like the Chenhall brothers, and others, have taken the shilling before the war started. Assuming that he sailed for India with the Battalion in August 1914, the '4 years and 9 months' period of service in the East, referred to in the press notice, would suggest a return home in the early summer of 1919.

By trade William was a printer and compositor, and he certainly resumed that trade when he returned home, and continued it for the year that elapsed between his demobilisation and his untimely death. There were, at that period, two printing businesses in the town, one operated by Thomas Greenfield, the publisher of the *Tavistock Gazette*, in Bedford Square, and the other, the firm of Jolliffe and Son, in Taylor Square, soon to launch itself into publishing the *Tavistock Times*, in competition with the *Gazette*. William would have worked for one of these. He also, on his return, renewed his pre-war role as a brass player with the local Salvation Army Band, playing cornet and trombone in an ensemble whose reputation extended far beyond the small hall on Kilworthy Hill. Bill Tucker, a fellow-bandsman during that period, was later to recall how William's health had deteriorated during his war service, and how illness finally forced him to give up playing.

Young William had been given, not uncommonly, three Christian names. The first two, William and John, were the names of his father. The third, Thomas, was a nod in the direction of his paternal grandfather. Old Thomas Exworthy had been born at Broadwood in 1832, had married Maria Walters from Milton Abbot, and had earned his living as a farm labourer. Thomas and Maria spent the early years of their married life at Rumleigh Bridge, in the parish of Bere Ferrers, and it was there, in February 1863, that their son, William John, was born. Within three years they had moved into Tavistock, where they had a daughter called Mary. The 1881 census recorded the family as living at 20 Trelawny Cottages, with Thomas, now forty-eight, working as a dairyman, and William John, at the age of eighteen, being described as a gentleman's servant. In 1889, having changed career direction from domestic service to house painting, William John married Selina Elizabeth Bending. The Bendings were a Plymouth family who, in 1881, were living in Cambridge Street, in the Ford district of the city. George, the head of the household, was a plumber and gas fitter, who had married Rosala, from St Helier, Jersey. By April 1881 they had six children, of whom the two eldest daughters, Selina and Rosala, were both unemployed domestic servants. Eight years later, when she was twenty-nine, Selina married William John Exworthy.

The marriage between William Exworthy and Selina Bending took place in Tavistock Parish Church on 9 November 1889. The bride, who was three years older than her husband, gave her address as 'The Hawthorns'. This was the house in Glanville Road, Tavistock, where Selina had been working for some time as a servant in the household of Augustus Barton. One of her employer's family, Marie Louise Barton, acted as one of the witnesses at the wedding. William and Selina had three children whom they named William, Selina, and Annie. William junior was born on 6 January 1891, at 49 Brook Street. In 1901 the family moved to 26 Trelawny Road, the address with which they were to continue to be associated.

Young William attended school in the town and then went into the printing trade, giving as much of his spare time as he could to the Salvation Army and its music. Meanwhile his father carried on his work as a decorator, and his sister Annie supplemented the family income by running a dressmaking business from No. 26.

William was in India, in uniform, when he received news of his father's death. William senior died at his home in August 1916, at the age of fifty-three. His son succumbed to pneumonia on 14 May 1920. Widow and mother Selina, outliving not only husband but son, died in June 1929, a week short of her sixty-ninth birthday. All three deaths occurred at the family home on Trelawny Road. All three burials took place at the Plymouth Road cemetery.

SAMUEL MILES
Died Sunday 30 May 1920. Aged 37.

Tavistock Bowling Club 1919. Samuel Miles second from left in back row

The small town of Millom lies close to the Cumberland coast, on the southern edge of the Lake District. There, at Moor House, on 27 September 1882, Samuel Daniel Miles was born. His father, John, was an iron ore miner. His mother, usually named Johanna but occasionally Hannah, was herself the daughter of a miner called Samuel Daniels. The new arrival, who thus took both his Christian names from his mother's side of the family, might be a Cumbrian, but both his parents hailed from the other end of the kingdom. John Miles, aged thirty, had married Johanna Daniels, aged twenty-seven, in Tavistock. Their move to the north-west had come four years after their wedding, in 1881.

Members of the Miles family were among the original occupants of the West Bridge Cottages. The 1851 census identified, at No. 40, five year old John Miles, along with mother, father, and five sisters. Mother was Maria, who was forty at the time of the census, and who was to die, nine years later, of apoplexy. Father was Samuel, who worked as a brewer's labourer, and was four years younger than his wife. Ten years on, and the family had lost both mother and youngest daughter. Father and three of the remaining children were now labouring in the mines. They included young John. At the same time, across town, Samuel Daniels, a miner, and his wife Elizabeth were bringing up their five children in Exeter Street. Johanna was the third of the five. In June 1877 at Tavistock Parish Church she married John Miles. They lived at 16 Chapel Street. The couple's departure for the north four years later was noted in the records of the membership of the Tavistock Congregational Church.

John and Johanna Miles were back living in Tavistock in 1901. The census of that year listed John as an arsenic miner. He and Johanna were living in Chapel

Cottage, the first house in Chapel Street, with their eighteen year old son Samuel, who was described as a grocer's apprentice. In April 1910, at the Congregational Church, Samuel married Evelyn Taunton, who for some time worked as a domestic servant for the family of the Duke Street grocer Albert Kennard. Evelyn had been born at Middlemoor on 8 December 1881. She was one of the younger members of a family which comprised seven children. Her parents, Thomas and Emma, nee Heale, appear to have started out on their married life at Northam and to have moved to Middlemoor, then to Parkwood, and finally to Bannawell Street. It was natural that it was to this Bannawell Street home, and to the tender mercies of her mother, who had been recently widowed, Thomas having died in November 1909, that the newly-married Evelyn returned for her first confinement in September 1910. Twin girls were born, and were named Evelyn and Elsie. They were both dead within a year. Two sons, Bernard John in 1913 and Leslie Roy in 1916, were subsequently born at 19 Bannawell Street, where Samuel and Evelyn had now set up home.

Soon after the deaths of his twin daughters, Samuel found himself required to register the demise of his father. John Miles died at Chapel Cottage on 30 December 1912. He was sixty-five, and was described as 'formerly an overlooker at a gold mine', a description that might help to explain his death, the cause of which was given as haemoptysis, a lung disease akin to tuberculosis, which was known and feared in mining communities.

Johanna, John's widow and Samuel's mother, spent the last years of her life at the family home, 19 Bannawell Street, now shared with her daughter Mary Ann and her daughter-in-law Evelyn, and she died there in June 1924 at the age of seventy-four. Her death was registered by a son-in-law called John Fogerty, who had married Mary Ann.

Samuel Miles enlisted at Plymouth as a gunner, No 91795, in the Royal Garrison Artillery, in June 1916. His first posting was to Ireland where attention was concentrated on the consequences of the Easter Rising. He served in France from January 1918 until he was demobilised in March 1919. Back home, his former employer offered him his old job as a grocer's assistant, but this did not work out. His military papers described him as having been discharged with a disability categorised as 'confusional insanity', and he was subsequently committed to the County Asylum. Such conditions, popularly termed 'shellshock', were among the many distressing consequences of the war, and a gunner would have been more susceptible than most to their effects.

Samuel died at his Bannawell Street home on 30 May 1920, epilepsy being recorded as the official cause of death. Described then as 'an army pensioner of no occupation', he was thirty-seven years old. His widow, Evelyn, continued to live in Bannawell Street for some time, before moving to a house near the foot of Callington Road, and finally to a Brown's Memorial Cottage, where she died in 1962. The younger of her two sons, Leslie Roy, familiarly known as Dixie, was killed in the Second World War. His name, one of forty Tavistock casualties of that war who are commemorated on the Town Memorial, appears quite close to that of his father, a victim of the earlier conflict.

RICHARD STRANGER
Died Monday 16 August 1920. Aged 29.

The Stranger Emporium 1906–37. Manchester House, Pym Street, Tavistock

In the 1840s a young man from Woodland, near Ashburton, moved to Holsworthy, married a local girl called Mary, and set up in business as a seed merchant. His name was John Stranger. He had two sons, Richard and John. The former became a draper, the latter a grocer. Richard, born in Holsworthy in 1854, established a successful business in his native town, married Edith Paddon, had three children, and then, in his forties, moved to Tavistock. For a short time he had a shop in Market Street. Then he took over substantial premises in Pym Street formerly occupied by Charles Harris. This became Manchester House, the town's principal drapery emporium. Richard shared his time between this high-profile business concern and the family home, originally Abbey Mead but later Watts Road. He also found time to establish a reputation as an active campaigner for those causes that related particularly to the trinity of concerns that guided his private and public life: Wesleyanisn, Liberalism, and Temperance. He sat, for five years, on the Urban District Council, and was a local magistrate. The *Tavistock Gazette* was to summon up a graphic image when it wrote, in its obituary, 'Mr Stranger struck social evil with a heavy broadsword'.

   Richard Northcott Stranger arrived in Tavistock in the mid 1890s with his wife Edith, originally a Penzance girl, and their three children, two sons and a daughter. He died, forty years later, a successful but a lonely man. Edith had died in 1908, at the age of forty-four, of Graves Disease. His younger son, called Richard Northcott after him, had, in 1920, when he was twenty-nine, succumbed, half a world away, to the effects of wartime wounds. The only daughter of the family, Annie, had died in 1924 at the age of thirty-seven, following an operation for appendicitis. This series of domestic tragedies cast a dark shadow over the last part of the life of Richard Northcott senior, as did his deteriorating eyesight. Of his immediate family, only the elder son, Edwin, had survived, and he had emigrated to Australia. The old man died, in November 1937, in his eighty-fourth year.

Young Richard Stranger was born, on 8 June 1891, in Holsworthy, but all his later memories were of growing up in Tavistock. At the age of ten he was admitted to the Grammar School. He later began to work as a draper in the family business, the idea no doubt being that, his brother Edwin's interests appearing to lie elsewhere, he, Richard, was the heir apparent to Manchester House.

In February 1913, at the age of twenty-one and the height of 6′ 2½″, Richard joined the ranks of the 3rd Devon Battery. Eighteen months of peacetime part-time soldiering were followed by mobilisation on the first day of the war and speedy departure for India. Meanwhile, his brother's career took him to various places in the service of the Royal Flying Corps, and, later, to Russia, where his anti-bolshevik activities earned him the Order of St. Stanislas. For his part, Richard saw service in India and Mesopotomia, before being discharged in November 1915, having been appointed to a commission as 2nd Lieutenant with the Royal Field Artillery Special Reserve. His new role took him to the Western Front. There, serving with the 36th Trench Mortar Battery RFA, he came close, in August 1917, to receiving fatal injuries. He had just returned from a home leave, and had emerged unscathed from some fierce combat on 31 July. A few days later he suffered several leg wounds, and was shipped back to Britain for treatment at the London Hospital. The *Tavistock Gazette* of 28 September gave the news that he had 'had his right leg taken off below the knee at the London Hospital last Saturday. He was very ill after the operation, but we were informed yesterday that he was holding his own, although still in a very weak condition'. Recovery was slow. A Medical Board, sitting some months later, was able to report that he was walking satisfactorily on his artificial leg, but that while he had been in hospital he had had a recurrence of the tuberculosis that he had originally contracted in 1909. Declared permanently unfit to resume his service, he was demobilised, and returned to Tavistock to convalesce.

In September 1919, in London, Richard married Caroline Ellen, the daughter of Richard and Katherine Spry, who farmed at Land Hill in Halwill, near Holsworthy. Caroline had been born in 1889, the second child in a family of five. Five months after her wedding she and Richard sailed for Australia. They arrived in March 1920, to be greeted by his brother, Edwin, who now lived in New South Wales. After travelling for a time, the couple settled in the town of Sandgate near Brisbane, in Queensland. Here Richard fell ill at the beginning of August. He died in the Brisbane General Hospital on the 15th. His father was 'informed by cablegram'. A local doctor gave his opinion that 'the cause of death was due to injuries received and to gassing while on active service'. Richard was buried in Toowong Cemetery. The chief mourners were his widow and his brother. Two months later the *Tavistock Gazette* carried the following announcement in the Births column: 'At Brisbane, Australia, to Mrs R.N. Stranger, a son'.

ARTHUR WHITTOME
Died Friday 27 August 1920. Aged 24.

Members of the Tavistock Battery, Barrackpore, India

Formally, the Armistice in November 1918 ended hostilites, and the Treaty in June 1919 brought to an end the war itself. Given, however, the power and resonance of some of the movements and ideas that had come to the fore during the turmoil of the war years, it is not surprising that much unfinished business remained. Of no area was this more true than the Middle East. The defeat of Turkey left a vacuum, for which temporary solutions were provided by imposing French control over Syria and Lebanon and British authority in Palestine and Mesopotamia. These settlements were immediately challenged by Arab nationalist movements. In Mesopotomia a revolt spread, to the extent that, by the Summer of 1920, only the three main cities, which were heavily garrisoned, were unaffected. It was in the violence of that Summer that Arthur George Whittome lost his life. He was the last of six Tavistock men to be buried or commemorated in cemeteries in Mesopotamia, present-day Iraq. He was also the last of the four fatal casualties of the Tavistock Battery, that happy band of pre-war part-time gunners who exchanged Crelake for Barrackpore in 1914. But his connection with India pre-dated the war, and had its origins in the early life of his father, John Thomas Whittome.

John Thomas was an engineer. He was born in Norfolk in 1864. In the early 1890s he and his new wife Jane, who was a native of Macclesfield, emigrated to India, where they spent some years working at one of the earliest Wesleyan Missions in that country, at Karur. Here, both their children were born, Elsie in 1893 and Arthur in 1895, before the decision was taken to return to England. In

1897 the family arrived at Tavistock, after a short stay at Hartlepool. Moving into No. 3 Parkwood Villas, which was to remain the permanent family home, John Thomas took over a business there that had previously been run by a Philip Veal. John Thomas was to run it until his death in 1935, when it was sold to Gilbert J. White. According to his press obituary, Mr Whittome was 'an engineer and wheelwright, and was responsible for designing and making many agricultural implements, motor trailers, and caravans'. He also lost no time in establishing himself as a figure on the wider stage of local affairs, becoming involved in a range of organisations, as well as serving a long period as a Wesleyan local preacher. He died at his home in Parkwood Villas, in November 1935, and was buried in the Plymouth Road cemetery, as was his widow Jane just one year later. Their daughter, Elsie, who married Ernest Scott, was to die in 1969. All three of them had to suffer the anguish of the loss of Arthur, son, heir, and brother, in 1920, at the age of twenty-four.

Arthur George Whittome was born on 31 August 1895. The move to Tavistock came just two years later. His education began at the Spring Hill House School. Then, at the age of ten, he was admitted to the town Grammar School. He was finally to attend the Dockyard Prep School in Plymouth. His pre-war involvement with the Tavistock Battery led directly to his enlistment on the first day of the war. He spent his nineteenth birthday waiting to be shipped to India. Following his arrival there, he spent some time at Kasauli in the Simla Hills, where he gained a signalling qualification. He was also involved in operations on the Afghan border, and was in one of the drafts that left occasionally for spells of service in Mesopotamia. After four years in the ranks with the Royal Field Artillery, he was, in November 1918, appointed to a commission in the Indian Army. The attachment was to the 2nd Battalion, 123rd Outram's Rifles, a unit that commemorated Sir James Outram, the British General who was a major public figure in the India of the mid nineteenth century.

In July 1920 the British authorities in Mesopotamia sent to India for reinforcements to deal with the insurrection, which was then at its height. Lieutenant Whittome sailed with his battalion from Bombay, arriving at the beginning of August. His first assignment was to command one of two river boats to be despatched up the Euphrates from Nasiriyah to relieve a vessel that had gone aground. His was the leading boat, and the first to come under heavy fire from hostile forces on the riverbanks. It was 27 August, and firing began at about noon. Rifleman Bhur Singh was later to explain what happened:

The whole time we were being fired at from both banks, and we fired in return. Whittome Sahib who was in command of us had been wounded in the arm. The enemy commenced to fire harder. We replied until all our ammunition had been expended. At about 16.00 hours Whittome Sahib was hit in the head and killed. Nearly every man had been wounded, and only a few were able to put up a fight.

The Basra Memorial, originally erected in the City's War Cemetery, commemorates more than 40,000 who died in operations in Iraq between 1914 and 1921 and who, like Lieut. Whittome, have no known grave. In 1997 the Memorial was, by presidential decree, moved twenty miles, to be re-erected on the site of a Gulf War battlefield.

WILLIAM TUCKER
Died 11 February 1964. Aged 78.

No. 40 Bannawell Street, Tavistock

A sturdy terrace that adorns the top reaches of Bannawell Street, and was built in the middle of the nineteenth century, has for some time gloried in the name of 'Gold Diggings'. One of these houses, that looked across the road to the Workhouse, was No 40 Bannawell Street. Here, in 1879, a young saddler called John Thomas Sambles Tucker brought his new wife, Mary Jane, the daughter of Samuel Dodd of Exeter Street. John was an employee of John Williams, who ran a successful saddlery business in West Street. He remained in the same employment throughout a working life that stretched almost to his death in 1923. His widow, Mary, died ten years later. They both lived into their seventies, and outlived two of their sons, Samuel and William.

John was twenty-seven and Mary twenty-five when they were married at Tavistock Register Office. Over the course of the next twelve years they had six children, Ellen, John, William, May, Ernest, and Samuel. The last of these arrivals, in January 1893, seems to have acted as a reminder to the parents that they had fallen behind in the programme of baptisms. Samuel shared his christening celebration, on 15 May, with brothers William and Ernest and sister May.

William was the third child in what was, by the standards of the time, not a large family. He was born on 14 February 1885, and, like his brothers and sisters, attended the Dolvin Road School. He then became a barber. In 1910 he and his brother John decided to join the wave of emigration to Canada that had, in those early years of the new century, become something of a flood tide. They emigrated to Manitoba, where, in 1915, William was living at 622 9th Street in the city of Brandon, some 150 miles west of Winnipeg, and still earning his living as a barber. Here, on 16 August 1915, having recently received details of the death, in uniform, of his younger brother, Samuel, he enlisted. Like every other Canadian recruit to the cause, he made, before a magistrate, an oath of attestation. After affirming his loyalty to the King, he 'agreed to serve in the Canadian Overseas Expeditionary Force for the term of one year, or during the war now existing between Great Britain and Germany should that war last longer than one year, and for six months after the termination of that war.'

At the time of his enlistment, William was described as being 5' 8" tall, with a dark compexion, black hair, and blue eyes, and weighing 135 lbs. He declared himself to be a member of the Church of England, a barber with fifteen years experience, and a bachelor whose next of kin was his father over there at 40 Bannawell Street, Tavistock. Crossing to England in September 1915, he began to experience, soon after his arrival, trouble with his feet which caused distress on long marches. The condition was said to have its origins in the long hours that he had spent standing in the barber's shop. The military authorities decided that he should be assigned to appropriate duties in England such as security work at army installations, since the flat feet and weakened arches rendered him unfit for combat duties. His work gave satisfaction and was rewarded with a stripe. His medical state, however, deteriorated, and by the Summer of 1918 a report was describing him as 'a not very well nourished adult male', whose breathing sounded feeble. His final discharge came through on 22 August 1919. Two addresses appear, in succession, in his military papers, as potential post-discharge residences. One was 9 Ford Street, Tavistock. The other was 156 High Street, Sandgate, Kent. The key to this was that William Tucker had, during his long period of service in England, married a wife.

Olive Hynes was born in March 1889, the illegitimate daughter of a servant called Bessie, who probably subsequently married Olive's likely father, a sailor called William Burrows. No. 9 Ford Street, where Olive was born, was the home of her grandparents, Nicholas and Elizabeth Hynes. Olive was still living there in 1917 when, at the age of twenty-eight, she married Private Tucker. The wedding took place on 8 September 1917, during a period when William was doing duty in Kent.

William returned to Canada in September 1919, with his wife, and took a construction job with Canadian Pacific Railways. Olive, however, found it difficult to adjust to her new life. There was a divorce. By 1923 she was back in England, where she remained. In February of that year she attended the funeral in Tavistock of her father-in-law, John Thomas Tucker. William was not present. His name had, by now, been included on the War Memorial. He lived the rest of his life in Brandon, did not re-marry, and died there on 11 February 1964, three days before what would have been his seventy-ninth birthday. In 1941, at the age of fifty-two, Olive married a thirty year old quarry worker called Douglas Oates. Their married home was, where else but No. 9 Ford Street.

The explanation for the mistake or deception that has lain hidden for the best part of a century must lie with Olive Hynes/Tucker/Oates. And she probably took it with her to the grave. She died, in Mount Gould Hospital, Plymouth, on 24 October 1977.

SOURCES

BOOKS

Aggett, W.J.P.	History of The Devonshire Regiment Vol 3.
Atkinson, C.T.	The Devonshire Regiment 1914–1918.
Blumberg, H.E.	Britain's Sea Soldiers.
Booker, F.	Industrial Archaeology of the Tamar Valley.
Collacott, R.A.	The Collacotts of Devon.
De Ruvigny, Marquis	The Roll of Honour.
Douglas, J.	H.M.S. 'Ganges'.
Dyer, G.	The Missing of the Somme.
Edmonds, J.	Military Operations in France and Belgium.
Edwards, T.	Regimental Insignia.
Gliddon, G.	The Battle of the Somme.
Graves, R.	Goodbye to all that.
Gulworthy W.I.	Gulworthy – A Crossroads in Time.
Halpern, P.	A Naval History of World War One.
Hoehling, A.A.	The Great War at Sea.
Holt, T.	Battlefields of the First World War.
Jarvis, S.D. and D.B.	Naval Officers Who Died in Service 1914–19.
Jarvis, S.D. and D.B.	Naval NCOs and Men Died in Service 1914–20.
Keegan, J.	The First World War.
Kemp, P.	British Warship Losses of the 20th Century.
Laffin, J.	Panorama of the Western Front.
Lloyd George, D.	War Memoirs.
Macdonald, L.	The Somme.
Macdonald, L.	They Called it Passchendaele.
Middlebrook, M.	The First Day on The Somme.
Nowell, F.T.	Record of the Third Devonshire Battery.
Parkes, O.	British Battleships.
Pevsner, N.	Buildings of England.
Pope and Wheal	The Macmillam Dictionary of World War One.
Richardson, R.	Through War to Peace 1914–1918.
Stacke, H.F.	The Worcestershire Regiment.
Thompson, J.	Imperial War Museum Book of War at Sea.
Warlow, B.	Shore Establishments of the Royal Navy.
War Office	Statistics of the Military Effort 1914–20.
Wasley Gerald	Devon in the Great War.
Winton, J.	The Submariners.
Wise, J.	A Guide to Military Museums.
Woodcock, G.	Tavistock's Yesterdays No. 5.

DIRECTORIES

Admiralty Instructions 1914.
Annual Navy Lists.
Bennett's Business Directory of Devon.
Billing's Directory of Devon.

Conway's All the World's Fighting Ships.
Dictionary of National Biography.
Hammond's Plymouth Directory.
Harrod's Directory of Devon.
History of the Corps of Royal Engineers.
Kelly's Directories of Devon and Cornwall.
King's Regulations 1914.
Morris's Directory of Devon.
Officers Died in the Great War.
Old Kelleins Who Died in the Great War.
Pigot's Directory of Cornwall and Devon.
Post Office Directory of Devon.
Registers of the Naval Memorials at Chatham, Plymouth, Portsmouth.
Slater's Directory of Devon.
Soldiers Died in the Great War.
Tavistock Directories.
White's Directory of Devon.
Who Was Who.

REGIMENTAL OFFICES AND ARCHIVES

Cheshire Regiment.
Coldstream Guards.
Devonshire Regiment.
Duke of Cornwall's Light Infantry.
Essex Regiment.
Gloucestershire Hussars.
Grenadier Guards.
Hampshire Regiment.
Lancashire Fusiliers.
London Scottish Regiment.
Manchester Regiment.
Middlesex Regiment.
Monmouthshire Regiment.
Northumberland Fusiliers.
Prince of Wales's Own West Yorkshire Regiment.
Queen's Lancashire Regiment.
Royal Army Medical Corps.
Royal Artillery.
Royal Engineers.
Royal Flying Corps.
Royal Fusiliers.
Royal Garrison Artillery.
Royal Marines (Fleet Air Arm Museum).
Royal Welsh Fusiliers.
Sherwood Foresters.
Somerset Light Infantry.
South Wales Borderers.
Worcestershire Regiment.

ORGANISATIONS

Ancient Order of Foresters Friendly Society.
Commonwealth War Graves Commission.
Devon Family History Society.
Exeter College, Oxford.
Machine Gun Corps Old Comrades Association.
Tavistock Town Council.
Womens Institute: Gulworthy Branch.
Womens Institute: Tavistock Branch.
Womens Institute: Whitchurch Branch.

NEWSPAPERS AND PERIODICALS

Brandon Sun, Manitoba, Canada.
Brisbane Courier, Australia.
Devon Family Historian.
Kelly College Chronicle.
Salisbury Times.
Tavistock Gazette.
Tavistock Times.
The Times.
Western Morning News.
Wipers Times.

MEMORIAL INSCRIPTIONS

Individual Grave or Memorial Inscriptions (most listed by Commonwealth War Graves Commission).
Parish War Memorials:
   Devon: Tavistock, Gulworthy, Whitchurch, Bere Ferrers.
   Cornwall: Calstock, Launceston, Bodmin.
   Gloucestershire: Ebrington.
   Suffolk: Easton.
   Warwickshire: Rugby.
Tavistock Parish Church War Memorial.
Grave inscriptions in Dolvin Road Cemetery, Tavistock.
Grave inscriptions in Plymouth Road Cemetery, Tavistock.
Grave inscriptions in Gulworthy Churchyard.
Tavistock Grammar School War Memorial.
Kelly College War Memorial.

DOCUMENTS

Public Records Office:
   Army Service Documents – First World War.
   Census Reports for 1851, 1861, 1871, 1881, 1891, 1901.
   General Register Office Records of Births, Deaths, Marriages.
   Services Records of Births, Deaths, Marriages.
   Consular Records of Births, Deaths, Marriages.
   Regimental War Diaries.

World War One Medal Record Cards.
Devon County Record Office:
　　　Devon County Roll of Honour.
　　　Gulworthy School Admissions Registers.
　　　Sale of Duke of Bedford's Estates 1911: Particulars.
　　　Tavistock Church of England School Log Books.
　　　Tavistock Congregational Church Record Book.
　　　Tavistock Council School Log Books.
　　　Tavistock Grammar School: Admissions Registers.
　　　Tavistock Men Who Served in the Great War (manuscript).
　　　Tavistock Parish Records.
　　　Tavistock Parliamentary Constituency: Electoral Registers.
　　　Tavistock Urban District Council; Minutes of meetings.
　　　Tavistock Workhouse: Register of Births.
　　　Tavistock Workhouse: Register of Deaths.
Tavistock Town Council:
　　　Tavistock Burial Registers.
　　　Council Minute Books.
　　　Council Misc. Papers.
Exeter Cathedral:
　　　Devonshire Regiment Roll of Honour.
Kelly College:
　　　Kelly College School Registers.
Canadian Archives:
　　　Canadian Army Service Documents.
　　　Canadian National Archives.

MUSEUMS, LIBRARIES, RECORD OFFICES

Bermuda Maritime Museum.
Bodmin Town Library.
British Library Newspaper Library.
Cornish Studies Library.
Cornwall County Record Office.
Devon County Library.
Devon County Record Office.
Devon Family History Archive (Tree House, Exeter).
Devon Local Studies Library.
Fleet Air Arm Museum.
Imperial War Museum.
North Devon Local Studies Library.
Plymouth City Library.
Plymouth and West Devon Record Office.
Plymouth Maritime Studies Library.
Public Record Office.
Somerset County Record Office.
Suffolk County Record Office.
Tavistock Subscription Library.
Tavistock Public Library.
Westcountry Studies Library.

SURNAME INDEX

Bold numbers denote primary articles

Abel 178
Abell 89
Abels 44
Ackford **170–1**
Acton 199
Adams **12–3**, 15, 24, 140, **154–5**
Addicott 191
Alderson 20
Alexander 69, 105, 153
Alford 72
Amos 35
Anderson 141, 202
Arbuthnot 51
Astbury 121
Attewill **102–3**

Backwell 31, 85, 139, 171
Bailey 57
Baker 111
Bale 127, 159
Balman 44
Barkell 54
Barkwill **44–5**
Barton 235
Bassett 24, 25, **28–9**
Bath 99, 124, **140–1**, 143, 209
Bawden 86
Beatty 53
Bending 235
Bennett 135
Betjeman 128, 181
Bickle 69, **146–7**
Bilkey 78, 206
Blythe **200–1**
Bolt 123
Boon 39, 108, 109
Botterill 222
Branch 72
Bray 120
Brenton **8–9**, **182–3**
Brock 64
Brook 4, 226
Brooks **118–9**, 124, 143
Brown 16, 95
Browne 190
Buckingham 80
Buckley 182
Budge 98
Burgoyne 81
Burnard 217
Burrows 243
Buscall 210, 211

Camozzi 146
Cardwell 17
Carter 48, 228
Caunter 197
Chatfield 53
Chenhall **66–7**, **68–9**, 131, 144, 234
Chowen 115
Churchill 23
Clark 154
Clarke 12, 100, 225
Cleave 219
Clifton 115
Cloak **150–1**
Cobbledick 213
Coles **24–5**, 26, **226–7**
Collacott **62–3**
Collins **186–7**, 203
Colwill 50
Cook 62
Coombe 15, 20, **54–5**
Coombs 39, 221
Cornish 179, 209
Couch 117
Cousins 175
Cowling 166
Cox 73, 120
Cradock 13
Cranch 64
Craze 27, **130–1**
Creber 48, 228
Creeper 219
Crook 17
Cross 33
Crossing 100
Cruze **222–3**

Damerell 125
Daniels 236
Dashper 73
Davey **58–9**, **60–1**, 88
David 35
Davies 24
Davy **80–1**, 212
Dawe 216
Dennis 89, 116
Dickens 226
Dillon 129
Dingle 31, 80, 84
Dodd 18, 242
Doidge 97, 183, **184–5**, 195, 217
Down 27, 89, 126
Drake 13, 24, 120

Dudley 132
Duke 10, 113
Dunstone 40

Easterbrook 47
Eddy 220
Edmonds 1
Edwards 69, **144–5**, 146, 202
Endacott 45, 139
Essery 201
Everett 67
Exworthy **234–5**

Fay 15
Ferryman 6
Fogerty 237
Foot 52, 53
Fortescue 79
Foster 143, 201, 218
Frayn 108
French 37
Friend **88–9**, 170, **178–9**, 217
Frost 93
Fuge 181
Furness 153

Gallie **34–5**
Garland **46–7**
Gawman **92–3**
Geake 75, 111, 205
Geddes 167
Geist 71
Gerry 177
Gibbings 166
Gilbert 166
Giles 72
Glanville 35
Gloyne 18
Golding 233
Goldsworthy 75
Goodeve 122
Goodman 124, **126–7**, 132, 143
Gordon 35
Gosling 206
Gould 24, **152–3**, 174
Grainger **136–7**
Graves 37
Greenfield 235
Greening **164–5**
Gregory 303
Gundry 232

249

Haig 37, 59, 104, 124, 143, 175, 176
Haldane 19
Hale 66
Hamilton 67
Hammond 106
Handy 197
Hardwick 24
Harper 89
Harris **56–7**, 131, **148–9**, **192–3**, 238
Harry **120–1**, 124, **138–9**, 143, 223
Harvey **64–5**, **214–5**
Hawke 232
Hawker 68
Hawkins **224–5**
Hayman **166–7**, 171
Heale 237
Hearne 147
Heath 75
Heller 189
Hellier 69, 140, **162–3**
Hicks **220–1**, 223
Higginson 35
Higman 83, 93
Hill **90–1**, 159, 171
Hindenburg 204
Hockaday 231
Hodge 220
Hodgins 24, 25, **26–7**
Hoehling 25
Holman **158–9**, 160
Horne **190–1**
Horrell 219
Hoskyns–Abrahall 21, **22–3**, 24, **156–7**
Huggins 219
Hurrell 136
Hutchings 209
Hynes 92, 243

Jago **116–7**, **176–7**
Joll 199
Jolliffe 235
Jones 90, 141, 208
Justham 27

Kellaway 170
Kelly 21, 58, 107
Kennard 237
Kennedy 55
Kerslake 185
Kerswill 20, **122–3**
Kiggell 124
Kingdon 186
Kipling 35, 61, 201
Kitchener 3
Kittow 230

Knight 9, 40, 182
Knott 151

Lambert 67, 69
Lane 135
Lang 15, 139
Laundry 82
Lavis 213
Lean 82
Legg 152
Lendon 181
Lethbridge **36–7**, 39
Lewis **110–1**
Lipscombe 155
Lloyd George 74
Love 219
Lucas 135
Lucy 155
Luscombe 179
Lutyens 34, 45, 59, 112

Maistre 185
Maker **38–9**, **78–9**, **108–9**, 140, **206–7**, 228
Mallett 33
Marshall 71, 91
Martin **30–1**, 53, **72–3**, 75, **84–5**, 114, 178, 218
Masters 129, 165
Mathews 158, **160–1**
May 137
Medland 119
Merrifield 24, **48–9**, 51, **228–9**
Metherell 140
Metters 16, 17, 45
Miles 72, **236–7**
Mitchell 38, 189, **198–9**
Mockler 6
Mockler-Ferryman **6–7**, 8
Moyle 162
Mudge 175
Mulvihill 27

Nettle 208
Northey 66, 96
Northway 89, 124, **134–5**

Oates 121, 243
Osborne 116
Owen 5, 63
Oxenham 203

Paddon 106, 238
Paige 53
Palk 14
Palmer **86–7**, 97, 122, 203, **210–1**
Parsons **96–7**
Payne 82

Paynter 148
Peacock 215
Pearce 152
Peard 115
Pendry 69, 183, **194–5**, 197
Pengelly **94–5**
Penny 209
Perkin **20–1**, **124–5**, 127
Perrot 61
Peters 214
Pethick 98, **180–1**
Pevsner 34
Phillips 191
Philp **70–1**, 223
Phipps 181
Pike 64, 92
Pine 191
Pitcher 198
Plumer 119
Plummer **82–3**
Postlethwaite 21
Pott 41
Potter 86
Price 73

Raleigh 199
Rawlinson 89
Raymont **114–5**
Reddicliffe 139
Rich 186, **212–3**, 223
Richards 131, 209
Richardson 28, 32
Rixon 184
Roberts 69, 194, **196–7**
Rodda 233
Rogers 2
Rooke **100–1**
Rouse 43

Sanders 227
Sands 79
Sargent 20, 63, **202–3**
Sassoon 124
Scheer 48, 49
Scott 241
Seager 83
Shepherd 84
Simmons 12, 13, **14–5**, 24, 197, 220
Simonds 151
Singh 241
Skinner 20, 21, **104–5**, 124, **132–3**, 230
Sleeman 103, 121
Slocombe 116
Smale 76, 99
Smith 115, **232–3**
Snell 66
Soper 25

Southcombe 71
Spooner 69, **172–3**
Spry 142, 239
Spurway **188–9**
Squire 211
Stacey **42–3**
Standlake 151
Stephens 148
Stranger **238–9**
Sussex 139
Symons 14, **98–9**, 181

Tarner 139
Taunton 237
Tebb 85
Teglio 21, **106–7**, 131
Thomas 149
Thorne 165
Tonkin 121
Townshend 56
Towsey 119
Tozer 177, 185
Trefry 193
Trelawny 228
Treliving 40
Trick **32–3**, **208–9**
Truscott 31, 85, 97

Tucker **18–9**, 20, 140, 187, 235, **242–3**
Turner **216–7**
Tyrrell **16–7**, 87

Veal 241
Veale 201
Vinson **218–9**
von Spee 13

Wainwright 129
Waken 28
Waldron 97, 121
Walk 103
Walke 79
Walkem 124, **128–9**, 133
Walters 235
Ward 21, 115
Warren 72, 73, **74–5**, 120, 138
Watt 227
Watts **10–1**, **112–3**, 124, **142–3**
Waye 45, **168–9**
Weaver **76–7**
West 121
Westaway 161

Westlake **40–1**, 213
Weston 229
Wevill 75
Whistlecraft 147
White 27, 147, **230–1**, 241
Whitehead 6
Whittome 131, **240–1**
Wilkinson **174–5**
Willey 37
Williams 18, 41, 90, 93, 108, 110, 195, 209, 230, 242
Willis 31, 84
Willoughby 229
Wills 105
Wilson 24, 49, **50–1**
Winney 105, 152
Wonnacott 45
Woodley 150
Woodrow **204–5**
Wooldridge 90
Woolley 105
Woolridge 52
Worth 44, 80, 97

Yard 24, 49, **52–3**

Zappert 13